Norman
And
Me

Julie Savage

ISBN:0615952011
ISBN-13:9780615952017

FOREWORD

I believe that everything happens for a reason and that there are few coincidences in life. Our lives are, to a certain extent, preordained, and the people who happen along on our path are meant to. My nana used to say that "what's meant for you won't go by you" – and she was always right. I believe that now is the right time to tell my story. Why should my story be such a big deal? I hear you thinking; or who's interested? Well, my life has been a little bit extraordinary; so much so that people seem interested in the tales I have to tell. So here it is: my first attempt at writing and, thankfully, some divine guidance helping me articulate the events of my (to some people) bizarre life so far.

I suppose my story begins on the day I was born. We are blessed, if we are lucky, with parents who love and nurture us. The usual deal being that our folks give us guidance and instruction on how to live our lives and deal with the things that come along. I am lucky: my parents tried their best to do just that. I know how much they loved me, even though I was difficult at times. Most of us become, to a certain degree, how our folks would want us to be. Not me – I was born different.

CONTENTS

ACKNOWLEDGEMENTS

My heartfelt thanks to Tom Roberts for designing an awesome cover, and to Steve Horn for pointing me in the right direction. I thank God every day for my children: Daniel for the joy and humour he brings into my life; Rebecca – my rock and my best friend – without whom none of this would have been possible. Thank you, Michael, for your patience, encouragement, and for loving me enough to allow me to grow and realise my dreams. The people in my life are not in it by accident. I chose you all.

1

MONDAYS

I hate Mondays! Every Monday except a Bank Holiday, that is. I have always hated them. Mondays at school were unbearable. I can remember as far back as primary school – to the mid 1960s, when tables and spelling tests were always the first lessons after assembly. Surely this was tantamount to child cruelty. It was in my opinion. Then later, at secondary school, Monday was a day that used to consist of double lessons of either Science or Math. Yuk! I figured that teachers too must have hated Mondays and, as revenge for having to work them, doled out even more homework on that day than on any other. I have spoken to lots of other people about my dislike of Mondays and, I have to say, many agree with me.

Well, here we are; it's Monday again. (They seem to come around far too fast for my liking; much faster than Fridays or Saturdays for sure.) I am on my way to work. I don't mind working; I have always worked and, because my job is part of who I am, it's much easier to get out of bed and go there. The people that say my job isn't a proper job should know that I have always viewed it as one; I think I need to in order to make sure that my feet are kept securely on the ground. Sometimes, this business can make you lose your temper, your faith, your mind – even the plot! So I always endeavour, sometimes successfully, to maintain my sense of humour. After all, jobs are less of a chore if, in my opinion, you tackle them with a happy heart.

I work as a professional psychic. Saying that always makes me feel awkward and I'm not really sure why. I realized early on in life that I was psychic; but I learned to hide that fact and now, here I am, admitting it. Nevertheless, I enjoy the fact that I am different. So, here I am at 8:25 on a Monday morning driving to work, not even bothering to wonder what's in store today. Each day is so unpredictable, colourful and thought-provoking that I remain completely interested in what I do. The 'normal' jobs that I once had in administration and retail were so different to what I do now. The years of organized planning, target-chasing and structure that I was used to were an insignificant training ground for my present working day in the 'cupboard', as I like to call the lovely room where I hold my consultations.

This little room is only a small part of who I am and what I do. It's quite an important part though, and very popular with the people who come to see me, especially those who are searching for something. My room is one of many in our holistic centre (called this only because we couldn't think of how best to describe what we do here). The centre runs efficiently and effectively, mostly due to the fact that it is managed expertly, by my beautiful daughter Rebecca and my dear friend Michelle. The centre has another reading room like mine – available to the other readers who work with us. It also has a 'treatment room.' This room is shared by our resident acupuncturist, our beauty therapist, and our food sensitivity and allergy tester. We also have a small room named the 'Zen Den': this is where our various healers, including a palmist and a psychic artist, perform their miracles of healing. You can appreciate that it is a hive of industry most days at the centre. The reception and waiting area are often like King's Cross station, yet still Rebecca and Michelle manage to keep fuss to a minimum. They are somehow able to run all of our diaries and manage our time expertly. How we all came together is interesting in itself, but, for now, here is just a small insight into what goes on most Mondays in my world.

Most of our working mornings we meet for a cup of tea in the reception area of the centre, and on Mondays we drink our tea while catching up on where we went and what we did over the weekend. Just a normal Monday morning gathering of staff; the only difference is that our tea break is before we start work. At around 9:45, I go into my room where I meditate to tune into my guide. Rebecca goes to work answering emails and dealing with the numerous answer-phone messages that have been left over the weekend, before greeting our clients and ensuring that everything runs smoothly. I try to keep my little room warm and cosy. It is important to me that it feels good; so, I light candles, burn incense and put on some soft background music. My room always has such a nice vibe. (If you can comprehend that rooms have feelings.) It has in it a table and chairs at which I sit to read cards, a bookshelf, a cream leather sofa and various knick-knacks and books that are sentimental to me. It's a comfortable room, and I like to remain here until I have my first client at 10 A.M. I don't often look in the diary to see who my appointments are with; it doesn't matter really as Rebecca manages the diary for me. I am lucky in that my diary is usually booked up to a year in advance.

At 10 A.M. prompt I open my door and see that the reception area is now busy with people here for their appointments. The atmosphere is now totally different to how it was an hour ago; the nervous anticipation of our clients is tangible. It always feels to me a little like a dentist's waiting room, and this usually makes me want to giggle. If clients have booked their readings with friends and have come together to support one another, then there is usually a "you go first" argument which takes place. This, I think, would indicate that a reading is not always just 'for entertainment purposes only', as the poster which we are forced to display for legal reasons suggests.

My first appointment this particular Monday is with Paul. Paul is a big guy; I guess about 6'2" and weighing around 18 stones. He has had his appointment with me booked for about ten months. I must say that the ten minutes he has been in reception (he arrived early) seem to have set his nerves on edge. When I appear from my room, which leads out into the reception area, he glances up looking like a rabbit caught in headlights. My name is on the door of my room, and I figure he knows that it's me that he's going to be seeing. Paul and I have never met before, and I sense that I am not what he expected to see. A lot of people are surprised when they see me apparently. I suppose people have ideas of what a psychic should look like – usually a cross between Mystic Meg and Doris Stokes. I am 5'1", blonde and, I think, normal looking. A reporter from the *News of the World* once said that I was the most unlikely looking medium he had ever set eyes upon. I took that as a compliment.

Anyway back to Monday, and as I enter reception I look across and smile at Rebecca as she sits behind her desk, groomed to perfection; this lovely young woman, who I once held as a baby in my arms, and I feel so proud when she announces, so efficiently: "Julie, this is Paul, your first client." Paul's face, I notice, reddens when she introduces him. And when he stands up, he shuffles awkwardly. He doesn't give me eye contact, nor does he speak. I smile again and invite him into my room. He walks in ahead of me, closely followed by a small lady who smiles at me. "I'm Pat, pet – Paul's mum," she says. Paul doesn't acknowledge her. She follows him into my room – unseen by everyone but me!

I ask Paul to take a seat, opposite me, at my table. His little mum stands behind him, looking over his shoulder at me. She looks concerned for him. I don't pay too much attention to her at this point. I introduce myself again: "Hi Paul. I'm Julie. I don't think we have met before, so I will run through what is going to happen today." I explain to him that I will be reading cards for him this morning: two sets of different cards. The first, I say to him, will tell me all about him as a person, and his life. "These cards will outline any problems around you and, hopefully, provide some solutions. Then I read these cards," I say, pointing to the larger deck of cards on the table. "These give insight into your future and tell me what's in store for you. I also work as a medium, and will try to connect with the family and friends around you who have passed away." He seems totally unmoved by this synopsis of my services and has kept his head bowed; looking at the table the whole time I am talking to him.

He is completely silent; not uncommon, though a little unusual. I guess that the best thing to do is to get on with his reading. I ask him to shuffle the first set of cards that I hand him. I watch as he tries to shuffle quickly so that I won't notice how badly his hands are shaking. Then I take the cards from him, span them out face down like a large fan and invite him to choose ten. As he chooses his cards I mention that a lady came into the room with him. I tell him that she is standing behind him, and is telling me that she is his mother – Pat. He stops selecting his cards and then looks at me – looks at me for the first time. A long look into my eyes, as though he wants to find something; to see what I can see. He doesn't either acknowledge or answer me. Pat seems embarrassed by this and adds: "Tell him that his granddad, Bob, will be here in a minute." So I tell him what she has just said and this big man looks down as a tear leaves his eye and runs down his cheek. In silence, I offer him a tissue. He accepts and I lay down the cards he has chosen – in the formation that I have always used.

The cards he has selected tell his story, and I start to read his life as if the cards are a book. I begin by telling him what has happened in his life recently; fairly insignificant things about his new car, his recent house move, changes at work. He has pulled himself together by now, regained his composure. I notice that he is shaking his head incredulously. I guess that the things I'm telling him must be right. My own guide,

Norman, tells me to continue and helps me to analyse further Paul's chosen cards, and how they correspond to him.

My God! This guy's had an awful life. No luck or love. He feels so low, isolated, lost and, very recently, suicidal. I chatter on through the reading, listening and then repeating what my guide has said. Sometimes I talk so much that it makes me breathless, and often I am not always aware of the effect that my words are having. Today Norman tells me to stop and give Paul time to take in what I have said so far. I do. Paul looks a little bit shocked at my revelations. I ask him if he is okay. He nods, I carry on. When the first card reading is complete, Paul is till shaking his head. He can't believe what has happened. "I know that you don't believe in all of this stuff," I say. "You probably didn't know what to expect. Do you want me to continue?" He just nods and I hand him the second deck of cards. As he shuffles them, this time with a bit more confidence, he speaks for the first time in twenty minutes. "My God!" is all he says.

As he is shuffling these, his future cards, I begin to see a mist building up in the corner of my room. This mist gets a little thicker and then begins to form into the shape of a person – this time a man. Very soon I can see through this mist much clearer. It's an older man. "Your granddad, Bob, is here," I say. "He's telling me that he didn't believe in any of this either." I describe Bob, and what he is wearing, and then carry on with what he wants me to tell Paul. Bob tells me how much he loves Paul, and how difficult things have been for him. Going right back into Paul's past to when Bob's own son (Paul's father) Joe, left his family and moved away. Bob said how he had stepped in and willingly become the father figure in Paul's life. Paul at the time was only four years old. Bob went on to tell me that they had had great fun together – fishing, going for walks – and he smiled while he reminisced that some of the happiest times he could remember were spent with just Paul, together in his shed each Saturday. Here they would spend their time eating corned beef sandwiches and drinking tea out of their flasks while listening to football on Bob's radio. Bob enquired of me to ask Paul if he could remember the shiny blue flask that he had bought him for his eighth birthday.

Bob described how close they had become and how hard it was for him to leave Paul when his "number was up"; after all, this was what his "waster of a son" had done to the lad, too. But poor Bob had no choice in the matter and he went on to tell me how he had passed away one Saturday, on the way home from fishing with Paul. They had been walking home through a field when all of a sudden Bob was gripped by pain – a really intense pain in his chest. Bob was seldom ill and this pain really took him by surprise. He didn't want to alarm Paul, so he continued walking. Soon after the initial pain other searing pains started to spread across his chest and down his arm and poor Bob collapsed. He remembered how he had started to float out of his body. He said he felt no pain, just pure joy. That was until he became aware that he was floating above his body, watching all that was happening below. He described how awful it was to watch Paul, as he stood there first staring and then screaming at the empty shell of a body that had once held his beloved granddad – the only man he had ever loved. Paul was just ten years old.

Pat, Paul's mum, confirmed the story and went on to tell me that Paul had never really come to terms with losing his granddad. She said that he hadn't been able to move on. He had blamed himself for the death, especially after overhearing his uncle, on the day of Bob's funeral, say: "If my dad had been with someone who had first aid experience, then he might be alive today." Paul had been devastated and, unfortunately, his feelings had been somewhat overlooked at that sad time. After all he was just a kid. He took to spending long periods of time on his own, in his bedroom, refusing to talk about Bob or about anything else concerning that day, finding the pain of it all unbearable. This colossal event in Paul's childhood was to shape his future. He became isolated; a loner so introvert that even his mum couldn't reach him. He kept a low profile at school and started work at 16 on a production line at a factory. The noise in the factory was so loud that the workforce was ordered to wear earplugs. This suited Paul; it cut out the need for conversation, continuing his isolation.

So here was this big man, sitting in front of me, weeping out his grief; something he should have done a long time ago. Thinking about Bob and the event of his death, however, was good therapy for Paul. He needed the release. Bob told me: "This is what he has needed, pet." When Paul was a little calmer and his grief had abated, he managed to tell me how much he had loved Bob and even managed to laugh at some of the experiences they had shared. He was also able to tell me of the desperate loneliness he felt each and every day of his life since losing Bob 22 years ago. I just listened until he had finished talking, and then prompted him to choose some cards for his future from the deck he had just shuffled. These cards, thankfully, were much better. They held promise of a future that saw him settled with a girl – a soul mate. I saw Paul being embraced by another family, perhaps his future in-laws. Bob and Pat remained silent while I told him this. Paul himself seemed reluctant to even hope that this could happen. But when Bob and Pat nodded their heads in agreement, I was sure that this would come to pass. If they agreed with me, it was bound to be right.

Paul told me that he couldn't explain what had possessed him all those months ago to book to see me, and how he never intended to keep the appointment. I just told him that sometimes things were just meant to be, and to trust the invisible, divine intervention in life that endeavours to give us indicators and help every day – if we could only just accept it. I'm not sure that he bought that, but it gave him food for thought, I'm sure. Paul said that he was going to make some changes in his life and that he felt he had experienced something that morning which would ensure nothing would ever be the same again. Bob and Pat decided to leave. After passing on their "I love yous" to Paul, I thanked them and they went, far less concerned about him than they had been. Paul sat a few minutes longer to regain his composure and, when he stood up, he asked if he could hug me. This was progress indeed: Iron Man wanting a cuddle! I said yes; I don't think that Paul had been hugged in a very long time. I then opened the door of my room for him and told him to be good – something I always seem to say. He smiled and thanked me again. Paul left my room and returned to 'normal life' once again.

As he left my room I looked over to Rebecca. "Julie, this is Emma. She is your next lady," she said. "Hi Emma. Come in," I said, as I stood holding the door open for her to enter my room. "I am so nervous," Emma said, her hand in her pocket, clutching her dead grandmother's wedding ring. "No need," I said smiling, as Emma and her grandmother came into my room. "No need at all."

Emma's experience was about to start; mine started a long time ago. So I think it's only fair to take you back. To the beginning.

2

THE BEGINNING

I came into the world late – 17 days late, to be precise – on 25 November 1961, causing mayhem in the delivery room. My mother had a difficult time giving birth to me, resulting in a forceps delivery that left me looking somewhat peculiar. I was so ugly that my dad went home and sobbed. I was the first-born child of Bill and Ena Savage. I was very much wanted. My mum had previously suffered two miscarriages, one of which was particularly devastating: she lost a boy who was stillborn just two years before I came along. My parents were married seven years before I was born; so I guess they were ready for me. Or were they? Regardless, I always felt very much wanted and loved.

My dad Bill (George William, to be exact) Savage, was the seventh son of Richard and Florence Savage. My grandfather was a refuse collector. He was also a part-time lay-preacher and a full-time drunk and hypocrite. My dad had little in common with his father and, as a result, had very little to do with him. Dad didn't drink. He used to say that he didn't like the taste of alcohol very much or how it affected some people. I guess he witnessed first-hand the problems that his father's drinking caused at home. My granddad – Dick, as he was known – was married first to a woman called Lilly, apparently a lovely lady. They had two sons and a daughter, all of whom I knew as my aunt and uncles. Poor Lilly died of consumption just 12 years into their marriage. Dick was devastated. He turned from being a church-going family man into a depressed drunk who left his children to God and Providence (a term my nana often used). His life had changed forever. He had lost his beloved Lilly, his soul mate.

Florence, my dad's mother, was the only one of my grandparents that I ever knew. She was a real character. Born in 1900, her beloved father died when she was only 11 years old, and she felt as though her life was over. She was sent to work in a country house when she was just 13, after her mother re-married. She hated her new stepfather; they just didn't get on and Florence's rebellious nature pretty much ensured that she would be put into employment in a big house, away from home. This suited her; it gave her freedom and she fell in love when she was just 17. Whilst working as a dairymaid her attention was caught by John – one of the farmhands. It was love at first sight. Her lovely John was a local boy who, despite her pleas, signed up to fight in the First World War. They made love just once before he was sent off to fight in the Second World War. Like so many other young men of that time, John was killed in action, never to return home and never knowing that Florence was pregnant with his child. This was to shape her future and seal her fate.

Florence was sent away to her aunt's house to have her baby and was reminded every day, before and after the birth, of the disgrace she had brought to the family. She had her son, Alfie, when she was just 18, and her refusal to give him up resulted in her being put out on the streets with her baby and with nowhere to go. She went along to the local wash-house to enquire about work, but there was none available. A lady in the wash-house, overhearing her plight, caught hold of her as she was leaving. She told her of a man living nearby that needed a housekeeper. This man's wife had recently died of consumption and his children needed taking care of. Florence took his address, thanked the lady and sought out this man. What she found when she reached the house was disgraceful. The children were all ill and hungry and the house was dirty and bare. The man – Dick Savage – had sold what little furniture there had been to get beer money. The whole prospect of living there was grim. Dick told Florence that he couldn't pay her anything. All he could offer, in return for her cooking, cleaning and looking after his children, was a roof over her and her baby's heads. She was desperate; so she accepted. It was only ever meant to be temporary. Little did she know the sacrifices she was making that day.

She turned the house over and made the best of what there was, and the children came to respect and love her. Her brusque nature and her 'lets get on with it' attitude brought a little hope into what had been a bleak house with a grim future. Dick continued to drink, albeit not as much. But Florence didn't mind: if he was at the pub, then he was not under her feet. It wasn't long before she organised the household, and the children began to feel and look better for having been fed and cared for. The arrangement suited them all. Each night at bedtime, Florence would lay in her room with Alfie by her side and thank God for the small mercies bestowed upon her.

Dick was a morose character who frowned constantly. Not one for small-talk, he loved to preach about his beliefs to anyone who would listen to him. The whole household was different when he was at home: he was certainly the master in his own house. After all, Florence was no better than an unpaid housekeeper. But she didn't mind; she just kept her head down, her mouth shut and got on with it. One night, a few months after she had moved in, Dick came home from the pub one night in one of his sanctimonious moods, declaring that "people were talking" about the fact that they were living in sin. My nana always insisted that their relationship was solely based on a mutual need for one another. There had been no physical contact between them whatsoever, so she wondered at why people would think that. She worried that once again she was going to be put out on the streets with Alfie, who was the only sunshine in her life. "What do you want to do about that then?" she asked, bracing herself for his reply. "Well, it will stop tongues wagging if we get wed," he said. "Alright then," she said, more than a little surprised at what had just left her mouth. So, that was that. She told me once of the feeling of dread that came over her as she lay in her bed the night that Dick had proposed. Not surprising, given the type of man he was. Her only thoughts were of Dick's three children that she had come to love and did not want to be parted from, and her beautiful son who now, at least, would have a roof over his head. The fact that Dick would never acknowledge Alfie or even call him by name seemed to escape her thinking that night. She thought that this offer of marriage and security was the best she could hope for. Love didn't come into it.

Within months they got married. Theirs was a very strange relationship: a completely loveless union, their mutual dislike seemed to keep them at least talking, if only to criticize each other. Dick was still out a lot, so home life remained bearable. Florence loved her brood and, soon after the marriage, found that she was pregnant. She made the most of whatever she had, which was minimal, and became sought after as the local nurse, midwife and undertaker, using the healing skills she had learned from her mother to earn her a few extra pennies. And she made sure that Dick did not get his hands on her money. Florence was always of such interest to me. She was well versed in witchcraft and pagan ways, yet she read the Bible every night. She was the hub of the family, feared by most, respected by all – a complex woman. My dad, Bill, was the youngest of her children, yet she never seemed to like him very much. I used to think that being her baby, her youngest, she would love him a little bit more than the rest. But no. She constantly reminded him of how traumatic his birth had been – she had been bed-ridden for nearly a year after he was born due to severe haemorrhaging – and that it was his fault. My dad got all the worst chores, and was used as the neighbourhood messenger for most of his young life. Despite all this, he was a loyal and obedient son who was always good to her. He became a wonderful man in spite – not because – of his childhood.

My mum Ena (or Thomasina, as she was christened) was the daughter of Thomas (Tom) and Ellen Fairbairn. Ellen had three children before she met Tom, and then had four girls to him. Mum was the third girl, and she told me that her mother desperately hoped for a boy this time to name after Tom. My grandma was to be disappointed when, in February 1934, another girl came along. So my mum was christened Thomasina. She always hated her name with a passion and much preferred the shortened version – Ena. This new, shortened name came about when she started work in a grocer's shop. She was 15 years old and had just left school. The manager of the shop declared, much to mum's embarrassment, that Thomasina was such a mouthful and that would she mind being called Ena. This seemed so much better than the original version that my mum jumped at the chance. My grandma would tut on hearing my mum being called Ena, reminding her that she was named after a wonderful man, so therefore should be proud of her name.

Grandma Ellen had had a hard life; she was the only girl in her family and had two younger brothers. Her parents owned a milliner's shop in Newcastle. They were quite successful in business and would keep young Ellen off school, to see to her brothers and keep house for them while they worked. Subsequently, my grandma lost lots of schooling and was illiterate. This was always a huge handicap to her. She was quite a tough little lady who had not known much affection as a child. She was also quite rebellious and left home in her teens to be with a man who had already been married. He was considerably older than her, but she loved him and they had three children together. He, like Florence's first love, was killed in action and it broke her heart. She eventually met Tom Fairbairn who was, I am told, the loveliest man you could ever hope to meet. Tom got offered a job at ICI, the big chemical plant in Billingham, so they moved lock, stock and barrel from Gateshead to set up home near Tom's work. Home seemed a million miles away to Ellen, and she never really felt at home in Billingham. My granddad Tom was a hard working, well respected, family man, who was anything for a peaceful life. He adored his children and was an excellent stepfather to Ellen's children: Ellen, Jimmy and Billy. Mum and her sisters loved their father so much. He often acted as the buffer for their mother, who could be very strict. Her daily mantra was "little girls should be seen and not heard" and, as a result, her children were quiet and respectful. They seemed to get all their affection from their father. Ellen was quite aloof emotionally; she didn't have time for kisses and cuddles. My mum's theory was that because her mother wasn't shown much affection as a child, she found it hard to be affectionate with her own children. I can't make a judgment on that; Ellen died when I was just two years old and I can barely remember her.

Granddad Tom died of a cerebral haemorrhage when my mum was 19. Ellen and her girls were devastated. He just got up one morning and collapsed. Their lives had changed forever. Ellen was very psychic and used to hold conversations with Tom long after he had died. Mum never really got over losing her lovely dad. He was so special and so important in her life. Long after his death in 1953, his goodness and the impression he left on his girls – my aunts – lives on.

Mum hated school and couldn't wait to leave. She left school one Friday and started work the following Monday. She loved her first job in a local grocery shop. She was always good with figures and people, and loved being busy; so it was the perfect job for her. She paid her mother her weekly board and lodge, and the rest of her wages were spent on clothes, make-up, and going to the local dances. Her two older sisters May and Olive, and her younger sister Violet, were all quite close in age so they often went out together. The sisters shared clothes and make-up, and were always very well thought of in their neighbourhood. They were the Glamorous Fairbairn Girls: all small, blonde and slim, and so elegant in spite of their humble upbringing. The four of them were so alike that they were often mistaken for one another. Old age has seen mum's sisters resorting to pushing trolleys, around the local town centre in order to carry their shopping. They are known to most locally as the 'Trolley Dollies.' Still so feminine and elegant, you can imagine how stunning they must have been as young women.

My dad, left school at 15 and got a job in a local bakery – a huge family-owned business that employed hundreds of local men and women. He hated the job from the start. The only saving grace was that it was near to home, paid him a wage, and he worked with a lot of great people, some of whom became his lifelong friends. Dad would tell us funny stories of some of the antics that would happen in the factory. He was a brilliant storyteller who could make most stories hilarious. Florence, his mother, took the best part of his wages from him, and the rest he spent on his passion – cars.

All dad ever wanted to do was drive. Nana bought him an old clapped out Austin when he was 17, and took extra money out of his wages each week until he had paid her back. Dad didn't mind; he tinkered for hours, often till late at night, teaching himself the workings of the car's engine. Once the car was paid for and slightly more road-worthy, nana arranged for a local man to give dad driving lessons. Naturally, he had to pay weekly out of his wages for the lessons, but he didn't mind. I think that his obsession with cars was perhaps born of his need to escape from the noisy household he lived in. The crudeness, vulgarity, and criticism directed at him from his father seemed to matter less when he had his head stuck under the bonnet of a car. In his own world of motor cars and engines, his dreams of driving away from home were his way of escaping the bedlam that existed in the Savage household. He soon passed his test and, as a result, was expected to be a chauffeur for my nana, who would remind him how that if it hadn't been for her he would never have been able to buy a car in the first place.

Dad was a handsome chap: tall and dark, with piercing blue eyes. Despite this, he always seemed to lack confidence – perhaps due to the constant criticism and lack of compliments from those around him. He also lived in an environment where there was no room for vanity or glamour. The house was always threadbare. The Savages had gone from living in poverty, to just living with the basics in life. Nana didn't care too much whether things matched or looked pretty; she was completely un-materialistic. She was herself: a very plain looking woman who never wore make-up or perfume. The only soap in the house was carbolic; she preached cleanliness next to Godliness, so it was no surprise that dad was never really sure of himself. He once told me that his saving grace was that he was always able to make people laugh. His warm personality and giving nature made him a popular lad and he liked nothing better than to entertain others with his huge store of jokes, often making himself the brunt of them. He met mum at a local dance when they were both 19. She had an instant effect on him. He was bowled over by her beauty, femininity, the sheer loveliness of her. He couldn't believe his luck when she allowed him to walk her home. She had just lost her father, and her vulnerability stirred something in dad. He made it his job to look after her. She became the focus in his life; something to love even more than his car. He adored this quiet doll-like girl, and couldn't quite believe that she would be interested in him. He fell in love with her the first time he saw her and loved her with all of his heart until his untimely death at 54.

Their coming together must have been quite an education for both of them. Dad went for tea at Grandma Ellen's house one Sunday. The table was set beautifully, and there was a feeling of such peace in the house he had never experienced before. Nobody shouted to get attention. Ellen liked him immediately and her intuition was always right. Dad felt like a fish out of water on this his first visit to our mum's mother's house; and he was desperate to make the right impression. As often happened in his life, humour saved the day. The lacy tablecloth Ellen had put on the table for tea got caught on Dad's waistcoat button, so that when he stood up to leave, the tablecloth left with him – causing carnage on the table. The sugar spilled, the tea cups toppled, my aunts gasped, everyone rushed to stand up to save their clothes and to prevent any further damage. Luckily, no harm was done and, after the initial shock, everyone laughed and the ice was broken. I remember that dad once said he was never so glad to be out of a room in his life!

For the first few months of the courtship, dad would take mum not to his mother's house, but to his sister Freda's house. His half-sister, the only girl to Dick and Lilly, Freda was married to George, and their son Ronnie was just a few years younger than dad. Mum got on well with Freda and her family, but often wondered why she hadn't met dad's parents. After broaching the subject a few times to him, he told her that there was no reason, and that if she wanted to, she was welcome to come along the following Sunday and have tea. The experience of having tea with the Savages stayed with my mum forever. She went the following Sunday, all dressed up, as usual, and couldn't believe her eyes. Florence was always honest, to the point of cruelty sometimes, and put on airs and graces for nobody. The house was full of family, all of them shouting over one another to be heard. This table was nothing like she had ever seen before. There were no small cut sandwiches on this table, just big old pieces of ham stuck between two rather large slices of bread, newly cut home- baked cakes, and tea that was so well stewed it looked like treacle. Most of the family smoked, and they did so at the table. Plates were in short supply, so everyone was expected to just grab a sandwich and get on with it. Mum chose a sandwich just to be polite, and as she did so the bread came away in her hand while the ham remained, hanging off her lips stuck to her lipstick. She was mortified. Thankfully, nobody seemed to notice her embarrassment. She realized now why Dad had had his reservations about taking her to his home. Florence didn't have much time for pleasantries; she saw Mum as a painted doll that needed to toughen up. She didn't always sympathise with nervousness or vulnerability. Her belief was that you had to be strong to survive, and those who weren't didn't.

So that is it: a brief outline of dad, mum, and how they came to be. I think I probably chose them as my parents. They were so different from each other in so many ways, yet fabulous parents who worked together as a team. When mum had me, she had to give up work. Dad still worked at the bakery and his wage was a pittance. They seemed to struggle financially all their married life. That, I'm sure, made me a better person. I was taught to value things. They both always made me feel special. I was mum's little helper and dad's little princess. I was so like Dad. I even looked like him, which isn't such an enamouring trait when you're a little girl, especially when your dad is a man and your mother looks like a beauty queen. I learned early in life to frown very hard at anyone who mentioned my likeness to him. I loved my parents with all of my heart and always will.

3

EARLY YEARS

My earliest childhood memory is of sitting on the couch surrounded by cushions, unable to sit up by myself. I was just months old. By this time we were living in Billingham, a town in the north-east of England, famous for ICI – Imperial Chemical Industries – and the town that mum was born in. We lived in a house owned by the local council. Our house was on a corner and it always seemed to be full of sunshine; probably due to the fact that the lounge had two large windows which let in lots of light. I remember feeling happy and sunny there. I can also recall my first birthday and can still describe in detail the presents I got for Christmas in 1962. I was exactly 13 months old. I remember how Christmas 1963 was better – I seemed to get far more presents. I also got lots of attention then and everything seemed perfect in my world.

The following year was strange. My paternal grandfather, Dick, died in March. I can't really recall much about it other than there was very little fuss made. Ellen, my maternal grandma, died just two months later. That must have been terrible for mum, who was heavily pregnant with my brother. Mark was born just 15 days later at home. I think it is safe to say that mum wasn't really good with childbirth. Who is? Even so, her GP had persuaded her to have a home delivery, explaining that just because her experience of having me was traumatic, there was no reason why this birth shouldn't go swimmingly. Big Mistake! She had a horrendous labour that the doctor was called upon to attend, and my brother was born with the umbilical cord wrapped around his little neck. He needed to be resuscitated. Mum would always say that he was worth it. He was the most beautiful baby anyone had ever seen in the family. Lots of dark hair crowned a perfect little face; his apparent serenity guaranteeing that he wouldn't ever be any bother. He was adored. I hated him!

What was the point of this horrible little individual interfering in our family life? I was, even at that young age, aware that mum wasn't very well after the birth and even my doting dad seemed to have less time for me. This little bundle of perfection was spoiling my life. These parents of mine, who had showered me with all their attention, were now giving more of it to little wrinkle features. There was nothing else for it – he had to go. I asked George, the man next door, if I could borrow a box of matches from him. When he asked what for, I replied: "to set that new baby on fire". This story, I seem to remember, was told at every available family meeting in the following few weeks. People would just look at me and smile. I would scowl very hard at them. My acceptance of Mark was a long time coming, and as he would lie in his beautiful shiny blue silver cross pram, I would climb on the wheels and prod and poke him awake. That pram had been mine! Why didn't he have his own pram? One day as a thunder storm rattled through the house, I felt quite happy when mum and I hid under the stairs while little precious boy lay in his pram; unprotected, I thought, and sure to be a goner. Not so, little "golden balls", as he would later be called, was to be a permanent feature in my life.

Sixteen months after the arrival of this little alien brother, my sister Alison was born. She was beautiful, the perfect baby. With rosebud lips and gorgeous curls, her happy-happy disposition made her so endearing. It was sickening. Even the neighbours loved Alison. She was the ultimate perfect baby girl who looked like something from a Pear's soap advert. Nice, if you like that sort of thing.

I was nearly four years old by now and already taking an interest in my appearance. I loved watching anything musical on television and I particularly loved Sandie Shaw. I took to walking around with no shoes on (something she did) and decided that, rather than have a fringe, I wanted a middle parting in my hair just like Sandie. So one afternoon, while Mum was seeing to the rug rats, I borrowed the kitchen scissors and took the middle section of my fringe between my fingers and chopped it right off down to the roots of my hair. This just left a huge gap in my fringe which looked really peculiar. I didn't mind it at all. I liked being different. Needless to say, looking as I did, my beautiful sister Alison was always going to be the one of us that was cooed over. I enjoyed the whole hair-cutting incident tremendously. I felt quite proud to have managed it all by myself. I got into big trouble with mum and dad though, who explained that I must never do anything like that again, especially as I had been asked to be bridesmaid for my cousin Margaret the next year. I was apparently going to be a beautiful little bridesmaid that everyone would look at. My parents told me that I would look really pretty, and that everyone would be looking at how cute I was. Yuk! I couldn't think of anything worse. Nevertheless, I behaved myself because it seemed to them that it was more important to look like myself than Sandie Shaw. They were stupid!

Cousin Margaret's wedding was a big event in the family in August 1966. A big church wedding that sent the whole family into debt for new outfits and wedding presents. I was bought a beautiful pink bridesmaid dress that made me feel like a princess. Well, it did while I was at home in the privacy of my own bedroom. Having to go to the church in a taxi with my other young cousins and without my mum was so daunting that I sobbed until my nose ran, my curls dropped, and my face puffed up like a chipmunk. The photographs of me, as you will imagine, were pretty awful; but how I loved that dress. I remember frowning so hard at people who looked at me that it made my little head ache. The only bonus was that when the wedding was over, I got to keep the dress.

The following month I started school. I loved it! I really didn't see the point in going home at lunchtime. Why spoil a good day? Yes, school was fantastic! I was a big girl now. I soon made friends and couldn't wait to go and see them each morning. It seemed only natural to me that in November I should have a party for my fifth birthday. This would give me the chance to invite all my new friends to our house, wear again my fabulous pink bridesmaid dress, and be the centre of attention for a change. I would show them rug rats!

By this time, we had moved to Stockton – just four miles from Billingham. Dad had managed to get another job – as a driver – but it meant he had to spend nights away from home. Mum was persuaded by nana to move nearer to her so that she could be on hand to help should she be needed. She never was. It seemed to make sense though; so they applied for a transfer from our beautiful sunshine house to an estate in Stockton. This house always seemed really grey. We lived at the bottom of a cul-de-sac. The neighbours seemed a lot rougher than where we had lived previously, but they were friendly enough. The back garden of the house was huge. This was a bit of a nuisance to my parents who were never keen on gardening, and in no time it became like a jungle. Hours of fun for me though; making mud pies and creating farmyards with plastic animals, using old lollipop sticks for fences. There were far more children living here in this neighbourhood than there were in Billingham; so that was a bonus. There were always plenty of kids to play with.

By now, Mark was three and Alison, the crowd puller, the angelic one, was 14 months old. Mark was adorable and even I had grown to like him. He was so loving; so utterly giving and pleasant, that you could not help but like him. I was finding myself increasingly out of favour with my mum these days; you see, even at this young age, I had a voice. I had an opinion on most things and was so clearly a daddy's girl that I felt I often got on her nerves. Well anyway, my big day – my birthday – was looming, and here was my opportunity to shine. I remember how the idea of throwing a birthday party for me absolutely filled mum with dread. There were two reasons: my parents were really hard pressed to find some spare money, and this, twinned with the fact that mum had never baked before (she could barely cook, really), were good enough reasons to, at first, refuse my request. The thought of catering for a kids' party must have been her worst nightmare. I wanted the whole works too: cakes, sausage rolls, and trifles – all the necessary ingredients for the perfect party. She was having the vapours even just considering it.

I would not be moved on this, though. If I couldn't have a party, then I didn't want anything. Dad, as always, gave in to me and then had the task of persuading mum that it would be okay. After all, we were only kids – the good food guide wasn't going to review the catering here. She was still not happy. So dad asked Florrie, the lady next door, if she would help mum out. She was a good baker and organizer. I always called her "Auntie". Her two daughters were close in age to me and would be invited to my party anyway. Florrie often popped in to our house for a cuppa and she said yes, of course she would help, and that it would be no bother. See – job done. No need for all that stress, mum! So, thanks to Auntie Florrie, the party was going ahead. I was reminded on numerous occasions leading up to my party just how lucky I was, and how much effort was going into this celebration.

At last my big day came. It didn't start off too grand really. You see, I thought, in my infinite wisdom, that now that I was five, that all the clothes that I had that were labelled ' Age 4 ' were no longer appropriate and I refused point blank to wear my 'Age 4' vest. Mum gave in to me eventually. She was no match for my stubbornness, and off we went to school. The whole day was fantastic! My birthday was mentioned in the morning assembly. I blushed, but loved it all the same. That day, I felt so different, so special, as if something big was about to happen that would change my life forever. Little did I know!

After school, I went home to begin the process of getting ready for my party. Mum had bought me some pretty pink ribbons to wear in my hair. I was pirouetting around my bedroom, making my beautiful dress flair out and float down like fairies' wings, while Florrie and mum were downstairs preparing things for the party. Florrie had brought her kitchen table into our house and had put it alongside ours. She then covered them both in a white tablecloth. It looked amazing. The table was then set with everything imaginable necessary for a child's birthday party. The whole thing was made even more special by virtue of the fact that these tables had been set in our front room. Both tables, when put together, were too big for the kitchen.

When I came down the stairs and saw how the table looked I was spellbound. There were cakes, sausage rolls, sandwiches with various fillings cut into little triangles, crisps, chocolate rolls, jelly in little fluted paper dishes, and a lovely pink and white birthday cake in the middle of the table with five pink candles on it. I was completely overwhelmed. I felt dizzy with happiness. I sat at the head of the table on my own, savouring the untouched beauty of this veritable feast. I will never, ever forget that view or how I felt at that moment.

As I was staring at the beautiful kaleidoscope of colours before me, something really strange happened. I slowly began to float upwards, out of my body towards the ceiling. Amazing! I was now looking down from the ceiling and I could actually see myself sitting where I had been, in the chair at the head of the table. I could see the top of my own head. It felt bizarre. I seemed to be floating above another me who was sitting where I had been down below. I remember thinking, 'Wow, it's great being five; it means that I can fly." After floating around peacefully for what seemed an age, but was probably only a few minutes, I looked down again. It was then that I noticed that there was a man standing next to the other - the sitting down – me. He was holding his arms up towards me, beckoning me to come down. I thought that perhaps I had better go back down; after all, my friends would be arriving soon. I would have another go of that flying later. Almost as soon as this thought had entered my head, I began to float slowly back down into my other body. When I finally landed back in it, I did so with a jolt that rocked the table a little. The man who seemed to have helped me down just stood next to me and smiled. He had a lovely face; I liked him immediately.

Mum came dashing through from the kitchen on hearing the table judder. She told me that if I must sit at the table, then I had to sit still. She didn't even acknowledge the man with the lovely face who was standing beside me. I figured he must be the gasman who had come to read and empty the meter. Mum and dad used to have to put shillings in a meter to get the cooker to work or the lights to stay on. That's good, I thought; mum usually gets a few shillings rebate back off him and that will go towards what my party must have cost her. How thoughtful of me! Unfortunately for mum, he wasn't the meter man.

My friends soon started to arrive and the house became a hive of activity: noisy and chaotic. Florrie's daughter, Karen, sat to my right and my friend Beverley sat to my left. The lovely man stood between Karen and me. He made no attempt to read or empty the meter, nor did it look like he was going to leave. Not to worry. I really liked him. He had a lovely face and nobody seemed to notice that he was there.

As we tucked into our party tea, this lovely man, who still hadn't left my side, started playing funny games with me. He kept telling me what my birthday presents were before I opened them. And he was making me giggle by predicting, correctly, what each of my pals would choose next to eat. At some point over the next couple of hours, I realised that nobody else seemed to be able to see him and that only I could hear him. I say I could hear him; he didn't actually talk or indeed even move his lips. He just looked at me and I knew his thoughts. Likewise, he seemed to be able to hear my thoughts. This was excellent – what a birthday bonus! Instinctively, I knew that this man was the 'something special' that was meant for me today.

Just before the candles were lit on my birthday cake, the lovely man told me that my dad had bought me a lovely present that he would bring home with him when he came in from work. I was ecstatic. It had been drummed into me, on more than one occasion, that if I was having a party, then a present was out of the question. My folks couldn't afford both. I was fine with that. I wanted my party so much that a present wasn't important. Until now! A present, too – oh wow! Could this day get any better?

I started to fidget – something that still happens to this day when I get excited. I began clapping, and Karen next to me asked what was wrong. "Oh nothing," I replied. "When my daddy comes in, I'm getting a special present." "What is it?" she asked. I looked at the lovely man, who told me that it was a projector. So I told her. "What's a projector?" asked Karen. I told her that I wasn't sure, but the lovely man told me that it was some kind of film show that had Disney slides to watch. "What's Disney?" Karen asked. Enlightened by the lovely man, I told her that Disney was Mickey Mouse, Donald Duck, and Goofy. Karen joined in with my excitement, and the good news spread quickly around the table. We were all going to be able to watch a Disney slide show later!

On hearing this, my mother was mortified. She grabbed me unceremoniously from my chair and frogmarched me into the kitchen. Once there, she lifted me up under the arms and sat me on the cold draining board. I can still remember the coolness of it on my legs. It made me shiver. She told me that I had not to tell lies and that I wasn't getting anything off dad, that my party was my present and I ought to be grateful. She then said that if I told lies again, she would send everyone home before the party games. I frowned really hard at her. The lovely man had followed me into the kitchen and stood behind her while she admonished me. He just winked at me and I knew to keep quiet.

Later that afternoon, as the pass-the-parcel game was on its last round, dad came home from work with a new red projector under his arm. I was elated. The lovely man nodded as if to say "I told you so". And my mum? Well, I could never tell whether she was furious, gobsmacked, or both.

4

DOCTOR DREAD

Such a lot happened in the next year that it's difficult to remember what happened first. My relationship with the lovely man flourished, and we soon became best friends. Mum and dad became aware that I was a little bit odd, and their views were justified by a series of events. The first was in spring 1967. Mum's older sister, Auntie May, came to visit one day with her daughter, my favourite cousin, Lynn. I absolutely adored Lynn. She was blonde, pretty, and always immaculately dressed. Lynn is three and a half years older than me, so, as you would expect, she became my role model and idol. I remember loving the clothes that she wore, which was just as well as I had them handed down to me when she had outgrown them. I was a grateful recipient, much preferring her hand-me-downs to new clothes. At five years old, I so wanted to be like Lynn. Everything she did was perfect, and whatever she wanted to play with or do was fine by me. I was only too happy to follow her lead.

May is my godmother and my favourite aunt. She always looked and smelled lovely, and sometimes, if I was lucky, she would let me go and stay at her house in the school holidays. That was brilliant; an escape from the rug rats. Lynn had a brother, Paul, who was great. He was just 11 months younger than me, and I always found him to be absolutely hilarious. His antics were often quite naughty, but he was a born entertainer and I loved him, too. When May and her husband, my uncle Stan, went to bed, Lynn, Paul, and me would sneak downstairs and watch horror films. Paul would imitate the Hunchback of Notre Dame by leaping around the furniture with a cushion under his pyjamas. He could walk like Frankenstein and make out that he was Dracula coming for our blood. Going to Auntie May's house was better than going anywhere.

Well, back to 1967, and their visit on this lovely spring day. Lynn and I went out to play in our scruffy back garden, and Lynn decided that we would play twizzies. This game consisted of her holding me by my wrists while she spun round faster and faster, until eventually my feet would leave the ground. I have to be honest, I didn't really like the experience; but Lynn seemed to really enjoy it. This, I felt, was a good enough reason to continue. After she stopped spinning, I would land back on Earth and feel so dizzy and sick, that I could hardly stand up without falling down. Lynn recovered from this dizziness much quicker than me, and wanted to repeat the process again and again. I hated it, but was only too pleased to oblige if it made her happy. On about the third go, or possibly the 27th rotation, I must have become a little heavy for her, and she let go of me in mid-flight. I flew through the air like a human rag doll and landed awkwardly against the garden fence. I screamed like a banshee, long howling screams that brought mum and May out into the garden, running towards me, faces full of concern. I was lying against the fence, crying. My arm really hurt. It hurt even more when I moved, so I tried to lie still until the pain lessened. It didn't. So I was picked up and carried into the house. Poor Lynn was crying too. Mum went for the man next door, who took us in his car to the local hospital. My arm was x-rayed and I was sent home with instructions to be given Junior Dispirin every four hours. Junior Dispirin! My God, this was agony. Surely a kid could die from pain such as this. Junior Dispirin failed to work its magic this time and later, when dad came home from work, even he couldn't cheer me up.

The next morning, after giving my folks a sleepless night, dad told my mum to take me to the doctor to get me re-examined. This request in itself sent her into a panic. Our GP was the grumpiest, scariest, most abrupt man on the planet. Mum hated going to see him even when she was poorly herself. The surgery was in the doctor's big, old house; a foreboding building that resembled the Addams family house. Grey clouds seemed to hover above it. The sun seldom shone on that house. Everything about it was grey: the stone, the mood, and the way it made you feel. Grey! Nevertheless, it was evident that I needed further attention and dad managed to convince mum that it was the best course of action. The next day, an emergency appointment was made and we got the bus – just mum and me – to the doctor's house.

The doorway to the waiting room was at the side of the house; this meant that you had to walk down a long path to get to it. Poison ivy probably lined the pathway. The path had lots of trees at the side of it. I have always loved trees, so I guess that this was probably the only nice thing about the pathway. Each step I took seemed to make the journey darker. There was a large square waiting room. The walls were a pale green and around the room, on each wall, were wooden benches. These oak benches had dark green leather seats and backrests. In the middle of the room was a big old oak desk. This desk belonged to the doctor's receptionist – Mrs Brown. She was brown by name and brown by nature. Everything from the tweed suit she wore, her shoes, her spectacles, her hair, her face, even her aura, was brown. She looked almost wooden. She seldom smiled and if she ever did, then her smiles were saved for the doctor. She had the most demeaning look. She had a man's face, really, and an ugly man at that! You really had to be poorly to want to sit facing her bulldog expression.

Mrs Brown spoke of the doctor as if he were the god of all doctors. She spoke of him with such reverence, letting all the poor waiting sick people know that his time was precious. Nobody dared speak in the waiting room; it was as if it were a holy place. She almost genuflected each time the doctor's – her master's – buzzer rang. This buzzer usually rang to signal that Doctor God himself was ready for his next victim, or patient, whichever the case may be. The buzzer made most people jump, not in a nice ding-dong way, but in a harsh, let's give them some wake-up volts fashion. Whenever Mrs Brown left the room, probably to plug some poor unsuspecting patient into the mains, those waiting would talk hurriedly and quietly to one another, often asking of each other questions like "what kind of mood's he in today?" ('he' being the doctor), or "have you heard him shouting much this morning?" Whenever someone came out of the doctor's room, once his big green door had opened, and the patient had been released, everyone in the waiting room would scrutinize the lucky escapee, looking for any tell-tale expression that would perhaps show what was to come. Then the waiting room vibe would become charged with tension, everyone offering sympathetic looks or reassuring smiles to encourage each other before entering the 'room of doom.'

Since my birthday, and the appearance of lovely man, I had noticed that I seemed to be able to feel other people's moods and emotions, especially if I touched them. So when my mum grasped my little hand that day in the doctor's waiting room, I felt the anxiety and panic that she was feeling in anticipation of our encounter with Doctor Dread. Alongside this ability, I also seemed to be able to summon lovely man whenever I felt a negative emotion. He would just appear at my side as if by magic. That day, thankfully, was no exception. I felt much less scared or bothered by things when he was near me. So, here we were: mum, lovely man, and me. And apart from this searing pain that was now all along my left side, I felt a little better.

Soon it was our turn. My name was called and we made our way into the room of doom. Dr Dread seemed really old, probably about 96, and way too old to be doing this job for sure. He sat behind another large oak desk, his spectacles resting on the end of his nose. He, I decided, was green. I had started to categorise people by colour. He was most definitely verdant. He wore a green suit, green shirt, green waistcoat and tie. He had grey hair, but even that seemed to be tinged with green. He matched his room – which was also green. In his room there was a bookcase full of dusty old books, a hand basin in the corner, and a picture of a skeleton on the wall, which I liked a lot. He never made eye contact with his patients – ever. He is the only doctor I have ever met who would diagnose a condition without looking at, not to mention examining, you. He just sat there behind his big brown desk pretending to write. His big bellowing voice made him sound like the bully he was. His greeting was always the same: "Yes?"

Mum, of course, first apologised for our being there, almost as if we were not worthy of his time, and then garbled her account of my accident the previous day. She explained how it had happened, the hospital, the Dispirin, the sleepless night, the crying. She went on to say that dad (yes, poor old dad, blame him) had insisted she brought me along this morning to make sure that I was okay. At this point he put down his pen, gave an exasperated sigh, and looked over his spectacles at me. I, of course, frowned at him – very hard. He was horrible, a big bully. "I suggest," he boomed, " that you continue as instructed by the hospital, with Junior Dispirin and accept that she's had a bit of a knock that is bound to hurt for a few days." "A bit of a knock!" My God, I had flown through the air like a practising trapeze artist, hitting the fence at 70 miles per hour, and he was calling it a "bit of a knock." I was furious and I could feel the anger welling up inside me.

I looked at my little mum, who looked ready to cry, and then at lovely man. He nodded. This was something he did those days. This nod was to let me know that I was to speak, and that he would tell me what to say. When this happened, I always repeated verbatim what he said; though I was never quite sure what the words meant. They were usually big words about things that I didn't always understand. So I opened my mouth. I looked Doc Dread right in the face. He was completely unaware of this, of course, and had gone back to writing his imaginary important message on his pad – a sure sign that this appointment was terminated and we were dismissed. I continued to stare at him until he looked up at me and then I said, in my most serious voice: "You're not a very good doctor, are you?" "I beg your pardon, young lady," he boomed. "I have a broken clavicle," I said calmly. Mum gasped, and I held my breath. My little heart was beating so fast it was making my arm hurt more and my head throb. "Young lady," he said, "Do you know what a clavicle is?" "No," I replied. "I just know that mine is broken." He looked at mum, scribbled a real note while we waited in silence. He then tore the note from his pad, put it into an envelope, and gave it to mum, saying: "Take this letter with you back to the hospital, where she is to have another x-ray." That was it – we were dismissed back out into the waiting room: mum, lovely man, and me. I made a point of letting Mrs Brown have my hardest frown. She frowned back at me and we left the surgery.

We caught the next available bus to the hospital. I was x-rayed again and it was discovered that I had indeed broken my clavicle (collar bone). My arm was put into a sling (something I was quite happy about). Mum seemed to cheer up immensely. She bought me a toy that day and some cherries to eat on the bus on the way home. Poor thing: she was obviously shaken. My collarbone healed quickly, and in the summer of that year the lovely man's visits continued. He taught me about nature and the names of birds, trees, and flowers. He knew everything about the weather and the clouds. He knew everything. Everything there was to know. My education in life continued.

5

LISTEN TO ME

One Saturday lunchtime, a few months later, I was out making mud-pies in our jungle of a back garden with my friend Lesley who lived next door. It was a lovely sunny day and we had been playing all morning. For no reason, I started to feel really cold. So cold, that I went inside to get a cardigan to wear. It was a strange kind of coldness: my bones felt cold, colder than they had ever felt before. The cardigan didn't seem to make much difference. I went inside and asked mum if I could have the fire on. She of course, said no. I started to feel as though I wanted to cry. I also knew that I had no reason to cry. I just seemed to feel that there were going to be tears.

My dad, who usually had two jobs because money was tight, had just come in from working a morning shift. He only had one job now, so was working any overtime that was available. Mum was in the kitchen making some tea. He followed her into the kitchen and I could hear them talking. His voice was low and sad sounding, and mum had gone silent. I walked into the kitchen and she was sitting at the kitchen table, crying, her hands covering her face. I stood in the doorway and asked what was wrong; why was she crying? They both ignored me! Dad put his arm around mum and told her not to worry. He went on to say that he would sort everything out, and that something would come along. I asked again what was wrong, but they still ignored me. I felt quite indignant; grown ups were stupid! What was mum crying for? I tried to prise her hands away from her face. She patted my arm and told me not to worry, that she was alright and for me to go and play. Dad also told me to go and play. So I went upstairs, still feeling cold, and now concerned, too.

I wandered upstairs into my bedroom. My curious nature getting the better of me, I decided to try and think very hard about lovely man. Sometimes when I did this he would appear. Sure enough, within a few minutes of my concentrating, he arrived. I told him, without using words, just by talking in my head, that mum was crying and wouldn't tell me why, and that dad was not his happy self either. I also told him how cold I was and that this whole situation was making me feel scared. "Don't worry," he said. "Your dad's been laid off work, your mum is having another baby, and they don't have much money at the moment. Your mum's just worried about how they will manage." "Oh no," I said. It sounded serious. "Everything will be alright," said lovely man. "Your dad will get offered a job tomorrow and all will be well." "Thanks," I beamed. The coldness lifted immediately and I went downstairs to spread the good news. Mum's lovely face was all blotchy, and dad looked tired and worn out. "Don't worry, everyone," I declared, "because tomorrow you, dad, are going to get a new job!" I clapped my hands. They didn't. Mum just smiled weakly and dad patted my head. Neither of them believed me, I could tell. That was until the following day, a Sunday, when an old mate of dad's knocked on our front door. He asked if there was any chance that dad was looking for work. This man had recently started working for a new firm who were looking for good lads. My dad was thrilled. Worry over. Mum was overjoyed. And me? Well, I was unmoved by the whole experience. Grown-ups cried for nothing sometimes!

Another crying experience happened later that year. My Auntie June cried loads. She wasn't my real aunt; just a good friend of mum's who we all called 'Auntie' out of respect. I liked it when she visited, she always brought us sweets. She and mum had been friends since childhood, and she was usually such a happy-go-lucky woman. Not today though. Boy was she unhappy. She was hollering her head off, big belly cries that you could hear all over the house. Mum was comforting her, holding her, and allowing her to cry into her shoulder, making her cardigan all wet. I was transfixed by the whole scene. How could someone, usually so happy and jolly, change into this state? What, for God's sake, had happened?

Mum was saying things like "don't worry, June, it will be okay," and then "just let it all out." Let what out, for Heaven's sake? If something inside was making her this sad, then I wasn't hanging around to watch it emerge. I went over to her and gently touched her knee. I didn't feel any coldness, so I knew she was going to be fine. I then went up to my bedroom. This crying was making my head ache. Once again, my curious nature got the better of me, and I wanted to know what on Earth was going on with Auntie June. I concentrated hard until lovely man came.

I told him about Auntie June. He just nodded as if he knew anyway. I had decided by now that lovely man lived somewhere up in the sky – probably heaven. He looked like one of the people in Nana Florrie's Bible and whenever he left me, he always floated up through the ceiling, vanishing into the sky. Well, Auntie June's crying must be loud if he could hear it all the way up there. He explained that her heart was aching. Ouch! God, it's serious then, I thought. He went on to explain how heartache came when someone was sad, because something was wrong with someone they loved. Mm. "Complicated," I said. "It must be my Uncle Joe – Auntie June's husband." Lovely man nodded. I didn't really like Uncle Joe very much. I suppose I didn't really like very many people, really. Uncle Joe was sneaky, or at least I always thought so. I had heard dad saying that he was hard work sometimes. He was no where near as nice as Auntie June. Lovely man said that Uncle Joe had a girlfriend. I knew that this was wrong. Mum was dad's girlfriend, and you should only ever have one girlfriend at a time. If you happened to marry your girlfriend, well, that was it – forever. Lovely man confirmed this to be right, even if he did laugh at the way that I explained it. "Who is Uncle Joe's girlfriend then?" I asked. Lovely man said it was a lady called Irene, who worked in a café. I was furious and jumped off my bed. I wanted to fight Uncle Joe, to hit him very hard or, at the very least, shout at him a very bad word like 'bloody'. (Dad said this word sometimes when he banged his finger with the hammer or hurt himself when he was mending the car.) I also felt really sad for Auntie June and thought that I would cheer her up by showing her that I was on her side.

Thankfully, by now, the crying had stopped, or at least the noisy crying had. Auntie June just kept blowing her nose and rubbing her eyes. She looked terrible. Mum had made her some of her magic tea that always made you feel better. "Why don't you come and live here with us?" I offered June. "You can sleep in my bed, if you like." She smiled at me, and then she looked at mum, who told me to go and play upstairs again. "I don't want to," I said. "It's boring up there. I want to stay down here with you." "Run along Julie," said mum. "Auntie June is just a bit sad and we are having a grown-ups talk." "About Uncle Joe and Irene?" I asked. Mum gasped, June nearly spat her tea out. "About Uncle Joe and who did you say?" Auntie June asked. "Irene," I said. "Uncle Joe's girlfriend, the one who works in the café." Mum got off her chair like lightning and ushered me upstairs, my little feet not touching the ground. It wasn't until some years later, when I was an adult myself, that I found out that I had been right. June had found out that Joe was having an affair. What she hadn't known, until that day, was with whom. He, of course, was denying it. I had somehow provided the missing jigsaw piece. I was right, or rather lovely man was right, once again, and when she confronted him with the name Irene, and the fact that this woman worked in a café, he confessed. They sorted their differences out and stayed together. I liked Uncle Joe even less from that day.

Lovely man told me later that night not to worry about what had happened that day. He explained that some people just didn't like the truth. Well, that was silly, wasn't it? He also said that your sins always find you out. I wasn't very sure what that meant, really, other than sin was a bad thing. It was mentioned a lot in nana's bible. Uncle Joe had obviously done some sin or something by having two girlfriends. Lovely man laughed a lot at what I thought. I liked making him laugh. It made his face all beautiful.

JULIE SAVAGE

6

HEALING NANA

The coldness came again several weeks later. My nana, dad's mum, who was by now my only living grandparent, took ill. Dad had come home early from work one day and I heard him asking Florrie next-door if she would look after us for a few hours while he went with mum to the hospital to see his mother. On overhearing this, I began to feel colder and colder and just knew that I had to go with them. Nana didn't like many people, but she loved me. She didn't like dad, her own son, very much, or mum. She loved me and my brother Mark, but she didn't like my little sister Alison much at all. How odd. Everyone loved Alison. She was so pretty to look at and she smiled all the time. She didn't ever frown like I did. Nana wasn't fussed on her at all; she preferred me, with my odd looks, my peculiar ways, and my strange behaviour. When I told dad that I wanted to go with them to the hospital, he said no, that hospital was no place for little girls. Mm. This was going to be tricky, I thought. Dad never, ever refused me anything, and his saying that I couldn't go just strengthened my resolve. I also knew that if I could just get to nana, and touch her, that I could make her better.

The coldness was getting worse. I devised a plan, and threw myself down in front of dad's car face down, arms and legs spread wide like a starfish, and cried. Not just a little insignificant cry, but a big gut-wrenching sob worthy of an Oscar. Mum came running out and asked what was wrong. I explained that dad wouldn't let me go to the hospital to see my nana. She tried several times to coax me, to pick me up, to get me indoors, but she was heavily pregnant, and unable to move me very far. Dad was adamant that I couldn't go. I was going to have to persevere for ages if he was to crack and change his mind. He started to get exasperated, and then annoyed with my naughty behaviour. I pulled out all the stops and wailed: "I love my nana, and if she dies," pointing at my parents, "then it will be your fault – and I shan't ever speak to either of you again. I will run away, if you go to the hospital without me." I had their attention now, so I continued my performance, saying: "I just need to see nana, I need to, to make her better." Dad sighed and said that although nana was poorly, she wasn't going to die, and that I would be able to see her when she was better and back home. "No!" I shouted. "You don't understand. Pneumonia is a killer!" This last statement seemed to stop them in their tracks. They looked at one another, and then at me. This gave me time to think about what I'd just said. Pneumonia: heck that must be something really bad if it kills you. I hoped that I would never get it. "Did you tell her it was pneumonia?" Dad asked mum. "Of course not," she replied. I saw my chance. "Please, pleeeaaase, Daddy. I'll be a good girl. Please let me come with you." He looked at mum. She shrugged, and the three of us got into the car and headed for the hospital.

It seemed to take ages to get to the hospital. Nana was in an old hospital, out of town, that specialised in chest conditions. She always seemed to have a bad chest – probably because she smoked Woodbine cigarettes every day. Once she had lit her cigarette, she left it in her mouth until it was finished. She would cough, sneeze, and pass wind and still, the cigarette would stay put between her lips. She didn't take it out of her mouth until it had burned down to the tip. It hung out of her mouth, even while she did her chores. She would clean the fire grate and wash the hearth with it hanging from her mouth. Often the cigarette ash would drop on whatever she was doing, but this didn't ever bother her. When baking, the ash would fall into pastry, Yorkshire pudding mix, and sometimes even cake mixture. Nobody dared to comment on this, of course. Nana was a scary woman, who could practically wither you with just a look.

The hospital was quite pleasant inside. Although it was old, the wards were bright and cheery. A line of beds either side of the ward, perhaps about 20 of them altogether, were in this long sunny room, and behind every other bed there were French doors. This meant that the staff could wheel the beds out onto patio areas, both sides of the ward, allowing patients, in whatever stage of illness, to have some fresh air each day. The nurse's desk was as you walked in, on the left of the room. Considering all the people in the room were quite poorly, the atmosphere felt cheerful. Dad stopped at the desk to ask the nurse on duty where his mother was. The nurse then took him, mum, and me to where the curtains were drawn around a bed, not far from the desk. Behind the curtains, in her bed, lay nana. She appeared to be asleep. She looked terrible. As I mentioned earlier, nana was never a good-looking woman, but that day, in that bed, she looked worse than I had ever seen anyone look.

My parents exchanged looks, and I knew that they were both shocked at how ill she looked. Dad placed a chair at nana's bedside for mum to sit on. He stood awkwardly at the end of the bed with his hands in his pockets. He was biting his lip. Nana was lying in bed, minus her teeth, which in itself wasn't unusual. She always preferred to leave them in a glass in her bathroom. Each and every day, she would change the water they were floating in; which was just as well, as us kids would often take them out of the glass when she wasn't close by and chase each other, threatening to bite each other's bums with them. Today her skin seemed really yellow, too. It matched the nightdress she was wearing: a sort of primrose, brushed nylon affair with daisies on it. Her breathing was really raspy, worse than usual, and there seemed to be a rattle coming from her chest. This was the first time in my life I had ever seen nana lying down, and she looked ready to die.

I went and stood at her bedside, at the opposite side to mum. I got hold of her hand – the hand that nobody ever seemed to hold, the hand that had delivered numerous good hidings in her time, the hand that most of us, as children, feared. She was a domineering woman, who was honest to the point of cruelty, foreboding and scary. She had an aura about her that was tangible. She was a short, heavy lady – 4'10" (cubed). Not your stereotypical grandmother, never affectionate or loving, she seldom seemed happy, but I loved her. I think I was the only one of her twenty odd grandchildren that did. I felt so connected, so linked to nana; we had an unexplainable bond. She never treated me like a child; we completely understood one another. She was fascinating. She would look into her coal fire and tell you who was going to visit her that day. I looked into that same fire, hundreds of times, and couldn't see anything other than coal, fire, and cinders. Her lotions, potions, and cure-alls were sought after by family and neighbours alike. Nana was a real anchor in the family, who didn't seem to need anything or anybody. So, why now, for the first time in all my five years, was I holding her hand? I don't know. I just knew that I had to; so I did.

Soon after I took hold of her hand, the coldness I had been feeling ceased. I started to feel warmer and warmer, and then my hand felt as though it was on fire. I could feel little static shocks in my fingers. This lovely warmth seemed to be coming from above my head; it was entering the top of my head, running down my neck, into my shoulders, and then down into my hands. I knew that this warmth was going into nana, and that this was what I was meant to be doing. I had a feeling of such peace; I felt special, as though this great happening was going to make a difference to her. Dad and mum were talking to each other in soft tones, but I was oblivious to what they were saying. I was so absorbed in this beautiful warmth that I seemed to be getting from somewhere. I stayed in the same position for a long time, right up until lovely man put his hands on my shoulders, and I knew then to stop. I felt somehow satisfied, that I had finished a job that I was meant to do. I knew in that moment that nana was going to be alright. She would get better soon, and our special bond, our unspoken link was forged. Sure enough, she made a quick recovery, and went home the very next week. This left the doctors and nurses who were looking after her a little perplexed. I was glad that I had insisted on going to see her. Well worth the dramatics, methinks.

7

DON'T JUDGE A BOOK BY ITS COVER

My life had changed in so many ways since my fifth birthday. Even so, I was just a child and hadn't quite grasped the concept of keeping things to myself. I said what I saw, told what I knew, and it didn't really occur to me that lovely man was invisible to everyone other than me. What I had noticed, though, was that dad and mum sometimes talked about my "funny ways". I knew this because there were times when I walked into the room that their conversations would stop awkwardly. I was naturally very astute, so I just knew that I had been their topic of discussion.

I was a kid that was always looking to find out things. I think that's supposed to be a good trait in children, but I think that I was just naturally nosey. One day, dad announced that he would have to go to the library. I really didn't know what a library was, but I was interested in finding out, so I asked if I could go along with him. As a self-taught mechanic, dad in his spare time tinkered with old cars. He would buy an old car, usually one that was ready for the scrap yard, and spend hours rebuilding and repairing it. He would then sell it, making a few extra pounds to go into the household kitty. He was poorly educated. (Nana reckoned it was because of the War, and nobody dared argue with her.) He was never able to spell properly and wasn't much of a reader either. But he was clever in lots of other ways. He had been working on a car this day and was trying to solve a problem with the starter motor. After all his attempts to rectify the problem had failed, he decided that there was nothing else for it: he was off to the library to borrow a workshop manual. Me in tow!

I loved the library. It was awesome; so lovely and warm (that in itself was always a bonus for me), full of interesting books. It was an old building, with polished wood floors that smelled like our school hall. The peace and quiet was amazing. I loved it! Dad headed over to the motoring section and I went over to a corner where another girl a little older than me sat reading. The books were all different shapes and sizes, and they stood on the shelves like colourful soldiers all facing the same way. I chose a book from the shelf: it was about a farm. I sat on a little chair, at the same table as the other girl, and opened the book. I began looking at the pictures. It was really well illustrated – a lovely book. The pages were quite big and showed wonderful scenes of lush green fields, heavenly blue skies, and a really jolly-looking farmer, who had red cheeks that matched his shiny red tractor. This seemed such a lovely farm and I day-dreamed about living on it. Even the animals seemed happy and contented.

Once dad had found what he was looking for, he came to collect me. I asked him if I could take the farm book home. He explained to me that if you borrowed a book from the library then you had to look after it carefully. He went on to explain that the book would also have to be returned within two weeks. That seemed fair to me. I was more than happy with that arrangement; it meant that I would get to come back in two weeks and choose another book. So with our books under our arms, we made our way to the lady behind the big desk in the centre of the room. She took our books and then asked dad who the farm book was for. "My daughter here," said dad, looking down at me. "And how old is she?" she asked, talking about me as though I were invisible. "I'm five," I said quite confidently. "Oh you can't have this book dear," she said with a patronising look on her face. "This book is from the age seven and over section." Turning to dad, she added: "She won't be able to read this." She further justified her spitefulness. "Let's go and look in the infants' section," she said, adding insult to injury. "I want this book," I said. "I can read it easily," I lied. She didn't seem at all convinced. I didn't like her; she had a yellow twinset on that matched her yellow teeth and her lips looked tight and thin like those of lizards. "Right then, dear," she said, looking at dad as if to communicate to him that I was about to show myself up. "If you can read this book to me, I will let you take it home." Oh God, now I'd done it; my big mouth had got me in trouble again. I cleared my throat convincingly. My hands were clammy and my little heart was beating so loud, that I felt sure that she could hear it. Dad looked at me expectantly. She opened the book and pointed with her index finger to the first word on the first page.

Enter my saviour – lovely man. In true Superman fashion, he had come to save my day once again. I almost wanted to laugh out loud. I didn't laugh, though. Instead, I started to repeat what lovely man was saying, reading the words that the librarian was pointing to; slowly at first, but as my confidence grew, I read faster and faster. At the end of the second page, she halted me. "Fine...fine. That's fine dear," she said, only this time, not so smugly. Her face was all pink and she was fidgeting nervously. "That's a bright little spark you've got there," she said to dad. "Mm," he muttered, looking puzzled. I was thrilled! The farmyard book was mine for a whole two weeks!

In September that year mum gave birth to my brother Andrew. He was gorgeous – like a Tiny Tears doll with personality. I really liked Andrew. I was allowed to stay up a little later than Mark and Alison to help bathe him. And for being so helpful, I was told to sit back in the chair while mum surrounded me with cushions and put baby Andrew into my arms. I felt so special – I was holding him all by myself. I noticed that night a beautiful yellow glow around Andrew's little head – just like the glow that shone around baby Jesus in the crib at Christmas time. That moment was magical. I felt that our family was complete. My complete happiness seemed to summon lovely man, who sat at my side while looking down on baby Andrew. He told me all about this new addition to our family, about what he would be like when he was older, and told me that when he grew up, Andrew would go into the Army. He seemed to know lots of things that were going to happen in the future. He could tell, he said, that Andrew would be loving, giving, and kind, and that he would probably have to wear glasses for most of his childhood.

Naturally I relayed these things to dad and mum, who kept glancing at one another as I repeated, parrot fashion, what I was hearing from lovely man. "Who is telling you all this, Julie?" dad asked. "Oh, just my friend," I replied. "Where is this friend now?" he continued. "Just here," I said, pointing with my chin to the side that lovely man was at, while I continued to hold baby Andrew. Dad wanted to know if this friend was a girl, woman, boy, man. I told him that he was a man, who only came to see me sometimes. "Who is he? Where is he from? What's his name?" asked mum. The lovely man just winked, and then smiled at me and said: "Just tell them I'm normal." I misheard him and told her: "He is lovely, he's just Norman." "Oh, right," dad said. "Norman, eh? Norman." So from that day, my lovely man became known as Norman – our Julie's Norman. My Norman never was, and seldom is, wrong about anything. My dad came to recognize this in the years that followed, and quite often would refer to him as Norman Wisdom.

Norman wasn't the stereotypical unseen friend that some children seem to adopt at a pre-school age. I don't think that I ever insisted that a place be set at the table for him, nor did I blame him for spilled drinks and other acts of clumsiness on my part. He doesn't have blue hair, pointy ears, or red eyes. My overall behaviour as a child was quite normal, apparently. No night terrors or irrational fears marred my childhood, and I am pretty sure that I wasn't ritualistic or withdrawn. I mention all of these traits because these are just some of the things that sometimes occur when a child has an imaginary friend. My invisible friend has never been imaginary – he's very real to me. He looks the same today as he did when he first appeared to me all those years ago. The only weird thing about him is that he hasn't ever aged. He is tall, dark, and handsome, and if I had to say that he resembled someone, then it would still have to be one of the disciples in nana's old Bible. Norman is patient and mild mannered, always calm – he never loses control. His patience and tolerance have been sorely tested over the years he has spent nurturing me. I know I can be difficult at times, but he appears unperturbed by this. I am often asked if he is my Angel. I honestly don't know. He has protected me from harm on numerous occasions, forewarning me of danger. He helps me avoid hurtful situations if I am meant to avoid them, yet allows me to live my life in this world. I refer to him as my guide, and I feel that he helps me assist and guide others on a daily basis. Without him, I have no connection to the afterlife or the colourful spirits that I work with as a medium. He is a gatekeeper, a confidant, my mentor, my teacher, my guide. He is with me when I need or want him to be. I suppose with all this knowledge and wisdom to hand, I should be some sort of oracle. Not so! I acknowledge that I have a truly special gift, an ability to tap into something or somewhere inside of me that can access amazing things. Having studied other psychics and mediums, I have, I think, little in common with their mode of behaviour, work practice, or way of life. I'm just a normal woman with an extra radio channel in my head, some crazy wiring, and, sometimes, some unexplained abilities. I am, as an adult, very rational and logical thinking, born out of having to deal with unusual situations in my childhood, I think. Some of my past experiences have been funny, some sad, some happy, but most of them strange; and I conclude from this that this is just the path I was meant to walk. I hope the things that I have learnt have made me a better person. It wasn't easy being psychic as a child; my feelings of love, happiness, fear, anger, injustice have always been profound, and there are times that I haven't dealt with situations as I should have. But, I figure that if I was selected to carry these abilities, then they are there for the using. I just didn't always use them wisely as a child.

8

POWER

I accept that I can influence things; I'm just not sure why or how. I just know that if I want something badly enough, then I usually get it, and that positive thoughts generate positive things. Likewise, negative thoughts can be quite dangerous. My first experience of this was when I was seven years old. In my first year at junior school, I sat next to a boy called Nicholas Wilson. I was drawn to Nicholas probably because nobody else was. He was a bit scruffy and often smelled of urine. He told me that he shared his bed with his 3 brothers, one of which was a serial bed-wetter. His clothes were ill-fitting and grubby – his mum obviously hadn't mastered the art of ironing. Nicholas had hosted the dreaded head lice a few times and this had earned him the title of 'Nitty Nicholas'. I liked Nicholas Wilson. He was kind and funny, very bright, and I felt so sorry for him. He wore the same coat all year round: a thin navy jacket that seldom kept the wind or rain from beating his skinny body. Nick had no friends at school and spent playtime alone most days. The only time he was included in team games was either at the teachers' insistence or if there was no-one else to make up a team. Despite all this, he was hard-working in class, could draw just about anything, and was well behaved, never wanting to draw attention to himself. Being a little odd myself, I think I identified with Nicholas, and although I had no shortage of friends, I really enjoyed his company.

One particular day, our teacher, Mrs Kane, was off sick. So, after morning assembly, we were told that we would be taught for the day by the dreaded Mr Hardy. A feeling of impending doom seemed to accompany this information. Mr Hardy was a scary, scary man: tall and thin, he sported a too thick for his lips moustache that matched his too thick for his eyes eyebrows. His expression was always thunderous. He was the only male teacher in the school apart from the headmaster, and it was up to him to say grace in the dinner hall before our lunch. You could hear a pin drop when he spoke. Nobody dared speak while Mr Hardy was speaking. You can imagine the rumours that circulated the school about him, probably due to the fact that he was quick to punish any child from any classroom if they appeared the least bit insubordinate. His cupboard apparently held shoes, straps, canes and rulers, to be used as he saw fit. When he scanned the hall, I found it best not to give him eye contact. It was almost as if by looking at you, he was searching your soul for bad behaviour. We paraded to his classroom across the school yard, in twos holding hands. As I held Nick's hand, I could sense how nervous he was. "Don't worry, Nick," I said. "We'll be okay if we just do our work and keep quiet." Fortunately, we were able to pick our own desks. So Nick and I sat together at the edge of the classroom, near the door.

Mr Hardy began the lesson by pointing out his classroom rules: no talking, no fidgeting or breathing unless necessary, just heads down and work hard. He set us work in our arithmetic books. Everyone just got on with their number work. The silence was eerie. The classroom was Victorian and the high windows let in little light, which meant that the room lights were always on. The floors were wooden and the desks were old with inkwells in them. Unlike Mrs Kane's room, there were no bright pictures or charts gracing the walls; just a blackboard, his desk, the torture cupboard, and us kids.

Behind us sat Christine and David Johnson. They were cousins who lived across the road from each other. Christine was beautiful; her long dark hair always worn in a perfect ponytail with pretty ribbons. She went to a dance class and had perfect poise. I thought she acted like a prima donna. I didn't like her at all. She always had the biggest, reddest apple for break-time, and she would eat most of it then give the core to one of her friends to finish off. Some of these stupid girls saw her apple core as divine fruit. It got on my nerves that everything in the class seemed to centre on her: she was the class monitor, the leading voice in the choir, and it seemed that she always had to play the lead in the school play. The teachers obviously loved her. I thought of her as cold. She always got to be the team captain whenever we played games. This meant that she got to pick who was on her team. So, depending on whether she liked you or not that day, you were made to feel special or useless. Her cousin David was a beautiful boy, with his thick dark hair, his big brown eyes, and an all-year tan. They obviously came from the perfect family. David was a brilliant sportsman who could run faster, jump higher, and bat harder than any other boy in the class. He was also big headed, vain, and a bully.

Christine and David sat together that day because Mr Hardy had ordered that boys and girls were to pair up; and lets face it, neither one of the Johnsons would deign to sit with anyone other than each other. Unfortunately, they sat behind Nicholas and me. The big clock ticked away the minutes as we worked industriously in our math books. The silence was only interrupted when Nicholas put his hand up and requested that he may be excused to go to the toilet. "No boy, you should have gone after assembly!" horrible Hardy replied. Nick's cheeks reddened, he put his head down and continued to work. I nudged Nick when Mr Hardy's back was turned and made a face that showed what I thought of this horrible man. Nick just smiled. A little while later, I became aware that Nicholas couldn't seem to sit still – it was evident that he really did need to go to the toilet soon. My own tummy started to ache for him. All of a sudden, Nick made a dash for the door, running out of the classroom towards the cloakroom. This brave run, unfortunately, was a little too late and a wet trail of urine followed poor Nick's steps, indicating his poor bladder control. Christine Johnson looked on the floor and cried out: "Ugh, sir, there's water or something on the floor." Her cousin started to laugh, which encouraged his sheep-like friends to do the same. Mr Hardy shouted "enough," which was sufficiently loud to silence everyone again, and then marched out of the room following the trail of pee. Christine tapped me on my shoulder. I turned around and saw the smirk appear on her face as she said: "What are you sitting with him for? You'll start to smell like him soon." I told her to shut up and gave her a withering look. Mr Hardy returned to the class with Nicholas, who looked so embarrassed, his head bent in shame. A slight titter of laughter broke out and Mr Hardy's head spun around looking for the source. This seemed to do the trick; order was restored. I put my hand on Nick's skinny back and mouthed at him not to worry. He just looked at me, such sadness in him.

Soon after it was playtime, and when the bell rang, we put our chairs under our desks, closed our books and filed out into the school yard like little soldiers. I stayed at Nick's side, sensing that he might need my support. Norman was there too, so something was about to happen. Sure enough, we had just got out into the yard, when David Johnson and his entourage approached us. These pathetic little followers who only laughed when he laughed and at what he deemed funny. David planted himself before us, looked Nicholas up and down several times, a look of pure malevolence on his face. He then started to chant "Pissy Pants, Pissy Pants". The other boys joined in. "Get lost," I said. Poor Nick just put his head down. This seemed to incite David and he spat: "You're disgusting; you should be made to wear nappies. You're a smelly get!" I shouted to David to leave Nicholas alone. "You shut up you. You smell like him," he replied, looking me up and down. Nick's head shot up and he said: "Leave her alone, she does not smell." David then started pushing Nick in the chest chanting: "Pissy Pants, Pissy Pants". The other boys joined in with this cruel mantra. "Shut up, all of you," I screamed. This alerted Christine, who jogged over with her friends in hot pursuit. "What's going on, Dave?" she asked. "Oh, the scruffs are getting upset," he replied. "He stinks that much that we shouldn't have to sit in the same class as him. From now on everyone should call him Pissy Pants." I was furious. Nick, however, was scared, and his little skinny knees started to tremble. David picked up on this and, pointing to Nick's legs, said: "Oh, look he's gonna piss himself again." Everyone started to laugh. David, encouraged by this, started again with this horrible chant. I started to feel more and more annoyed until I felt as though my head would explode. I stared hard at David Johnson, focusing really hard on his lovely cruel face. I realized that I couldn't actually hear him; I could see his lips moving but I couldn't hear anything at all. I stared and stared at him until all at once his nose began to bleed. Blood started pouring from his nose, gushing like a tap onto his pristine school jumper, flowing so fast that the girls around him started screaming. The look of alarm on his face was incredible, he was scared. His friends started to back away from him, fearing that they might be splashed with his blood. Christine also screamed, and then ran for a teacher, while David fell to his knees and bent over allowing the blood from his nose to form a red pool in the school yard. Nicholas looked on transfixed. "That's what you get!" I said. "Now leave us alone." I walked away and Nick followed me. I felt scared and really drained at what had just happened. This little drama was the talk of the class for the rest of the day. Everyone left Nick and me alone, and I felt thankful for being ignored. At lunch time one of Christine's friends came over to tell me that Christine blamed me for David's nose bleed and that she was going to get me after school. I ignored her. Nick was concerned, but I told him not to worry and that I wasn't finished with her either. I shadowed Nicholas all day, trying to make sure that he was kept from the cruelties of the school yard. As we sat in our last lesson that day, I prepared to teach Christine Johnson a lesson she wouldn't forget.

After school, I was ready for the big show down; not really knowing what was to come. While I was putting my coat on in the cloakroom, I noticed that Christine and her friends were standing together in a pack, waiting for me. I walked very straight towards her. She seemed a little surprised at this. "Go on then, get me!" I said. "You made our David's nose bleed," she said threateningly. "So what!" I said. "He's just a bully like you." I was quite scared at this point, but was determined not to show it. She then launched herself at me, catching me unaware. I fell to the ground and she pounced on top of me and started pulling my hair. I didn't fight back. I just told her "stop it, stop it now or you'll be sorry." My unwillingness to participate in this cat-fight just seemed to spur her on and she began slapping and punching me. All at once, I couldn't feel anything, or hear what she was saying. I just concentrated very hard on a picture of her face in my mind and imagined her nose bleeding, too. Then it did! It started to drip blood the same way that David's had. Her hand flew to her face trying to stem the flow. A useless act, really. I got up, looked around at the spectators, her friends, my classmates, then down at her kneeling on the floor trying helplessly to stop the nosebleed, and I said just one word – I said: "See!"

I often think about that particular childhood incident and wonder that if the nosebleeds were caused by me, was I bad for making them happen or good for protecting the very innocent Nicholas Wilson. My nana had a saying – "a hex only sticks on the guilty". This event ensured that I wasn't ever victimized again. The power of the mind is a wonderful thing.

9

JOHNNY EMBASSY IS NOT DEAD!

Some of the most profound psychic experiences in my childhood took place at my nana's house. Nana lived a few miles away from us, in a council-owned house that she had lived in since it was built in 1920. The house was always cosy and warm. It had a coal fire that she lit every morning come rain, hail, or shine. Her house was situated on a road that was quite wide and often busy. The houses in the neighbourhood all looked the same and, although it was only a council estate, most of the front gardens were well tended, lush, and green. It was a friendly neighbourhood, and nana was well known. The front gate to her house creaked constantly, despite everyone's efforts with oil and grease to quieten it. The gate also had a strong spring on it which ensured its closure once you were inside. In the front garden there was a large array of rose bushes, all different in colour and size. Nana loved roses, and each of these bushes marked something special: a person, an event, or a particular memory of hers. The front door was seldom used. Her visitors (mostly family), once through the creaking gate, walked the long path along the side of the house, round the corner to the back door which was always open. Nana was always in. She hardly ever went out – she was at her happiest at home. Her son, my uncle Harold, lived with her. He hadn't ever married, so she was hardly ever alone. Harold was lovely – our favourite uncle. He liked going to the pub and smoking.

The house had a warm, safe feeling about it. This was the house in which nana had given birth to her children – the house where she had also found two of them dead in their little beds. It smelled of Sunday roasts, Yorkshire puddings, and potatoes. I would often stay at nana's in the school holidays. I slept in her bed, on the side where granddad had once slept. The old feather mattress still had a slight indentation caused by the years he had slept in this bed. Nana taught me lots of things: how to cook, knit, and sew. She also helped me to understand things about me that nobody else could. We were alike – two of a kind she used to say. It was at nana's that I first experienced death.

Across the road from nana's lived a young family with small children and a beautiful golden Labrador dog called Brandy. They hadn't lived there very long, but nana said they were a nice family. Brandy was a lovely dog. She was only a few years old and was quite boisterous and playful, but so friendly. She used to stand behind their gate, wagging her tail and barking at anyone passing. The children in the family loved her and she adored them. I used to watch them playing with her in the front garden. They were sometimes a little rough with her, but she seldom got vexed. She would just yelp and walk away, her tail still wagging. I sometimes stroked her through their gate. She was one of the few dogs that I wasn't afraid of.

One day I was swinging on nana's gate, waiting for Uncle Harold to come home from work. He worked on a building site and was always dusty when he came home. He would pick me up off the gate as if I were no weight at all, and ask how his favourite girl was. Harold didn't ever learn to drive so he walked everywhere, usually whistling as he went. Nana was putting the final touches to tea and had reminded me that it wouldn't be long before he was home. So I took my usual place on the gate, looking down the road waiting for him. I looked across the road to where Brandy lived and felt a strange feeling of panic when I saw that their gate was open. It was never open, something was not right! While I was thinking about this I saw Brandy. She came running from the back of the house, along the side path, through the open gate, and straight into the road without stopping. She ran into the path of an oncoming car. It was impossible for either the dog or the driver to stop and they collided with a bang. The car skidded after it hit Brandy, and as it passed her, I noticed that she was lying inert on the road. The driver, a middle aged man got out of the car and put his hand to his mouth, saying repeatedly: "Oh my god! Oh my god!" He walked over and squatted down by Brandy who was laid very, very still. A nearby neighbour who had witnessed the whole thing whilst he was gardening, told the driver where the dog belonged, and the driver made his way to Brandy's house.

Poor Brandy. I was in shock, I think. Not knowing what to do, I just stared at where Brandy was lying and I started to cry. I stopped, however, when I saw what looked like an identical Brandy stand up from out of the lying down one, and happily trot away. I ran into nana's kitchen. "Nana, Nana! Brandy over the road has been knocked over and some of her is lying in the road but another 'see through' part of her has just got up and left the bones and skin, and has run away. Nana got me to stand still and repeat, slowly, what I'd just said. I did, and, after listening, she explained to me that Brandy's body must be dead, but that the part of her that I'd witnessed get up and leave her dead body was her soul. Nana said that everyone had a soul and that if we were good, then our souls would be good, and that when it was our time to die, we would all leave our bones behind but that good souls would go to heaven. I figured that this made perfect sense.

Later that night, at bedtime after our cocoa, nana and I put our hands together, closed our eyes and said prayers to help get Brandy to heaven. "Brandy was a lovely dog, so she was sure to get a good bed in paradise," Nana said. From that day, death became no big deal to me. It seemed that that wasn't the case for most other people, though. A fact that I discovered on the day that Johnny Embassy came to see me.

Johnny Embassy was my name for my Uncle John. He was married to my dad's sister, Dora. We didn't see much of him, really; mostly Christmas time and days when he came to nana's with his Embassy coupons. He smoked Embassy cigarettes, went to the local Embassy club (a workingmen's club), and saved Embassy coupons which he would bring to nana's. She would buy them off him for a few shillings, save them up, and then order goods from the Embassy Coupon Catalogue. I don't think he took much notice of his nieces and nephews. I don't think he even knew our individual names. He just called everyone "pet". I liked it when he came, because nana would let me help her count the coupons that he brought. We would count them into piles of 100, and then put elastic bands around piles of 1000. I was good with my numbers, and nana never needed to check that my counting was right. I was clever for my years, nana said.

It was a day in spring shortly after Brandy was knocked over, and I was joined at nana's by my brothers, sister, and several cousins. Apparently, the grown-ups were going to a funeral – whatever that was. It must be important, though, I thought, because my dad and the men in the family were all wearing suits. The ladies were very smart, too – all in black, my favourite colour. Because nana didn't go out, it was her job to look after us kids. We would, of course, all behave well for her. She was very strict and would clip ears, smack legs, and punish bad behaviour. Most of her grandchildren were afraid of her. She didn't like most of them very much, and because Mark and I were her favourites, we were treated totally differently to any of the others. Nobody ever dared comment on this in front of her, though. She was a scary little woman! So, on this sunny day, we were all told to play out in the garden together.

Nana's back garden was nearly all lawn. There were a few border flowers here and there which added a bit of colour. I thought that the most interesting part of the garden was at the bottom of the lawn. Here was a vegetable patch, nana's herb garden, and in the corner, an old disused greenhouse. The greenhouse had an aluminium frame and had been all glass. Several of the panes were missing now, and the door was permanently wedged open. I loved it in there. Nana used to call it my "crystal palace". I spent hours in there. It was always nice and warm; which was great for me because I still felt the 'coldness' often. Inside it were all my treasures: bottles of perfume that I had made from rose petals, my little china tea-set for when I was entertaining, lots of old jars, coffee, jam and meat paste jars that I had stacked neatly on a shelf for when I wanted to play shops, a book and pen for my writing practise, and a few old ornaments that I had taken from home, just to make this special place my own. So when I was bored of playing with my cousins this particular day, I wandered off into the crystal palace for some peace and quiet. I wouldn't let anyone in with me and nana told the other kids to play with each other and to leave me alone.

It was particularly interesting in the crystal palace that day. Harold had taken me for a walk the previous Sunday and had helped me collect some tadpoles from the pond we had gone to. We had carried them home and nana had given me an old plastic bowl to put them in. I just loved watching them swim about. I had also collected a caterpillar the previous day, and that was in one of my jars with some leaves. Harold had put some holes in the jar top so that it had air. I was quite absorbed in my nature project and watching the tadpoles. So much so, that I didn't notice Johnny Embassy come in. I jumped when I heard him say "Hello, pet." He was smart, too. He had a lovely grey suit on, a white shirt that was open-necked, and his usual unruly hair was combed back. "What you up to?" he asked. "I'm just watching my tadpoles," I said, and carried on looking in the bowl. I felt a little uncomfortable – I wasn't use to Johnny Embassy talking to me. "They will change soon," he said. "And before long they will grow legs and turn into frogs." I already knew this; Harold had told me. I also knew that they would have to be put back in the pond, too. I nodded and felt that I ought to say something, so I asked: "Do you want me to count some coupons for you?" "No thanks, pet," he said. "I'm not saving them now." "Oh," I said, and must have looked a little puzzled because he went on to say, "I have left my coupons in a shoebox in my wardrobe, all ready for Auntie Dora to give them to your nana. I've also put in the ten shillings I owe her." "Oh," I said again. He patted me on the head and said I was a good girl then left. I noticed as he went that he had no socks or shoes on. Strange!

I thought that if Johnny Embassy was back at nana's, then my mum and dad must be too. So I tidied up, put everything back in its place and came out of the greenhouse, just in time to see the grown-ups arriving. Down the path came Auntie Dora and my mum, who had her arm around Dora's shoulder. Dora's head was bent and she was walking slower than usual. Dad and the rest of the family followed behind looking really sad. Why wasn't anyone smiling? I followed them into nana's. The cousins and my siblings, by this time, were playing in the shed.

Nana had made two teapots full of tea and had set the table, which was in her living room, with all sorts of goodies. Like a party tea. There were sausage rolls and a large pie, some cakes she had baked earlier that morning (I had helped of course), and an array of pickles and sauces. I realised that it was a special occasion when I noticed that nana had taken her best tea-set out of the china cabinet and was using it to pour the hot strong tea into. Well if this was a party, what was everyone looking so sad about? I wandered into the kitchen where mum was taking clean tea-towels off plates, revealing sandwiches. "What's wrong with everyone?" I enquired. Mum looked at nana and then down at me and said: "Everyone is a little bit sad today, Julie, so be a good girl and be quiet." "Why?" I asked. She then told me that Uncle John had died and that everyone had just been to church to send him up to heaven and that that had made everyone a little sad. "Why though," I asked. She sighed and said: "Because we won't ever see him again." "Why?" I asked. "I've told you," she said a little exasperated by now. "He has gone to live with the angels in heaven." "Hah!" I declared. "You're wrong, mum." "Shush!" she said, and frowned as she went on. "Auntie Dora is very upset so you must be quiet and stop asking questions. Be a good girl and carry these sandwiches to the table with me." This was ridiculous; what was she talking about? Johnny Embassy dead? No way was he dead. I had been talking to him just a little while ago.

As I carried the sandwiches into the room, I noticed how sad Auntie Dora really was. She was sitting in Harold's chair, just staring into the fire. Her eyes were all red from crying and she had a handkerchief in her hand that she kept biting on. I wanted to make her feel better, so I went over to her, stood in front of her, and said, in a somewhat informative tone: "Auntie Dora, Uncle Johnny is not dead!" I had spoken quietly, thinking that it was best that only she should hear this first. She stopped staring into the fire, looked at me and said: "What?" "Uncle John isn't in heaven yet; he was in the greenhouse with me earlier." She looked puzzled, so I went on. "He had a nice grey suit on, no tie and his feet must have been freezing coz he had no socks and shoes on. He told me that he has left his coupons in a shoe box with ten shillings that he owes nana, and you are to give them to her." She gasped and then started to cry again. I think mum must have realised that I had said something, for she marched towards me, grabbed my hand, and led me quickly into the kitchen. I burst into tears. I didn't know why; probably because seeing Dora sad had made me sad, too. Nana sat me down in the kitchen and ran me a glass of water from the tap. She told me to sip it slowly. Dad came into the kitchen and I cried louder. He put his arm around me, and as he did, I felt him mouth something to nana over my head. "She can't help it, Bill" nana said. "Nor can she stop it. She sees them like I do. Don't worry she'll be fine." I was fine. Totally fine. I was crying because I sensed everyone else's sadness. I wasn't crying for Johnny Embassy. I knew he was alright. He had just left his bones behind. He was sure to be fine. I think I learned soon after this incident that it was best to just keep quiet about some things.

JULIE SAVAGE

10
LUCKY 7

When I was six years old, we moved house again. Mum had never really settled in Stockton, so was eager to move. Dad was, once again, working at Sparks – the large bakery that he had first worked at when he left school. This bakery supplied all of their local Sparks shops. It was a large company. Some of the Sparks shops had properties attached to them that also belonged to the company, and this was how we came to move. Dad enquired, was offered, and accepted a huge flat above one of their shops in Norton. Norton was only about two miles from Stockton, but it was nicer – much nicer. The flat was spacious: it had three lovely big bedrooms; most of the rooms were bright too – each room had nice big windows. There was obviously no garden, too, which was great for dad and mum, who hated gardening anyway. And, being above a parade of shops, there was always something to see or do. I made lots of nice new friends in the neighbourhood and in my new school, and enjoyed the time that I lived there.

Visits from Norman continued. He still endeavoured to educate me, answering all my questions, and explaining the whys and wherefores in my little life. I was a happy little girl despite the recent change and the continuous unexplainable events that occurred. The first of which was not long after we moved there, shortly after my seventh birthday – 25th November 1968. I felt even more grown up now that I was seven. I was unbearably bossy to my siblings, forcing them to play schools which allowed me to play teacher or shops, where I always had to be the shopkeeper. I was a control freak, even at that young age. I loved them all though and considered myself just motherly, whether they liked it or not.

Baby Andrew was, by now, toddling around and, because we had a coal fire, mum would put her big fireguard around it each day. This fireguard was placed around the hearth and it had a front and sides. The sides had hooks on them which were looped through other hooks on the walls either side of the fireplace. It was huge and only mum and dad could move it. This fireguard was multi-purposed: it aired our clothes, kept the kids safe from the fire, and provided me with something to lean against when I was cold, which was most of the time.

For my last birthday, Auntie May had bought me some lovely nylon panties – very different to the navy blue or white cotton ones that I was used to wearing. I felt even more grown up in these big girls' panties. They had lovely little frills on them, and I couldn't wait for them to be washed so that I could wear them again. I was wearing these lovely panties the night of my accident.

I had been playing alone in my bedroom while dad and mum bathed and fed the rug rats. I had by then realised, that if I played quietly and out of the way, they might forget I was still up and forget to put me to bed. I also figured that if I pretended not to be hungry when mum made supper, I got to stay up for a bit longer. I would say, just as my bedtime was announced, that I was hungry now and, usually, she would make me some tea and toast that I could eat with her and dad while the others were in bed. I'm sure that they knew exactly what I was doing. After all, I was the eldest and it was only fair that I should be allowed to stay up later than the others.

This particular night, I went along into the lounge, playing for time while mum was putting the kids to bed. Dad had taken the fireguard away from the fire to put the final shovel of coal on for the night. As usual, I was cold. So I went and stood against the hearth with my back to the fire. As always, the heat of the fire warmed my bones and I lifted my skirt up to let the fire warm my bum. It was okay to do this; mum often did it. I looked over at the television. Some variety show was on. It was good. Lovely dancing girls with feathers were high kicking on a glass staircase then Bruce Forsythe came on telling jokes. What happened next seemed to happen in slow motion. I was watching the television and I forgot that the fireguard wasn't there. I went to lean back against it and lost my balance. I fell into the fire in a sitting position. I felt a searing pain bite into the tops of my legs. Luckily, Dad heard me scream. He was on his way up the stairs from the coalhouse with a scuttle full of coal. He came running in, followed closely by mum. He pulled me by my arm out of the fire, picked me up, and ran along into the bathroom. Mum kept saying "What's happened? What's happened?" Fortunately, the bath hadn't been emptied from earlier when the rug rats had been bathed, and the water, by this time, had cooled considerably. I got a shock when dad plunged me into it – clothes and all – then proceeded to run even more cold water in. I started to shake violently. I don't know whether it was shock or the coldness of the water that caused this. The pain from the burns on my legs was horrendous. Mum sat with me, waist high in water, with a towel around my shoulders, rubbing my arms and cradling my head as I cried. Dad came back into the bathroom with his coat on and his car keys, and announced that he was taking me to hospital. I started to cry louder not wanting to go to hospital. I was so scared. He picked me out of the bath, wrapped me in a blanket, and carried me down to the car.

He took me to the accident and emergency department at the local hospital, who referred me to another hospital further away that had a specialist burns unit. It was there that a nurse and doctor painstakingly removed pieces of charred nylon (the remnants of my panties) out of my legs with tweezers. They sprayed the backs of my thighs with 'magic skin' to protect my sore legs. They then dressed them and put large bandages on before I could go home. I hadn't walked since the accident and these big bandages hampered me. So dad picked me up carefully, his arm under the back of my knees, and we went home. In the car on the way home, he told me how brave I had been, and told me that a nurse would be coming to see me each day to change the bandages until my legs were better. This meant that I had to stay off school, but I was far too exhausted to care. It was very late when we got back home and it was quiet when we got in. The television programmes had finished and mum was sitting, waiting for us. My legs were so sore that I had to go to sleep on my tummy. I had a fitful night and was aware, several times, of mum and dad coming in to the room to check on me.

The district nurse came the next day and every day after that to dress my legs. As she removed my dressings I would cry out in pain. I had to lay on my front and always had to have either a pillow or a cushion to hold on to. After about ten days, I had to go back to the hospital and see a different doctor to the one that I'd seen the night of the accident. He removed my dressings and thoroughly examined my legs. There was a long mirror in his room and I asked if I could see what my legs looked like. I got a shock when I saw how they were. The skin on the back of my upper thighs was a peculiar colour: it was purple and all puckered and funny, a bit like mum's quilted dressing gown. There were little black bits amongst all this horrible burned flesh. My legs were lumpy, bumpy, and ugly. The doctor said that he was happy with how I was healing. I certainly wasn't! He decided it would be better to leave my dressings off and let some air get to my legs. He sprayed some more magic skin on them and gave dad a prescription to get our own tin. This had to be sprayed onto my legs twice a day. It was good stuff, he said, and it protected against infection. My dad asked if my legs would heal back to normal and the doctor looked doubtful. "I don't think this little girl will be wearing mini skirts any time soon," I remember him saying. "As long as she's alright," dad reasoned, "then that won't matter." We left the hospital and, as we did, I smarted as the cold December air hit my bandage free legs. I don't know what felt worse: burning or freezing.

I was really upset at the prospect of my legs staying as they were, and when Norman visited me later that night, I told him as much. "Don't worry," he said. "I'll get some healing sent down for you." He did too. Each night at bedtime, I would lie on my tummy and wait for my healing. My legs would start to feel tingly – like pins and needles. These tingles would run up and down my legs. This experience felt wonderful and, although my legs were still very sore, I couldn't feel anything other than numbness while this was happening. I knew that my legs would be fixed in no time. They were! A year after the accident, I had no scars, skin puckering, or discolouration at all. It was as though the accident had never happened. I was seven years old. Perhaps this was what the grown-ups meant when they said "Lucky Seven!" I certainly had been lucky.

11

VIBES

I have always been strangely particular about the vibes of things. This began in my childhood. I was always touching and feeling things to see how they made me feel. I could differentiate between a good or bad vibe on most things: what I ate and drank, the toys I had, and, particularly, the clothes I wore. Feelings were very important to me. I have always loved clothes and have always known that certain items of clothing are lucky for me, while certain things are not. This must sound really bizarre; so let me try to explain. I believe that everything has a vibe – an aura. Inanimate objects have vibes and living things and people have auras. An aura is an energy field that surrounds us. It's around two to six inches wide, and it is more apparent around our heads and shoulders. Our own energy field, it is usually only visible to very intuitive people. Our auras can be affected by how we are feeling and they can quite often change colour. For those of us lucky enough to be able to see them, we can determine mood and character by looking at someone's aura. The aura will give indications of someone's mood, emotions, worries, even health problems. I've always thought of the aura as a portable mood detector. When an aura looks flat or grey around someone, it usually depicts that the person concerned is a little troubled, tired, or depressed. A spiky aura can indicate mischief or ill-temper. When we are happy and well, our auras glow. If there is a need for healing, then an aura will usually show a mist or grey area near the part of the body that needs healing. Someone with a headache will have a mass of grey around his or her head, usually.

I have always been very aware of my own aura; so much so that I refused to ever wear a hat as a child. Any hat made me feel as though my head was being pushed into my neck. I also hated having my hair done; this made me feel as if my personal space was being invaded and that, too, affected my aura. Whatever I wore seemed to affect my aura, too. My first recollection of this was when I was five, when dad and mum took me to get a new winter coat. They found me a beautiful pale blue coat with matching scarf and, nightmare of all nightmares, a hat! The hat and scarf were part of the whole ensemble and the nice lady in the department store decided that I really would suit this hat. Ha! If she could catch me to try it on. I took off, running around the children's wear department like an Olympian to avoid trying it on. There I went, weaving between fixtures and rails until she gave up the chase. Dad and mum bought me the coat which was parcelled up along with the scarf and hat. Needless to say, the hat never came out of the bag.

Obviously, at this age, mum chose my clothes. But even then she would ask me if I liked what she was about to buy for me. It gave me the chance to feel the vibe of it, and decide whether I liked the vibe or not. I remember I liked to wear the same clothes repeatedly; the clothes I felt lucky or happy in. Usually, if I was told to wear something that I didn't want to, something would happen to me: a rip, a tear, an accident on some occasions. Black was always my favourite colour. Sometimes, grown-ups on finding this out would frown at me. This didn't change my opinion. I still love black now. I remember being invited to a birthday party of a friend in class. She had a lovely big house, and her June birthday meant that we would be able to celebrate in the garden. Most of the girls there wore pretty floral dresses and white sandals. Not me! Dad and mum had to trail around town finding me a black velvet dress, after promising me a new dress for this party. They got one, eventually. I loved that dress. It had a white frilly collar and was just what I wanted.

Mum had a mail order catalogue that we kids used to spend hours looking at. We especially liked the autumn/winter edition that had pages and pages of toys. We would write our Christmas lists to Santa, citing our favourite toys, giving him the page and item number to make it easier for him. This also ensured that we got exactly what we wanted. Money was still always in short supply, so mum ordered things for us from it so that she could pay over a term for what we wanted. Once, for a surprise, she got me a bright red cape. It was horrid. Dad and she tried to convince me that it was a little Red Riding Hood cape. I was having none of it. I hated it. At the age of eight, what I wore mattered to me, and it was so un-cool. It didn't have any sleeves, just stupid arm holes. And when I tried it on, it made me feel funny. I was declared ungrateful, and was told that I would wear it, whether I liked it or not. The first few times I was made to wear it I got sent home from school with a poorly tummy or headache. This cape made me feel sick. I would tell my parents as much, but they took no notice. It seemed strange that the minute I took it off, I felt better. I would wear anything rather than this cape, and used to resort to hiding it behind other clothes in the wardrobe, hoping that they would forget that I had it.

We had, by now, got a pet – a small Pekingese dog that we called Ming. She was lovely; quite a temperamental little thing, who only liked certain people – really just me and mum. I had made a big deal before Christmas about being old enough to be responsible for a pet. So when Dad came home from work one January evening carrying her, I was thrilled. She was to be my dog and my responsibility. I took her for walks, fed her, and thought her adorable. She was a light blonde colour with a little squashed black nose and big brown eyes. I considered her to be the loveliest dog I'd ever seen. A little while after we got her, it was evident she was a duchess! Ming wouldn't eat dog food. Her diet consisted of scrambled eggs or tinned baby food. She hated being wet and had hysterics when we tried to bath her. She had tiny little legs and a long coat which meant that she trailed dust and debris along with her – a mobile duster, really. After a few months, we noticed that she had some knotted fur behind her ears. But she wouldn't let any of us brush or comb her, so this problem became worse. Mum had a word with someone who had the same breed of dog, and was told that the best thing to do was to take her to the vets and have the knotted fur cut away from her ears.

One day in the school holidays, mum set my brother Mark and me on the bus with Ming and to an appointment to the vet in the next town. Mum had made me wear the dreaded red cape. The conductress on the bus told us we had to sit upstairs because we had Ming with us. This was no problem, and no sooner had we sat down than it was time to get off the bus again. We made our way to the vets, which was an old converted Victorian house. There were five steps up to the main door, and a peculiar clinical smell hit you just as soon as you were inside the outer door. I gave the note I had to the lady receptionist, who told us to take a seat in the waiting room. I didn't like the feeling in this place, and felt a little afraid. I think Ming felt it too, for she became agitated and kept pulling on her leash to go, becoming more and more fidgety as the time was passing. My heart was beating really fast and I felt so hot in this awful room with this awful cape on.

We were soon called into the vet's own room, and Mark and I stood by the big table, upon which we had lifted Ming for the vet to see her ears. The vet was an older man with grey hair and wore a white coat. He wasn't very smiley or nice. A nurse kept hold of Ming while the vet took some scissors and started cutting the knots of fur from behind her ears. "Be careful, please," I said. "She's really frightened. Please don't hurt her." They both ignored me and the vet carried on cutting. In less than a minute, Ming yelped in pain and blood appeared on her lovely fur. The stupid vet had cut into her ear. He started grumbling, something about her ears shouldn't have been allowed to get into this state. He then told the nurse that he would to have to put some stitches in her ear, and for her to get a tray ready. I started to cry, which made him tut some more. We seemed to wait ages while he put some stitches into poor Ming's ear. I had been frowning so hard at the vet that I'd given myself a headache. He seemed totally unmoved by us, the dog, or his mistake.

Eventually, we were allowed to take her. I was given a note for mum with instructions on how to treat Ming, and when she was to return to get the stitches removed. Mark and I went straight to the bus stop with Ming. I carried her, apologizing to her, crying my eyes out. I felt angry, and when Mark told me that my face was all red like my cape I could have hit him. "Exactly," I said. "This wouldn't have happened if mum hadn't made me wear this stupid cape." We didn't have to wait long for the bus home. Once again we sat upstairs, me nursing poor Ming, trying not to look at the ugly black stitches in her little ear. I was really upset, sobbing quite loudly. Ming was shivering and was trying to get her head inside my cape. By the time it was time to get off the bus, she had opened her bowels all over my cape! We took her home and she was soon on the mend. Can you believe that mum actually had the cape dry cleaned?! I was only ever made to wear it one more time, some years later, and that time proved to be near fatal. After that, the cape, thankfully, was thrown away – too bloodstained to be cleaned. Never again have I worn anything that makes me feel the way that red cape did. And even to this day, I remain mindful of how the things I wear make me feel.

12

SEEING AND BELIEVING

1970 was quite an eventful year, as I recall. I loved school, and my school report had been good. I had started back at school after the long summer holidays, and was glad to do so. I had lots of friends at school and at home, who I had noticed could be easily enthralled by my imaginative ghost stories. It was a year at school that saw clubs springing up all over the place. If my peers weren't joining clubs, then they were forming them. The I Spy club, the Tufty club, book clubs, and various others were becoming really popular. A girl in my class called Carol was forming a club just as we returned to school. Carol was an only child; quite spoiled, but very creative, and, if you were invited and joined Carol's club, you were given a badge, pencil, notebook, and other goodies like homemade toffee cakes, courtesy of Carol's mum. In order to receive such benefits, one had to swear allegiance to Carol, play only the games she wanted to play, and mix with club members only. It was strictly forbidden to mix with anyone other than a fellow club member. She was, as you will imagine, bossy and overbearing, so when she invited me to join, I declined. I wasn't good at being ordered around or told what to do, so the club rules didn't really suit me – even if the fringe benefits did. Carol lived in the nicer part of town and was allowed to use her dad's garden shed as a clubhouse. I couldn't imagine anything worse than being stuck in there with Carol each night after school. She took my refusal to join quite personally and was really spiteful to me as a result. This only confirmed to me that I had made the right decision.

The pals I had at home were different to those at school; all differing in age and background, and all coming from different schools. I was always drawn to people and interested in their lives. I loved making new friends with kids in the neighbourhood. Deborah and Gary were my friends; a sister and brother who lived opposite me with their Auntie Jean. Auntie Jean was herself a widow with a grown up son who also lived with her. Mum and Jean got on really well and she often popped into ours for a cup of tea. Deborah and Gary were already living in the road when we moved there, and they were good fun to be with. Deborah was my age and her little curly-haired brother Gary was two years younger. Often when we played together, I would notice a lady watching us. Deborah and Gary didn't seem to notice or acknowledged her. She was young and slim and always looked sad. I felt sorry for her, yet I didn't know why. I once mentioned to them that I could see her. Deborah looked at Gary, and they both shrugged, seemingly ignorant to the fact that they were being watched. But they were – sometimes, really intently.

We were still living in Norton, in our flat above the shops. The shops were always busy, so there was always something to see or do. The end shop was a Spar grocer's, run by Mr and Mrs Wynn. They were a nice couple in their 50s, and they lived in the flat above their shop. Their front door was to the side of the shop, right at the end of the parade. Mr and Mrs Wynn knew everyone. They were friendly, even a little bit nosy, so were always up on the local gossip. It was a close community and everyone was friendly and open. As children, we all congregated outside the shops on the paved area in front. It was a meeting place that we used prior to going down to the school field to play our ball games, or practise our gymnastics. Everyone seemed to know everyone. It was a happy, safe environment, and I loved living there. Mr Wynn didn't like anyone playing with balls near his shop windows, and would often come out and move us on if he thought there could be some damage caused. For all they were quite a pair of nosy parkers, they kept themselves very much to themselves, working long hours in the shop. The only visitor I ever saw them have was a lad in his late teens who occasionally would visit them after the shop was closed. This tall youth usually came on his bike, and would stop and open the Wynn's front door, before wheeling his bike into their hallway.

One day, Mr Wynn was in a particularly grumpy mood. He was only small in height, about 5'5"; he was quite stocky though, and always smart with his white grey hair, and his pristine white overall. His wife wore the same kind of overall. She was even smaller than him, with black hair, glasses, and was always immaculately groomed. For all Mr Wynn's stature, he was very fiery, and we usually jumped to attention when he barked out an order, or told us to move on. So this particular day we stood and watched as he came out of his shop and chased away some boys. These boys were leaning their bikes against his shop window. "Go on, back to your own end!" he ordered. "These windows cost a fortune, and if you so much as scratch one with those handle-bars, I'll be asking your fathers for the money." This seemed to do the trick and the boys rode off with their heads down.

Later that day, I watched as their usual visitor arrived and parked his bike against the shop window, and then went to open their front door. The shop was now closed. Even so, I was in close proximity to him, so I said: "You best not let Mr Wynn see you doing that. He'll go mad, leaning your bike against his window." "That's okay," he said. "He's my dad." "Oh!" I said. "I didn't know." He just smiled, let himself in the flat, and took his bike in with him. He smiled at me and I smiled back. He seemed nice. A few days later, mum and I were in the Spar. I had gone with her to help her carry the shopping. Mr Wynn was telling her about the trouble he had been having with kids, their balls, their cheek, and their bikes. He was explaining how the last school holidays had seemed particularly troublesome, and that now there seemed to be lads coming from all over, purposely leaning against his shop windows, just to annoy him. I spoke up and told him how I had tried to help him by enforcing his message to all those who did just that, and how I had even reminded his son not to park against the window, even before I realised that it was his son. "What son?" he said. "I don't have a son!" "Well the lad that goes into your flat now and then reckons he's your son," I said. "He told me so last week. He said that you were his dad!" Mr Wynn looked puzzled and looked at mum, who looked down at me. "You must be getting mixed up, Julie," mum said. "I'm not," I said, frowning. "He definitely said that Mr Wynn was his dad!" "What did he look like, this lad?" Mr Wynn enquired. "Oh, tall with black hair. He's quite skinny and he has nice white teeth," I continued. "His bike is red and shiny and he just pushes it, instead of riding on it." Mr Wynn stared at me, not saying anything and then he looked at mum. She seemed embarrassed by the whole incident. She hurriedly paid for her groceries and we left shortly after, leaving Mr Wynn plenty to think about judging by the look on his face.

Later that evening, when the shops had closed, Mr Wynn came up to our flat and told mum how many years ago he had had a son. This son had been killed on a racing bike, shortly after Mr Wynn had bought him it. He went on to tell her that he had never forgiven himself for going against his better judgement and buying it for him. Apparently, the description I had given him of their visitor, matched that of their son. Mum didn't know what to say, other than how sorry she was. Later that night, when I was eating my toast for supper, she told me about Mr Wynn coming down and what he had said. When I went up to bed that night, I asked for Norman to come, and when he did, I told him about the whole episode. Norman explained to me that I was very lucky and that sometimes I was able to see "spirits". These spirits were people who had died and had come back here to look over or down on someone. I asked him about the lady who was always watching Deborah and Gary. He explained that she was their mother. She had been killed in a car accident when they were only young, and she came to make sure that they were alright.

The next day, I asked mum if this was true. She told me that it was, and that Deborah and Gary had to live with Auntie Jean because their mum had died years earlier. Apparently, they were in the same car as her when the crash happened, their dad was driving and had survived but their poor Mother had died instantly. Mum said that Deborah and Gary knew about it, but had been too young to remember her. Norman had also told me how to differentiate between spirits and real people. He told me to look at their feet. Spirit people hover a little above the ground and that if I could see some space between their feet and the ground, then they were spirit visitors. From time to time, I would also see people who appeared see-through, as though I were seeing them through tracing paper. These also were spirits. I liked being able to see spirits. And when I told my friends that I could, they were even more enthralled. That was the reason I felt that I should serve the school community, and form a Spooky club.

Everyone at school wanted to join my club. I had nothing to offer them as a membership token. However, a promise to visit a haunted house and see spirits was all that was necessary to ensure a healthy membership. My imagination was remarkable. I seemed to be able to make up the most amazing haunted house tales, often pretending that members of my family had lived in such houses. Due to the vast number of applicants, I was able to found a special exclusive club. I selected 12 of my favourite peers and told them they were in. I would sit in the school yard with a captive audience, promising them a "once in a lifetime" opportunity to visit a haunted house sometime in the near future. My club had only one rule: secrecy. I didn't want just anyone knowing what we were going to encounter or experience as valued club members. After a couple of weeks of assured popularity, due to the different aspect of my club, the members started to get impatient. They wanted action soon, especially the boys. There were four boys and, including me, nine girls. And the boys were hungry for adventure. They pressed me for a definite date for the expedition and, eventually, I buckled under pressure, promising that next Friday would be the perfect night for the trip. I declared, much more confidently than I felt: "Friday after school, we'll meet near my house, at the shops, at half past four."

This kept everyone happy for the week, and once again I was the esteemed leader of the pack. Friday, however, was looming far quicker than I had hoped. My nerves were jangling, for I had made the whole story of the haunted house up. It had sounded so convincing that I was even starting to believe it myself. What was I going to do? The story I had concocted was fantastic: it entailed a haunted house in the middle of a field, in the middle of nowhere. The house had a huge hole in the roof and had been deserted for years after a fire had claimed the young children who had lived there. Their souls, I assured any who would listen, could still be heard. I had guaranteed that not only would I take my club to this house, but that they would be able to hear the children, still haunting their last residence.

Each night leading up to Friday, I had trouble sleeping, worrying about how I was going to tell the group the truth. By this stage, I was really regretting the lies I'd told. I was sure that they wouldn't want to be friends with me after this, and had visions of being sent to Coventry for months. The shame of being branded a liar, once they found out that I'd fabricated the whole thing just to get their allegiance, was just too much to bear. I figured that I deserved all that I got for lying in the first place and each night I strengthened my resolve to come clean before Friday. But it just didn't happen!

Friday came all too soon; a nerve-wracking day for me. School playtimes consisted of nervous excitement from my club members, and assurances from me that it was really going to happen. Questions of what to wear and what to bring were thrown at me at every opportunity, and I called a brief meeting at afternoon break-time to answer questions, and reaffirm the meeting time and place. I also insisted that my club members kept secret where we were going; after all, I wasn't up for questions from parents that would totally blow my cover and expose me for the fabricator that I was. Everyone was to say that we were going to find conkers near the big school field. Those days, it was perfectly safe for children to play around the neighbourhood, unaccompanied by adults; so it was easy to be allowed to go to one another's houses without been given the third degree. At 4:30 exactly we met at our shops. I felt sick with worry and had been unable to eat my tea. Once we were all together, I set off, group in tow, around the estate, feeling more nervous by the minute, wondering how I was going to get out of this one.

When we reached the end of the estate, there was a road that I hadn't ever crossed before. On the other side of this road, there was a large privet hedge that concealed some fields that were overgrown and untouched. It was early autumn, and I was aware that the nights were getting darker much earlier lately, and by now we had been walking for a long time already. As we reached this road, everyone stopped and looked at me to direct where we went from here. "Over this road and along the fence," I said, with far more confidence than I felt. "Just along that road," I said, pointing into the distance. "We'll come to a dusty path that leads up to the house." What was I doing?! Why was I carrying on this façade? For all I had never been this far away from my house before, I felt compelled to carry on, and with this many people depending on me, I just had to brave it out.

Two of the boys went on ahead, confident that they would come to this dirt road as I had directed. I had decided, after crossing the road, that when we'd walked sufficiently far without encountering this path, I would declare that the haunted house must have been demolished recently; this, I reckoned would be the easiest way to try and salvage some kudos. About a hundred yards along the road, the boys up ahead had stopped. I guessed they had realised that the trek was futile and were sick of this wild goose chase I was taking them on. Not so! They had stopped because they had reached the dusty track that I had described and were waiting for us all to re-group. As we turned down the dirt road, nobody was more amazed than I that, looming up in the distance, at the end of the track, was the house I had described. Deserted and smoke damaged, in the middle of a field with a huge hole in the roof! Oh, my Lord. I was completely amazed. This was seriously lucky guessing on my part. The vibe of the group changed. My peers went from being mildly bored and perhaps a little disbelieving to nervous and excited, and a little in awe.

The whole group stood together quietly, gazing up ahead at what I had promised: that this would be the most amazing haunted house that they would ever get to see. "Is there anything we should do?" one of the girls asked. "We need to stick together, and stay safe," I responded in my best serious leader's voice. I told them that we should approach the house slowly and quietly, more for my benefit than theirs I think. I needed to get my thinking cap on. I wasn't prepared for this. There was to be no shouting, only whispering, and nobody was allowed to run off and leave the group. After this directive, our pilgrimage continued. Approaching the house was hazardous and difficult, for the grass was long and full of weeds. The boys went on ahead of us girls, trying to stamp on the long grass to forge an easier path for us. As we got to the house, the front door was shut tight, just as I predicted. So we went around the back, stepping carefully through the grass as we did. There was no back door, another thing I had guessed correctly, so we were able to walk into the house.

This dilapidated house was probably far too unsafe for children to be entering;

but we did, with a nervous excitement that was only topped by the tangible vibe in the house. It was so cold inside – the air seemed to have got even colder the further we went inside. Once inside the house, we noticed that there were walls missing. Only half of a staircase remained, different patterns of wallpaper still sat on the walls, reminding us that a family had once lived here. In the centre of the house was a huge hole in the ceiling, and, directly above that, an even bigger hole in the roof that showed the dusky sky and the clouds overhead. Everyone there was enthralled, looking to me for instructions. Staying close by, comforted by my imaginary previous knowledge about the place, I was really enjoying the whole experience and still shocked by my own powers of prediction. This whole bizarre scene seemed to me to have been conjured up out of my imagination. How could that happen? There was no way I could have ever seen this place before. It was completely hidden from everything. I was thrilled that my lies had turned into facts, and was determined to make the most of the power that gave me.

I was quite scared of the atmosphere in this shell of a house; it felt truly haunted. Haunted by past memories of events that had caused this much damage, or indeed by the children I had made up in my stories. I decided to honour my guarantee of ghostly encounters and instructed everyone to form a circle in the middle of the house, directly under the hole in the roof. We then looked heavenwards and held hands. It was a strange kind of moment. I asked everyone to be quiet, but to listen hard, and then asked, speaking out loud up into the darkening sky: "Is there anybody there? Are the children of the house here?" We waited, perhaps just a minute or two, before I repeated my question up to the sky. The second time there was a definite response. As we all stood together holding hands, each of us heard the distinct laughter of children. I am sure that if we were not all holding hands as we heard them that some of the club members would have made a run for it. The laughter was quite scary. But we held fast. All our little hands joined together. Each of us grasping the next palm tightly for reassurance. The laughter came again, followed by the sound of a smaller child – a baby – crying. One of the girls started to cry, saying that she didn't like it and wanted to go home. This unnerved the whole group, who were all a little scared by now. Even the boys suggested that we call it a day and go home. I was a bit scared myself, but wasn't going to show it. I nevertheless declared that ghosts didn't always like us to trespass for too long, so that now we'd heard them, we should leave them in peace. I told everyone to say "God Bless" out loud and stressed that it was important that we all left together, nobody was to run off. This was for my benefit as much as anyone else's.

We seemed to arrive back at my house far quicker than we had left it, perhaps spurred on by our ghostly encounter. Nobody spoke much on the way home. And once we had reached the shops, I told everyone that I had to go in now and sent them all home. All weekend I thought about that house; the children laughing, the feeling it gave me when I stood inside. The whole experience shook me greatly. So much so that at school the following Monday, I called a meeting to declare that I was disbanding the club. There were to be no more stories, no more ghost hunts. I told each of the club members that they had to keep secret the events of the previous Friday. They should never be talked about again. Nobody disagreed with me. The experience had obviously left its impression on them too. Years later, as I try to figure out where this house was, I can only guess that if my sense of direction and memory serve me right, the house stood on old farm land which was left for over 20 years, before a new prison was built there. The haunted house experience stopped me telling stories for a while. Tall ones, at least!

13

GREEN CAR SPELLS DANGER

For the time that we lived in Norton, I spent many hours in my little bedroom with lots of visits from Norman. He continued to re-educate and enlighten me, and would often bring spirit visitors with him. One day, he brought a young boy, who was perhaps two years older than me. Norman told me that his name was David, and that he was my older brother who had never breathed on the Earth plane. He explained to me that David had died before he was born; that he was mum and dad's son. David's spirit had continued to grow up in heaven hence his age now. I really liked David, and loved it when Norman would bring him along to see me. He looked like my brother Mark, but his colouring was fair, like my little brother Andrew. David's visits were random and he never stayed for long. Norman would tell me that David had jobs to do in heaven. I knew not to mention David to dad or mum at that time, and was starting to realise that keeping things to myself was the wisest thing to do when it came to my invisible friends. David came on his own one day while I was in my bedroom, and told me that dad would be buying a green car soon. He said that I wouldn't like this car, and it would cause something of an upset at home. I just shrugged. Dad was always buying cars, doing them up, and then selling them to boost the household kitty. So another car was no big deal.

Sure enough, the next week, Dad came home one evening with this shiny green car. Unlike his previous purchases, this car looked both roadworthy and smart, and he was delighted with it. He had picked it up for a good price at a motor auction out of town, and, as was the norm when he bought a car, mum and us four kids had to pile into it for a run around the estate to experience the smooth running of it. He was bristling with pride at such a good car – at a "give-away" price – and kept asking mum what she thought. She was making all the right comments, and this just added to his joy. He was so animated that night, explaining how this car didn't need any work doing on it at all, and how he was going to take us all for rides out at weekends rather than spend his spare time with his head under the bonnet. David was right. I hated this car! It had such a bad vibe about it. The whole of the time I was in it I felt claustrophobic, and by the time we got back home my legs were shaking and I felt sick. I thought it best not to say anything to Dad. I didn't want to burst his bubble. The car was indeed in excellent condition. It had beautiful leather seats, but these seats, however, made my legs restless. I could always smell something peculiar when I got into it. Usually, whenever dad went anywhere in the car, I would accompany him. But not anymore. Sitting in this car was no pleasure for me; in fact, it was torture. I hated our Sunday trips out, and on any other journey would try, whichever way I could, to stay at home rather travel in that car.

Every week – most often on a Saturday afternoon, dad, mum, and us kids would go to see nana. The four of us kids would sit in the back of the car, Mark and I looking forward to seeing nana, Alison and Andrew dreading it. Alison and Andrew hadn't ever grown on nana, and I think they sensed this. Nevertheless, they were good kids and didn't cause a fuss. Mum sensed her mother-in-law's dislike of them, though, and whenever she broached the subject with dad, he would say: "Oh, you know what she's like, pet. Take no notice." I think he was a little afraid of nana, too, and never did anything that would incur her wrath. Most times we went to nana's, Mark and I would sit near the windows in the car, and the two youngest between us. But in this car, I felt like I needed to see what was ahead so I used to insist on sitting in the middle looking ahead, watching the traffic. This particular Saturday, I felt really sick while we were travelling and I couldn't wait to get to nana's. By the time we got there, my legs were shaky and even nana remarked that I was as white as a ghost. Nana gave us some tea and jam and bread, and I started to feel better. But when dad announced that it was time to go home, I began to feel afraid of going in the car. I was cold, so I knew that something was going to happen!

As we were walking down nana's path towards the car, I saw a red-haired boy sitting in the back seat of the car looking at us through the window. I was holding Andrew's little hand and the sight of this boy stopped me in my tracks. He looked threatening and he pointed to Andrew, and mouthed the words "don't let him come in this car." Mum saw my face and asked what was wrong. "Can we get the bus home, mum?" I begged. "Stop being silly, Julie," she said. "We came in the car, there's no need for us to get the bus." "I don't like it." I started to cry. "You don't like what?" Dad said, trying to rationalize with me. "Your car, dad. I really don't like it." "That's daft. It's a lovely car. Come on now, be a good girl," he said, as he opened the back door for me to get in. Andrew climbed over first and sat by the window. But I was still hesitant. "Come on now," dad said. "You're holding every one up!" So, reluctantly, I climbed in, closely followed by Alison and Mark. I got hold of Andrew's hand tight and then I grasped Alison's hand, and told Mark to get hold of Alison's other hand. Mark didn't want to hold her hand, but I went on so much that mum turned round in her seat and asked Mark just to do it to make me feel better. We set off, us four kids like a human chain in the rear of the car. The red-haired boy had disappeared as we got into the car, but I still felt afraid. My heart was beating really fast, and I began praying in my head, saying the words "please God, let us get home safe, please God let us get home safe," over and over again like a mantra. As we were getting near to home, the boy appeared again. He popped up between mum and dad, scaring me. His skin looked an awful grey colour, and he had blood coming out of the side of his mouth. He started shaking his head at me. I closed my eyes tight to blot out the sight of him and kept up my prayers.

What happened next seemed to happen in slow motion. My eyes were still tightly closed, and I sensed dad driving round a corner. As he did, the door next to

Andrew flew open, and he was flung from the car. He screamed, I screamed, mum screamed. Luckily, I kept tight hold of his hand and I managed to drag him back into the car as dad was slowing down. Dad stopped and came running round our side of the car to check we were alright. Little Andrew's shoes had no toes left in them – the impact of the road on his feet had rubbed all the leather off his shoes. Fortunately, we were at the kerbside of the car, else things could have been far worse. I couldn't stop shivering and crying. We were all in a state, and even dad looked grey. He drove home slowly, and we arrived safe. Mum made us all some more hot sweet tea. My hatred of that car intensified.

My sightings of the red-haired boy continued. He was always in the back seat of the car, looking out of the window. Even when dad came home from work, I would watch as he sat there looking at me. The sight of him always scared me, and I would immediately look away when I spotted him. Dad was, of course, totally oblivious to his passenger. I would pray each night that dad would get rid of the car. Then, one night as I was doing so, my spirit brother David appeared at the side of my bed. He told me that it was just a matter of time before dad would sell it. I was not convinced. Dad seemed to like that car more and more each day. David also told me that the boy I kept seeing in the car meant me no harm. He explained that his soul was trapped in that car because of an accident that had happened to him, and that soon his soul would be free. I still didn't like him! He scared me. Apparently, his name was Thomas and that as soon as the mystery of his death had been cleared up he would be able to go up to heaven and rest. I wasn't sure why David was telling me all this. It didn't have much of an effect on me. If this information was meant to make me like Thomas or the car a little more, then it was not working. I didn't feel any different despite David's explanation. David told me to keep praying and that the car would go in three weeks. This seemed a long time to me, but he said that Norman and him were working on it and to trust.

Dad always parked his car at the front of the shops where we lived, and would look out of the window a few times during the evening to check it was okay. I would often look out of the same window waiting for dad to get home. I just needed to see that he was home safe. I would see him get out of that awful car, lock it up, and look at it as though he was really proud of owning such a car. Each Sunday morning he would wash and polish it, remarking how you could almost see your face in the bodywork. It was so shiny.

In the flat next door to us lived a young couple, Ken and Margaret, and their two sons, Peter and Martin. Margaret was really glamorous. She had lovely long blonde hair and wore really fashionable clothes, usually mini skirts that showed off her lovely legs. She worked in a local department store in sales, and she was always laughing and bubbly. Mum and dad always got on really well with their neighbours, and were particularly fond of Margaret. Who wasn't? She was so lovely! She often arrived home from work the same time as dad. She had a lovely little Mini Clubman, and she would always take her time parking it outside her flat, next to dad's car. Dad would often make jokes about her parking, but she took them in good humour. Dad made everyone laugh with his quick wit, and Margaret would laugh and tell him how cheeky he was. I was looking out of the window one day, when I saw dad and Margaret arrive home. As usual, it was taking her ages to park her car – a job that dad seemed to make look so easy. So as they got out of their cars, dad made some comment, and she nudged him and laughed. It looked as though Margaret was admiring dad's car, and he was obviously bristling with pride, patting the wing of the car and nodding his head. She made her way with dad towards the front door, and I heard as she accompanied him through our front door, up the stairs along the passageway, and into our lounge.

Mum was in the kitchen making tea and came through when she heard dad and Margaret. Mum offered Margaret a cup of tea, but she declined saying that she had to go and get Ken's tea on, and that she had only popped in for a minute to see if mum was interested in going next door, to her flat, the following Friday to a clothes party she was having. Mum hesitated; money was tight and I'm sure that she probably had to think about what she spent still. In true sales fashion, Margaret went on to say that this particular brand of clothing was really reasonably priced, that they did children's and adults clothes, and that nobody had to pay on the night of the party – there was a three-week period between ordering and paying. Mum looked more interested now and was hooked when Margaret mentioned that she had booked a fortune teller to come to the party to read tea leaves that night. This was obviously clever strategy on Margaret's part. People were fascinated in stuff like that, and she would attract far more women to spend at her party if a fortune teller were there. "Great. Thanks, Margaret, I would love to come," Mum said. She was hooked. Dad looked heavenwards, rolled his eyes, and said: "Load of rubbish. You women believe anything!" Margaret and mum just laughed. "No. Seriously, Ena," Margaret continued. "Even if you don't want to buy anything, at least come and have your tea leaves read. It will be a good girlie night in. I'm going to do some sandwiches and nibbles, make a night of it." I was so fascinated by the prospect of meeting a fortune teller that I butted into the conversation and asked: "Can I come please, Margaret." She looked towards me and smiled. "I could help you at the party. I will wash up for you or help you with the sandwiches." Margaret looked towards mum, who shrugged her shoulders. "Well if it's okay with your mum, then that's fine with me," she said. I looked at mum. "Can I mum, please?" I begged. "Well if it's alright with Margaret, it's okay with me." "Thanks," I said enthusiastically. I didn't often get chance to go places with mum on my own. It would be great; besides I was totally intrigued by this fortune teller woman who was going to be there.

Friday arrived and I couldn't wait to get home from school and get ready for Margaret's party. At around seven o'clock, mum and I went next door. We were a little earlier than the other guests, so we were able to help Margaret get things ready. She was busy making sandwiches and she let me help. Mum was emptying crisps, nuts, and other nibbles into small glass bowls, and we carried them out into the lounge. There was a coffee table in the middle of the floor at the front end of the lounge, and we put the dishes and plates on it. Pam, the lady who was demonstrating the goods for sale, was already there too, and she had set up a rail at the front end of the lounge and was busy taking clothes and lingerie items out of her suitcase and hanging them on coat hangers, on the rail. Pam was a work friend of Margaret's, and she was really nice. She let me help her hang things on hangers, too. I loved the feeling in the room that evening. Margaret's records were playing on her stereo; there were soft lamps on, and the whole feel of the place made me feel warm.

We had been there just a few minutes when Mrs Benson arrived. Mrs Benson was the special guest – the psychic fortune teller – who was always spoken of with reverence and awe. Her reputation was, apparently, fantastic. This lady knew things that she couldn't possibly know, and it was thought lucky to have your tea leaves read by her. Mum had talked about it all week, mentioning it to anyone who was interested, that she was going to have her tea leaves done by the said Mrs Benson on Friday night at Margaret's. This lady's reputation as a medium was remarkable. Everyone seemed to have heard of her. She looked, I have to say, disappointingly normal: just a middle-aged lady with a headscarf and coat on, she even had with her a shopping bag. Margaret welcomed her and escorted her into the lounge. We all looked towards her and she smiled. She then asked Margaret where she wanted her to sit. "I thought that if you sat at the dining end of the lounge, then you wouldn't be disturbed Mrs Benson," Margaret said. She made her way to the table, opened her shopping bag, and took out a small black square table cloth, and placed on it a crystal ball and some other little amulets that I couldn't make out. She fascinated me, and I kept stealing a look at her. Each time I did, she would be looking at me and I would hurriedly look away. The other guests arrived soon after, and the clothing demonstration began. While Pam was showing off the garments on the rail, carefully explaining the colours, sizes, and prices of them, Margaret's friends were taking it in turns to go to the rear of the lounge to have their cards and tea leaves read. I couldn't wait for it to be mum's turn and, typically, she waited till everyone else had had their turn before going herself. I asked if I could accompany her, but she said no. "You just stay up at this end. I won't be long," she said. I did, but I was dying to hear what mum was being told. I noticed at one point that mum and Mrs Benson were talking about me. I heard mum mention my name, and when I looked round she motioned for me to come and join her.

By this time her reading was finished, and Mrs Benson was just talking. As I got to the dining table, this strange woman took hold of my hand and said: "One day, Julie, you will be able to do what I can do." I didn't know what to say. I wanted to ask her loads of things, but instead, because I was a little embarrassed, I blurted out: "I like your crystal ball." She smiled and then said: "I have told your mum about the green car that your dad has. You don't like it either, do you?" Before I could answer, she continued saying "I have told your mum that dad needs to sell it." This made me feel so happy that I almost wanted to cuddle Mrs Benson. "Thank you," I said. "Thank you so much." She rubbed my shoulder and told me to be a good girl, then continued talking to mum. But I wasn't taking any notice. I was just so glad that, at last, something might be done about that horrible green car.

Mrs Benson left soon after that, and the rest of the party came to an end. When everyone had left, mum and I helped Margaret tidy up before going home. I was tired. It was well after ten o'clock, and as we made our way the short distance home, mum reiterated that she was going to speak to Dad about the car. Mrs Benson's words had obviously had a profound effect on her. Dad was still up when we got home, and he asked if we had enjoyed our evening. I looked towards mum before nodding. "Well, come on then," he said to mum. "What did the fortune teller tell you?" Mum hesitated for a second and then told him lots of things that Mrs Benson had said, things that she couldn't have known about. Dad seemed a little impressed until mum delivered the news about his car. "She asked me, Bill, if you had a green car. And when I told her you had, she shook her head vehemently before telling me that I had to insist you get rid of it!" "What a load of rubbish!" Dad said, shaking his head in disbelief. "It's not rubbish, Bill," mum continued. "She told me that there was a fatal accident linked to that car. She even told me that Julie didn't like it either, and that you would have no trouble selling it." "There's no way I'm selling that car," dad said. "No way at all. It's the first decent car we've had in a long time, and I am keeping it. This is all because our Andrew fell out, isn't it?" he added. "No, no, it isn't," mum assured him. I told her about that and she said that had nothing to do with it." "Well, I'm sorry," dad said resolutely. "But if you want to listen to some crank who obviously saw a green car parked outside when she came, and decided to be a scaremonger, then that's fine, but there's no way I'm getting rid of that car!" "Fine!" said mum. "But I'm telling you now, that there is no way either me or the kids are going in that car ever again!" And with that she stormed out of the lounge, taking me with her, and we made our way to bed. I went to bed that night and prayed even harder that dad would sell that car, and that mum wouldn't change her mind and let us get in that car ever again.

The atmosphere was very tense over the weekend that followed this little episode. No more was mentioned about the car, but we didn't go in it either. The following Wednesday, dad came home from work and announced that he had put an advert in the local paper, advertising his car for sale. Mum thanked him, and I could have sung for joy. The car was sold on the Friday of that week, and as the new owner shook hands with dad and got into the car, I caught my last sight of Thomas, who looked out of the back window sadly as the car was being driven away. The following day, dad bought a new blue Zodiac car that we all liked, me especially. The green car was gone and forgotten, or so we thought.

Two weeks later, two policemen knocked at our door looking for dad. He was due in from work, so mum asked if they wanted to come inside and wait for him. He arrived home shortly after, and the policemen said they wanted to ask some questions about a car he had previously owned. Not surprisingly their questions were about the dreaded green car. They asked dad where he bought it from, when he bought it, and if he had proof of purchase. Dad was always well organised with paperwork and went into the bedroom to get the documents they needed. I was sitting at the end of the lounge taking all of this in, staying quiet in the hope that I would go un-noticed. When dad came back with the paperwork, and the policeman asking the questions had checked it was in order, they thanked him and stood up to leave. "Is there a problem with the car?" dad asked. "Yes, but it's not your problem, Mr Savage," the bobby said. "What's the problem?" dad persevered. "It was involved in an accident, a hit and run accident before you bought it," the policeman explained. "Oh God. Was anyone seriously hurt?" dad enquired. "A young lad was killed," the policeman said. "We have reason to believe that the owner of the car panicked and sold the car at auction, out of town." "Thomas," I said aloud without thinking. "What did you say?" the policeman asked me, after exchanging glances with his colleague. "I said Thomas," I repeated. "The boy that was killed was called Thomas." "Yes, that's right," the bobby said. "How do you know that?" "I just guessed," I said. They looked at me strangely. One of the policemen shook his head and dad quickly asked if there was anything else he could help with. "No, not for now", the older of the two said. "Thanks for your time. That will be all." Dad saw them out and nothing further was mentioned. Later that night, at bedtime, I prayed to David and Norman that Thomas's sprit be allowed to rest and go to heaven, and I asked that all of dad's cars from now on would be safe and spirit free. Each time dad bought a car from that time on, he would take me for a run around the block in it and ask if I thought it was fine. They always were.

14

BAD BEHAVIOUR – BEST SHEET

One of the advantages of being the eldest of four children was that I seldom felt lonely. For all my younger siblings sometimes irked me, they were generally good kids, and did what I told them to do – most of the time. I used to feel as though I shared the responsibility of them, along with dad and mum. Mum suffered terribly from migraines, which really debilitated her. Whenever they came upon her, usually each month, she would have to go to bed and stay there for a couple of days until the pain subsided. She couldn't bear light or noise, and would only be able to sip water when she was ill with them. On these occasions, I would have to stay off school to ensure that Mark, Alison, and Andrew were washed, fed, and taken to school. I would then try my best to keep on top of the housework, and pop into her room to see if she needed anything. I imagine some kids would have welcomed the break from school. I hated it. I loved school, and missed my lessons and friends. Likewise, I hated the fact that my mum was poorly. Usually, on the third day of her malaise, she would get up, still not looking 100 per cent recovered, but she would sit with us and try to stomach some tea and toast. She always thanked me for my efforts to keep the house clean and tidy. Nana had taught me how to cook, so I was able from a young age to feed us all, and I endeavoured always to keep the others quiet when mum was poorly. Dad was equally appreciative of my efforts and would tell me how good I was. I loved earning his praise, and used to try and look after him, too; making sure that his tea was ready when he came in from work. Apparently, these dreaded migraines were hormone-related, so there wasn't much that could be done about them. My poor mum lost endless days of her life to these awful headaches.

When I was eight years old, I was sitting down one evening and dad me told that mum had to go into hospital. I was immediately concerned and it showed on my face. They both rushed to explain that everything was going to be fine. Apparently, she was to have a sterilization operation which would stop her having any more babies, and that she would have to stay in hospital after the operation until she felt strong enough to return home. During this time, we were to go and stay with nana. I fretted over this news for a few nights, and even Norman's reassurance that mum would be fine didn't seem to help. The word sterilization sounded barbaric to me, and I had visions of men in white coats cutting her tummy open and pulling out bits of God knows what! This, of course, was not the case, but even at that young age, my imagination would run away with me.

Mark, when given the news of mum's impending surgery, was calm and accepting. Alison and Andrew cried like hell! As my parents tried to comfort them, chasing away the worry of mum not being well, Alison admitted that she was crying at the prospect of having to stay at nana's! She knew that nana didn't like either her or Andrew. And she was right. Naturally, Mark and I weren't concerned at all about going to stay. I remember when mum would take the four of us to nana's; how she would greet Mark and me with open arms, and just nod at Alison and Andrew. This always baffled me. The two little ones were adorable, everyone liked them, and it was difficult to understand what nana disliked about them. That didn't matter. She just didn't like them and didn't bother to conceal the fact, often asking mum why she had bothered to bring "those two little buggers." Obviously, mum was upset at such remarks, but was too afraid of her mother-in-law to retaliate. As was dad, who seemed as reluctant to confront his mother about it, saying things like "take no notice of her, pet. You know what she's like!" So poor little Alison and Andrew were mortified at the prospect of staying with nana, probably much preferring the local children's home if given a choice!

The day for mum going into hospital soon arrived, and we all cried as we said goodbye to her. She had packed some clothes into a suitcase for each of us, hugged us, and told us that she would be home before we ever got chance to miss her. I wasn't so sure. By this time, Alison and Andrew were wailing again. Andrew was too young to know what he was crying for – he just did so because Alison was. Dad took the suitcase and put it, and us, into his car and set off for nana's house. None of us spoke on the journey, and dad tried in vain to make us laugh with his jokes. He soon gave up and then told us that we shouldn't worry, that Mum would be fine and so would we. He reminded us that he was staying at nana's, too, and would be there each night after work to look after us. Alison and Andrew had accepted their fate by this time. They had stopped crying when I told them how much nana hated whingers, so they had best cheer up soon. Dad and mum had spoken to me the previous evening, asking me to keep an eye on the others. They reminded me that, as the eldest, it was my job to take care of them in mum's absence. It made me feel important to have this undertaking and I assured them that I would do my best.

We soon arrived at nana's, and all seemed well. I had stayed there lots of times, so it was easy for me. Dad was instructed to put our suitcase in nana's bedroom. Apparently, the four of us were to sleep in her bed. Awesome! Dad was to sleep on the couch downstairs, and nana would sleep in the small back bedroom. I couldn't wait to sleep in nana's bed; it was so comfortable, and I immediately elected to sleep on her side of the bed. The others didn't care and said nothing, knowing better than to argue in front of her. The first three days we spent at nana's house were pretty uneventful. The days were long, and I tried to find things to keep the four of us amused in dad's absence. He would come home from work each night, have his tea, wash and change clothes, before going to visit mum in hospital. We would wait for him coming in from seeing her to ask how she was and would always ask when she would be allowed home. The reply was always the same: "When she is well enough." He would assure us that she was well on the mend, though, and it wouldn't be long. I wrote letters to her and enclosed pictures that Mark and Alison had drawn to cheer her up. We all missed her, and home, terribly.

By the fourth day of mum's stay in hospital, the boredom of staying at nana's had really set in. Nana reminded us each day of the sacrifices she was making for us. Having to sleep in the little bed wasn't doing her back any good, apparently. We just accepted her moaning and tried to stay out of her way as much as possible so as not to annoy her. Nana never went out, so neither could we. The back garden was as far as we were allowed. We were all going a little stir crazy. That evening, we only saw dad briefly. He had taken on extra work, driving a taxi, to supplement the poor wage that he got from his day job. We were reminded that after visiting mum in the hospital, he would have to go straight to work. When I pulled a face at the news, he tickled me under my chin and reminded me that mum would soon be home, and that I was doing a great job looking after my brothers and sister. I was really looking forward to going home. Nana hadn't been half as nice as she usually was when I stayed there on my own.

At 8:30, we were sent to bed after our supper of bread and jam with the warning to behave. Nana said this every night. We all got into bed and lay there awake. The others looked at me expectantly. I was the bedtime game creator and storyteller. I was so sick of I Spy, charades, and Chinese whispers, and couldn't for the life of me think of anymore bedtime stories. I missed my mum too, and was sick of being at nana's. When the kids became fidgety and restless, I thought it best to do something rather than let them get shouted at by nana for being noisy. I decided that we would play a new guessing game. Mark, Alison, and Andrew took turns to sit in front of me, and I traced a picture on their back with my finger. They then had to guess what I was drawing. Andrew went first. He didn't have a clue and was too small to understand; he just enjoyed participating and whatever he guessed I deemed to be correct. Alison was really good at this game and could easily establish what I was drawing. And Mark? Well, Mark was really ticklish and just writhed and giggled at my attempts to draw on him. His laughter made us all chuckle and he would try his hardest to brace himself and keep still when it was his turn. He never managed it, and we were all enjoying this simple game tremendously.

We must have been quite noisy, and on a number of occasions nana would come to the bottom of the stairs and shout up to us to be quiet, adding that if she had to come up the stairs to us, then we would be sorry. These warnings were sufficient to silence us for a few minutes, but did not stop our game. After our third warning from Nana, I took it upon myself to deem the game over, and after cries of disappointment from the others, reluctantly agreed that they could each have one more go. Little Andrew was getting used to the game and had started to take longer before guessing, enjoying the attention. Alison's easy guessing had stirred some competitiveness in me, and I took longer over a complicated windmill that she guessed eventually anyway. Poor Mark was worn out with laughing, and it had made his chest a little wheezy; nevertheless, he wanted his final turn. I really went to town on him, first drawing on his back until he laughed and then tickling his ribs and his armpits, sending him into hysterics. He was squealing, pleading with me to stop saying: "Julie, please stop. My toe is stuck." I took no notice and continued to torture him with tickles, so engrossed in making him laugh that I failed to notice nana's entrance into the bedroom. Her voice startled us. She shouted: "Right, that's enough!" We all jumped out of our skin. Alison and Andrew scurried behind me on the bed. "Look at the state of that bed," nana barked. "Out of it, all of you, and let me make it." We all got out of bed and stood against the wall. Nana threw back the counterpane and blankets, and gasped when she saw what we had done to the sheets. The sheets were flannelette and candy striped; these were the only sheets I had ever known her use. They were obviously old and well worn, but always clean. She pointed furiously to the rip in the bottom sheet; a small tear, about three inches long in the middle of the bed. "Who did that?" she asked venomously. "I did. Sorry, nana," Mark said. "It's my fault," I added. "I was tickling him and I didn't realize he had his toe stuck," I explained. "You're swines. All of you!" she spat, and I instinctively drew Alison and Andrew to me. In no time, she had stripped the bedding away from the bed, rolled the damaged sheet up into a ball, and replaced it with a pristine white linen sheet that she had taken from her bottom drawer. Once the bed was re-made, she ordered us back into it and warned us that if there was any more commotion, she would be getting dad home from work. We knew that we had gone far enough, had far outstretched her hospitality, and got into bed like little lambs. We didn't even dare whisper until we had heard her go downstairs and slam the lounge door behind her. The crisp cool sheet underneath our little bodies felt icy cold and peculiar, and it wasn't long before my siblings were in the land of nod.

I hardly slept at all that night; this sheet was chilling my bones. The only warmth I could feel was that from Alison's arms. She lay beside me fast asleep. I somehow managed to move her to the edge of the bed and positioned myself between her and Andrew, so that I could feel his body heat, too. My sleep was fitful; the coldness seemed to chill my bones, and whenever I turned over, it woke me up.

Early the next morning, I heard the murmur of conversation coming from the lounge below the bedroom. I crept out of bed and quietly made my way downstairs, careful not to wake the kids. I was halfway down the stairs, when I recognized my nana's voice moaning to my dad. "They're swines those kids of yours, our Billy," she was saying. "Buggers they are; no discipline. That's the problem." "They are good kids," dad said. "They're just missing Ena, that's all." "I'm telling you," she went on, "they're swines, and if it wasn't for the fact that you had nowhere else to go, I'd have put 'em out last night." "Don't be like that, mother" dad said calmly, obviously too tired after his night shift to argue with her. "Do you know what they did last night?" she went on. "They had me up and down those bloody stairs like a yoyo with their carrying on. And the last time I went up to them, the bed was in a terrible state." She went on to tell him that she had had to strip the bed to re-make it, and of how when she had, one of us had then ripped her bottom sheet. "Vandals they are, I'm telling you," she spat, and then said: "I've had to use my best laying out sheet on the bed!"

Oh my God! I stood on the stairs, frozen with shock at her last statement. Nana was known in the neighbourhood for attending to the dying, the dead, or anyone having a baby. She had told me stories of how she would wash down and lay out people when they had died at home. I ran upstairs immediately and shook the others awake yelling "Get out of bed, quick get up!" Their eyes full of sleep, they were alarmed at my manner. But they did as I asked. I was mortified to think that we had lain where dead bodies might have been. I ushered them downstairs, forgetting nana's recent opinion of us. We all piled into the lounge and towards dad, the two little ones clambered on to his knee, while Mark and I positioned ourselves on the chair arms either side of him. Nana tut-tutted and went into the kitchen to refill the kettle. Dad kissed us all and told us the good news that mum would be allowed home later that day. We were delighted. Apparently, she had made a good recovery after her operation and would be discharged at teatime. Dad said that he would collect us from nana's after work, and that mum would be at home by then, waiting for us. He asked me to pack our suitcase and be good for nana, reminding us that she had been kind enough to let us stay. Kind?! Ha! That was a laugh!

As we were dressing that morning, I reminded the kids to be good and got them excited at the thought that that evening we would all be home together with mum and dad. Everything would be back to normal. The day seemed endless, and at six o'clock, when dad came to collect us, we were all ready to go home. We dutifully thanked nana for her hospitality, and she lied and told us that we were welcome. I knew she was glad to see the back of us. I can still recall the coldness of that laying out sheet, and years later, when I reminded her of the night she'd put it on the bed, she denied it, saying that she would not have done such a thing. She did though and I would never forget it.

15

NANA'S ANGELS

In spite of that memorable visit, I still loved going to nana's house and especially liked the school holidays, when I was allowed to stay there with her on my own. Her house was always a place where strange things happened, and my understanding of it is that when like-minded souls come together, then special events unfold. I always had a great time when I had her sole attention. My Uncle Harold, who lived at nana's, spent most evenings and lunchtimes on Saturdays and Sundays at the pub. So most of the time, it was just me and nana. She used to tell me that she enjoyed my company and liked it when I spent time there, and this made me feel really special. Nana hardly liked anyone at all, so I felt honoured that she liked me.

We would sit after tea and knit or sew, then watch television together, and I wasn't ever made to go to bed before her. She would tear off strips of old sheeting and dampen my hair, then wrap my hair around these rags and, hey presto, after sleeping in them, I would have ringlets in my hair the next day. Bedtime was always after the ten o'clock news, when we would have two chocolate biscuits each, and nana would make us some cocoa with boiled milk. She would carefully carry our cocoa up the stairs, and we would drink it in bed. Her house was always cosy and warm. Nana didn't ever go out, so the fire was on constantly. This, she said, warmed the bricks, and regardless of the season, she liked the fire to be lit. It was even on when we went to bed. (She would leave it on low for Harold coming in from the pub.) She, like me, always felt the cold more than other people, and although she was a well built little woman, her chair was always near the fire. Nobody ever sat in nana's chair apart from her. She had her cushions strategically placed for comfort and, even if she was out of the room, her chair was left empty until she returned.

I always found her intriguing. She knew so much about many things: how to heal people, how to solve most dilemmas successfully, and, if she predicted the outcome of a situation, she was always right. One of her most astonishing traits, I thought, was her ability to read the fire. Often, she would look into the fire with an almost trance like stare and say: "Put the kettle on, Julie. Our Jean is coming." I would put the kettle on, and usually as it would boil, the said visitor would arrive. Nana didn't ever have a phone, so her visitors were always unannounced and, by virtue of the fact that she didn't ever go out, family would just visit her if and when, and would seldom say when they would be back to see her. One day, after she had told me that my cousin Margaret was on her way and to put the kettle on, when she arrived minutes later I was once again baffled and asked Margaret, without nana hearing, if nana had known she was coming. "No," said Margaret. "Well, she told me you were coming ten minutes ago," I said quizzically. "Doesn't surprise me with nana," Margaret said. She always knows who was coming. So the whole family just accepted that, most times, nana was beyond surprising.

I particularly loved her stories: tales of her childhood and young life, of the hardships that she had endured. Things that seemed unimaginable to me, her stories were so well told that you felt as though you were in them with her. She would talk about lots of different things: her beliefs, philosophies, and understanding of life. She was well versed in the pagan way of life. Her own mother had been a healer, midwife, and soothsayer, who had passed down her knowledge to nana. She knew how to make poultices and which herbs were best for healing. She had over the years attended many births and deaths. I always got the impression that nana's own psychic ability frightened her, and in order to keep her feet on the right path, she read her bible each night before going to sleep.

Nana's bedroom was really old fashioned and it never changed once in all the years I went there. The bedroom was at the front of the house, above the living room. Directly outside nana's house, there was a street lamp and its light shone directly into her bedroom on an evening. So the room was seldom dark, bathed instead in a lovely amber glow. The bedroom curtains were made of light brocade, so the light shone through easily. The old feather bed we both slept in had been the only bed that nana had ever owned in this house. The bed where she spent her wedding night, gave birth to her babies, and retired to each night of her life. It was an amazing bed; the feather mattress was so soft, and the bed itself seemed so high, that each night I would have to jump up to get on to it. Nana always slept at the same side, near the door. She got up early each morning, around six o'clock, to light the fire and get Harold's breakfast before he went to work. I slept by her side, in a slight indentation in the mattress, which she told me was caused by granddad sleeping in the same position for years and years. I didn't mind; the bed was always so comfortable, that I was seldom in it for long before sleep came. The bed's headboard was against the wall, and our feet were facing the window, where the light shone through, and in the facing corners were a matching set of ebony drawers and a dressing table. There was a large ebony wardrobe in the alcove to the right, and a little black lead fireplace against the wall at my side. On the mantelpiece was a picture of Jesus, his golden sacred heart shining forth from the picture. Often, when the amber glow of the streetlamp caught the picture, it seemed to illuminate that golden heart. Once, I remarked upon this, and nana told me: "He is always watching us, watching over us, shining his light on to the world." There was a bedside table at nana's side with a lamp and her bible on it. There was a rug at her side of the bed, too, which was on top of the linoleum. The only other thing in the bedroom was a large potty. This was kept under the bed. Nana's toilet was outside, so the potty served in emergencies. I never went on it, but I witnessed nana squatting on it during the wee small hours of the night. The sight always made me want to giggle, but I would not have dared. She carried it down with her each morning, and it was emptied and cleaned.

So each night, we would climb the stairs with our cocoa and get in to bed. Nana would get her Bible and I would lie, looking at the ceiling, the blankets pulled up under my chin, contemplating the day's events, and wondering what tomorrow would bring. When nana had finished reading, she would remind me to say my prayers before we drifted off to sleep. I always felt safe in that house, in that bed with nana; safe and content. I suppose it was the only other place, other than home, that I slept. Even so, I would often wake up in the middle of the night with the feeling that someone was watching over us. It didn't frighten me, but I was aware of it. I sensed that it was children who were visiting us. I could sense the height of them at the side or bottom of the bed.

Nobody ever had cause to go upstairs in nana's house. The toilet was outside, and the bathroom was downstairs next to the kitchen, so I always felt privileged to stay there. The house had three bedrooms. There was a medium-sized room at the back, which was Harold's room. It always smelled of stale smoke and beer. Next to it was a smaller room, which looked out on to the back garden. Nobody ever went into this room, but there was a small bed and a chest of drawers in there. I was never asked if I wanted to sleep in there, not that I would have wanted to. I much preferred sleeping in nana's bed. That room was peculiar, and often, as I was getting dressed on a morning, I would hear shuffling noises coming from there, as though there was somebody in moving about.

At home, when we got up each morning, we would go down to breakfast in our pyjamas and dressing gowns and get dressed after eating. But this wasn't allowed at nana's house. No. Nana believed that dressing gowns were to be worn only in emergencies or hospital, and she expected me to be dressed before I came downstairs each morning. The floorboards upstairs were old and noisy. They creaked when you walked on them, and when she heard me moving about, she would put me some bread on to toast so that it was ready by the time I came downstairs. One particular morning, the floorboards were creaking like mad in the little bedroom and, as I passed it on my way downstairs, I noticed that there was a lovely sunny glow coming from inside it. This light was also around the door, which was only slightly closed that day. I stole a look into this little bedroom and gasped when I saw two lovely little boys sitting on the bed. One of them was a few years older than the other, and the elder of the two was kneeling behind the younger one, on the bed combing his lovely golden hair. They looked to be around ten and seven, and when they saw me the little one smiled, then babbled something to the other one. I couldn't make out what he had said, but the older of the two boys put a finger to his lips gesturing for me to keep quiet about seeing them. I left the room and raced downstairs for breakfast, feeling a bit shaky at having seen these little ghost boys. I slipped down the final three stairs and was met at the lounge door by nana, who asked me whatever was wrong and why was I rushing. "Oh, no reason, nana," I smiled. "Well, don't run downstairs," she said Nana. "That's how accidents happen." "Sorry Nana," I said, and followed her into the front room.

My tea, toast, and jam were ready on the table, and Nana went about her chores while I ate my breakfast. I couldn't stop thinking about those two little boys and must have sat at the table ages thinking about them. Nana had finished hand-washing shirts, came into the room and said: "Come on, Dolly Daydream. You can help me peg this washing on the line. It's a lovely day and you look as though you could do with some fresh air." I carried my cup and plate into the kitchen and joined her in the garden to help with the washing. Nana was small and she struggled to reach the washing line. Each time she hung clothes out she cursed the line and huffed and puffed as she got on with the job of it. I handed her the pegs as she jumped in the air to catch the line and hold it down to peg the shirts onto it. It was, indeed, a lovely day and, as nana was pegging out the washing, I looked up at the small bedroom window and low and behold there were the two smiling faces of the boys, looking out watching us. The smaller boy waved at me. I waved my hand in front of my chest so that nana wouldn't see that I was waving at him; after all, I felt that their being up there was a secret.

It was a Saturday, and later that morning Harold came in from town declaring what a beautiful day it was. He had enjoyed his walk into town. He always loved walking and would walk the two miles to and from town every Saturday to get nana's shopping. He would always fetch something nice for our tea, and today was no exception. He had bought three lovely pieces of fresh cod fillet. He took off the newspaper they had been wrapped in and showed them to nana, then me, for our approval before putting them in the pantry on the cold shelf. Harold was always so kind. Each Friday night that he went to the pub, he would buy two newspapers from the local Salvation Army officer, who would go around the pubs selling them. He always bought the *War Cry* for nana and the *Young Soldier* for me, so that each Saturday I could sit and read the print off this, my own special paper, saving the crossword in it till last. I usually completed the crossword on my own, and Harold and nana would praise me, telling me how well I had done to complete it all by myself. After lunch each Saturday, Harold would go to the pub for a few pints, and nana and I would bake at the table in the front room; lots of goodies for Sunday's tea and usually a rice pudding for tea on Saturday. Harold would arrive home from the pub in time to watch on television the results of the football games. Each week, he would fill in a Littlewoods pools coupon, so he used to take down the results of the matches played to see if he had won anything.

This particular Saturday, I couldn't get the thought of the two boys out of my mind. I was dying to go upstairs to see if they were still there, but I didn't want nana to be suspicious – and she would be, if I had wanted to go upstairs. After our tea, Harold would usually have half an hour of sleep in his chair, and nana and I would clear the table and busy ourselves in the kitchen, preparing the vegetables for tomorrow's lunch. The peas had to be steeped, some vegetables peeled. The routine at nana's was always the same. She would say that if there was an order to jobs then everything would remain in order. I found the routine really comforting and I always knew what to expect when I stayed there. Saturday night was usually the best night on television, and Nana and I would sit, jobs finished, watching the box, waiting for her favourite programmes to start. Harold would come out of the bathroom after getting washed and shaved, put on a clean shirt and stand in front of the mirror that was above nana's fire to comb his hair. He always smelled of Palmolive soap and before going to the pub he would say: "There's plenty of coal in the scuttle, mum. Don't wait up. I have my key." Nana would always reply: "Alright, son." And he would be off, leaving us to have a cosy night in front of the television. During the commercial breaks, we would go to the toilet, make tea, and nana would put coal on the fire. At ten o'clock, we would watch the news before she would make our cocoa, put our chocolate biscuits on a plate, and lock the door before we went up to bed.

I couldn't wait to go to bed that night, hoping to catch a glimpse of the boys. Nana always suggested I go up before her and get ready for bed. This particular night, I went up before being told to and was quite disappointed when I peeped around the little bedroom door and saw that the boys weren't there. I felt sure though that I hadn't seen the last of them. Nana followed shortly after, our cocoa in her hands. I was already in bed, so she passed me the hot sweet cocoa and I cupped my hands around it, wishing as always that it would last longer than it did. I always finished mine while it was still hot – nana said that was the best way to drink it. I loved the warm feeling it left in my tummy. Nana put her lamp on, switched off the main light by pulling a cord above her bed, and set about reading her big blue bible. As usual, I stared up at the ceiling, thinking about my day, and then thought about God and Jesus, deciding that that night I would pray to God and ask if I would be able to see the two boys again. I had thought all day about them and had wished that I had spoken to them or spent more time with them. I must have fallen asleep shortly after.

The next thing I remember is being nudged awake by Norman, who was at my side of the bed, whispering to me to get up. "Come on, Julie," he said. "I've got something to show you." I was afraid of waking nana. "I can't," I said. "Nana will go mad if I get up in the dark." "Don't worry about your nana," he said, and then dared to touch her forehead. "She'll stay asleep." I carefully got out of bed, trying hard not to make a noise, which was difficult as I had to almost jump to get down from that bed. The little thud I made didn't appear to disturb her though, and I lightly crept past her as she slept. Each and every floorboard I stood on that night seemed to creak louder than the last, and as I was creeping past the door, my nightdress got caught on the door handle. It ricocheted me back into the bedroom; yet nana slept on. I'm always clumsy when I am trying to be either quiet or quick. We crossed the landing and passed Harold's bedroom door which was closed. The sound of his snoring reassured me that I wouldn't disturb him, at least. I followed Norman into the little bedroom and as we went through the door it creaked. Its hinges were obviously in need of some oil. The little bedroom that night looked totally different to how it had looked earlier on. The chest of drawers had gone and the little bed had vanished, too. In its place, however, was a larger bed that looked so much older. This bed had a wooden headboard and I looked to Norman, quite puzzled by what I saw. He gestured for me to get a little nearer to the bed, and as I did I noticed two little heads close together on a long pillow. These were the boys that I had seen earlier; they were sleeping so peacefully. The smaller of the boys was leaning into the older one, his little head almost a perfect fit into the neck of his companion "Who are they?" I whispered to Norman. "Angels," Norman said. "Two little souls lent to the earth-plane for a short time, now safe in God's keeping." I didn't really know what that meant, but I knew not to ask any further questions. I was just completely taken with the moment. He then told me to take notice of their auras: they were golden. "What are they doing here in nana's bed?" I asked. "They're your nana's little angels," he replied. "And one day, she will tell you all about them." The whole scene made me quite sad, and I didn't know why; after all, these children looked so contented. Why was I feeling so unhappy?

The room was really cold and, as usual, I started to shiver. Norman took my hand and led me back to nana's bed. I climbed back in and into granddad's delve. It still felt warm, as though I had just left it. And once I was settled back in, Norman touched my head, blessed me, and told me to go back to sleep. As he moved from the side of the bed, I whispered: "Norman." "Yes?" he said. I pointed to the picture of the sacred heart and said: "Be good. He's watching you." "I know, Julie," he smiled. "I know." I fell asleep immediately after, without time to ponder over what I had witnessed. When I woke up the next morning, I stayed in bed a little while thinking of nana's little angels, wondering if she even knew that she had them.

Sundays at nana's were fabulous: the smell of the meat roasting, the radio playing hymns, the whole atmosphere of the house seemed different. This was a day when the chores were forgotten and only the smallest of jobs got done. The day had an easier, more relaxed pace. I ate my breakfast and felt happy and contented, glad to be alive and happier for the knowledge that I was staying at nana's for yet another night. Dad wasn't picking me up until tomorrow afternoon as it was a half-term holiday from school. Nana was singing along to the hymns, and I sang, too. I tried to pick up the words as we sang and managed to remember the chorus most times. My nana's favourite song was The Old Rugged Cross; mine was All Things Bright and Beautiful. I knew all the words to this one – we usually sang it at school in assembly. Nana always encouraged me to sing, telling me how much God loved to hear his name praised, and that singing would always make us feel better and chase away the doldrums. The practise of this, however, had gotten me into trouble lately. Each time dad or mum told me off, I would sing. This seemed to make the grown-ups cross, even if it did make me feel better. Oh well, a time and a place for everything, I suppose! I always sang to cheer myself up, and I figured that if nana said it did you good, then it surely must.

I sensed that nana was in a good mood; she was singing loads, only stopping when she smoked her Woodbines. Lunch, as always, was delicious, and we all sat down to eat when Harold came in from the pub. The table always looked better on a Sunday:

the best crockery and cutlery were out, the vegetables each in their own tureens. Harold always brought home a bottle of lemonade on Sundays, too, and we would have some with our lunch. After we had eaten, I helped nana clear the table, and wash and clear up in the kitchen, while Harold had his half-hour nap in the chair. This particular Sunday, as we sat after all our jobs were done, I told nana that when we went back to school, I would be getting my photograph taken. I hated getting my photo taken and I told her as much. "Why?" she asked. "Because it's hard to smile if I don't feel happy," I reasoned. "Mm," she said. "I can see that, yes." I asked nana if she liked getting her picture taken, and she said no. "Have you any photographs of you when you were a girl?" I asked. "Oh, somewhere I have some, Julie," she said. "What about photos of dad and Harold, and everybody?" I continued. "Yes, I think so," she said, smiling slightly. "I don't think I have ever seen any of your photos, nana." "No, I don't suppose you have," she said. "I don't get them out very often." This last statement made me curious. "Can I see them?" I asked her. "Today." She thought for a moment before answering me, and then said: "We'll see. Maybe when Harold goes to the pub later. If there's nothing much on telly, I will look for them." "Great!" I enthused. "That'll be great!" I sincerely hoped there would be nothing on telly. I would much rather see some photographs and hopefully hear some more of nana's old stories.

Later that evening, when Harold had gone out and Songs of Praise had finished on the telly, I asked nana again if she wouldn't mind getting the old photos out. "Mm, let's see," she said. "Let's have a cup of tea, and I'll try and think where they are." "I will make the tea, nana," I said, and jumped up quick to put the kettle on. While I was in the kitchen, I could hear nana rustling about in the cupboard in the alcove. I was dying to know if she had found the photos, but I didn't want to pester her. Past experience had taught me that if I pestered her for things, then she wouldn't oblige. The kettle, as usual, took ages to boil, and when it finally began to whistle, I poured the water into the teapot, then carried it, tea-cosy and all, through to the living room and put it down on to the table. The table in the living room always had a cloth on it, and on the cloth a wooden board, especially for the teapot. I noticed nana sitting with an old shoebox, going through the contents of it, sorting out different piles of photos. I was so excited. I fetched the cups and saucers, milk jug, and sugar bowl, and put them on the table, leaving nana to pour the tea. Then I went and sat down beside her on the couch. She had put the black shoebox back on her lap, and on top of it was a pile of photos that she had put into age order. They were all black and white. The first photo was of herself, as a baby, sitting on her mother's knee. It seemed funny to think of nana as ever having been a baby. These photos were fascinating, and she passed them to me one by one, telling me who they were of and when they were taken. One of dad at just eighteen months old; it looked funny because he had a sort of dress on; then one of him as he was older, with his older brother Harold and my Auntie Dora, who was pushing him in a funny little pushchair. There were photos of nana as a young girl, and granddad, who I couldn't remember because I was only two years old when he died. There was a lovely photo of my Mum, her sister – my Auntie Olive – and nana standing in front of nana's front door. I loved these pictures and kept asking nana loads of questions about each photograph and the people in them. Subsequently, we spent hours going through them. Nana seemed to get more animated reminiscing about the past than about anything else. Needless to say, the tea in the pot went cold, and I was really sad when we came to the end of the pile she had on her lap. "Are there any more, nana?" I asked her. "Oh, just photos in here." She tapped the shoebox still on her lap. "People that you didn't ever know." "Am I allowed to see them?" I asked her. My interest was obvious, and perhaps the polite way I asked made nana appear to weaken her hold on the shoebox. "I am really enjoying tonight," I pressed. "Alright then," she said. "Maybe just a few more." She took the remainder of her photographs out of the box and starting passing me some of them, still carefully selecting ones that she wanted to keep to herself, separate from the rest. There were photographs of her son Alfie, her firstborn – her lovely Alfie, of whom she spoke with such pride. Alfie had been in the army and had fought in the battle at Arnhem. She told me how much he loved life and how cruel it was when he died of cancer at just 39 years of age. I could tell Alfie's character just by looking at his photo. I sensed that looking at these particular photos was quite hard for nana, but she seemed to be spurred on by my enthusiasm and interest. There were some pictures of her parents and her brothers, and one of her sister who died in her early teens. I was starting to realise just how hard her life had been – all that loss and sadness. My respect for her grew enormously.

I felt that while I was looking through these pictures, I was about to uncover something exciting. I started to feel tingly, and although I had no idea what it was, I didn't have much longer to wait. All of a sudden, a photograph fell off nana's knee. It landed on the floor at her feet, facing up. I bent down to pick it up for her and, as I did, I saw the faces of the two little boys that I had met – the boys whom Norman had shown me fast asleep in the little bedroom, the boys he had called "Nana's Angels". Without realising, I had uttered the words "Nana's Angels" out loud. "What did you say then, Julie?" Nana asked. "What?" I pleaded ignorance as I passed her the photo. "I asked you what you said just then," she said. "Nana's Angels," I said quietly, my head down, looking towards the carpet. I felt her eyes on me and then on the photograph in her hand, and she just remained silent. I felt uncomfortable when things were silent, so I asked her: "Who are those little boys, nana?" "They are my sons who died!" she said in a very flat voice, and without taking her eyes off their photo. "What were their names?" "Lenny and Maurice," she answered, almost mechanically. I just sat there, not knowing what to say or do, and I jumped when she took a deep breath and said: "Right then, time for some fresh tea. Look at the time. The news will be on soon." She quickly gathered up all the photos, put them back into the shoebox and then into the cupboard. She told me to put the kettle on while she went for the coal scuttle. Out in the kitchen, I refilled the kettle and set it on the gas, and swilled out the old tea from the teapot. Once it was made, nana poured it for us, and we sat with our tea and chocolate biscuits to watch the news. Everything seemed to go back to normal and our bedtime routine began again.

Nothing more was mentioned about the boys until later that night as I was praying. Nana had just finished reading her Bible, our cocoa was all gone, and the silence was broken when I opened my eyes after saying my prayers and nana said: "You're a good lass, Julie. Who were you praying for tonight?" "For you, nana," I replied. "For me?" she said. "Why for me, pet?" "Because you have had so much sadness in your life, nana, and it must have been so hard for you to let go of your little boys." "They're in God's care now," she said. "Our children are only ever on loan to us." That's not fair though," I reasoned. "They should be here with you." "Oh, some days they are. Some days I can feel them here with me," she said wistfully. "I know," I said. "I have seen them, too!" "Where did you see them?" she asked me. "In the little bedroom," I said sheepishly. She encouraged me to tell her all about it; so I did. I told her about the first time in the bedroom and how the older boy, Lenny, was combing the little one's hair; about seeing them from the garden as they looked out of the window; and then about during the night, how I had been allowed to see them snuggled together in bed. She wanted to know everything: what they were wearing, if they looked happy, what they had said. She seemed to be more attentive when I remarked that little Maurice seemed not to be able to talk.

She told me their story. Lenny was only three years old when Maurice was born, and from the first day of Maurice's life, Lenny seemed to take it upon himself to look after his little brother. So much so, that he would help with his feeding, bathing, and dressing. He constantly sat by him while he was in his crib, often just gazing at him. When Maurice was crabby, Lenny would soothe him by singing to him, or stroking his head and, as he got older, Lenny would make Maurice giggle. When he began to walk, it was Lenny who stood behind Maurice, gently guiding and steering him. As he learned to walk unaided, he would follow Lenny about. Maurice was of a gentle, quiet nature, and nana had noticed that he was slow in talking. Nobody in the family could understand his baby-like babble; but Lenny could, and would translate to his mother what Maurice wanted. Maurice was small for his age; with white blonde hair, he resembled an angel, and was very shy, even of his other siblings. The two of them seemed to be in their own little world, separate from the other children in the family. And they always slept together. One would fret for the other otherwise. They slept together each night.

One winter morning, nana went upstairs to wake her brood up for school. She called and called Lenny without any response at all from the little bedroom. When she went in to investigate, she saw Lenny lying very still, and Maurice clinging to him, silent tears running down his face. She knew immediately that Lenny was dead and had to prise Maurice away from him. Lenny felt very cold to the touch; he had been dead for some hours. The doctor was called and, after examination, he came downstairs announcing that it was silent pneumonia that had taken poor little Lenny. Nobody could have known that this would happen. He had appeared perfectly fit and well the previous day. His funeral was held the following week, and nana recounted how it had been one of the worst days of her life. After Lenny died, little Maurice became even more withdrawn. He cried most of the time, sobbing himself to sleep most nights. He was inconsolable, and it was difficult to understand what he was feeling because only Lenny had ever been able to connect with him. Nana found it difficult to get him to eat, and she worried as the months went by and his mood failed to lift. He was often to be found in the garden or in his bedroom, chattering away in his own little language. Nana remarked to granddad one day that she was afraid that Maurice was grieving his life away. Granddad just reasoned that it was a time thing, and that eventually Maurice would get over it.

Maurice didn't get over losing Lenny. The following year, lightening struck twice, and nana found him dead in bed one morning. The family doctor who attended remarked to nana that he felt that Maurice had died of a broken heart. Nana agreed. She told me that losing Maurice was terrible, but she had found solace in the fact that now he would be back together in heaven with Lenny. She went on to tell me that sometimes at Christmas, or on their birthdays or memorials, she would imagine that she could hear them or see them together. She really hoped that it was not her imagination or wishful thinking. That Sunday evening in bed, she said that she was glad that I had seen them and that it brought her great comfort to know that they were happy and, more importantly, together. It took me a long time to get to sleep that night. And although the story of Lenny and Maurice was a sad one, I felt happy that they were now angels. I looked over to the picture of Jesus on the mantelpiece, and asked him to look after my nana's angels. I don't know if it was my imagination, but I am sure that on that night, his sacred heart shone a little brighter.

16

BEST KEPT TO MYSELF

I was around nine years old when I realized that some things were perhaps best kept to myself. Norman still visited me on a regular basis, and I continued to see dead people. But I had started keeping quiet about it. I had learned that the truth didn't always suit grown-ups, and for some reason, I felt much wiser than the most of them anyway. Some things, however, were hard to keep to myself, and quite often I would just come out with things, without thinking about what kind of effect the facts I were about to spout were going to have on people. Subsequently, I was still raising eyebrows and being discussed by my parents. Three major experiences in 1970 forced my decision to stay mum about things for a while. They all occurred around nana. It seemed that whenever I was in her company, I became more attuned. I wonder now if that was because I felt more comfortable being different in nana's company than anyone else's.

My nana seldom went out of the house. She had once had a funny turn on a visiting bread van while she was shopping, and it really affected her. She had fainted or "blacked out", as she liked to call it, and this seemed to result in a lack of confidence and a little bit of agoraphobia on her part. As I mentioned a little earlier, most people in the family visited her and, having such a large family, she was seldom lonely. Two of her neighbours also used to call in from time to time, too: Meggie from the house directly opposite nana, and Mrs Mack from next door. Meggie was a funny woman whom I never really warmed to. She had yellow hair and a bright pink face, which didn't really make for an attractive look, and she moaned a lot, too. She whinged about the weather, the government, society, the television, her family, and anything else that took her fancy. I'm sure she only visited nana to have a good old moan. Nana would see her coming across the road and say: "Oh hell! Here comes half an hour of misery." Meggie didn't really ever acknowledge me – after all, I was just an insignificant kid. Nana would sit and listen to her whining and would glance in my direction when Meggie wasn't looking, and look heavenwards. The house used to almost audibly give a sigh of relief when Meggie left. Mrs Mack next door however was a different kettle of fish. She was a small Irish, Catholic lady, who had been widowed early in her life and had brought up her two sons, whom she adored, single-handedly. She was lovely.

One rainy day, I was staying at nana's again during the school holidays, and at around three o'clock in the afternoon, Mrs Mack popped in for a cup of tea. She warmed herself by the fire while nana put the kettle, and asked me how I was. I told her I was fine; fine but cold. She remarked how cold it was for autumn and that she felt sure we would have snow before Christmas that year. Nana carried the tea through, and we all settled down to drink it. Nana and Mrs Mack started to talk, and I felt so content. I loved listening to grown-ups talking; I was always interested in what people had to say. This particular day, Mrs Mack was telling nana how pleased she was for her youngest son. He had just been given a permanent position at work after finishing his apprenticeship. She was so proud of him and went on to say that he had a job for life with this firm. All of a sudden, I began to feel even colder and something really strange started to happen. Although I could see Mrs Mack and nana's mouths moving in conversation, I couldn't hear a word they were saying. All I kept hearing was Mrs Mack saying "job for life, job for life, job for life." I concentrated really hard and managed to get the words to stop and I began to think about Mrs Mack's son. I started to realize that he wouldn't live a long life and that made me start to feel really emotional. Nana and Mrs Mack continued their conversation, oblivious to my feelings and all I could think was how sorry I felt for lovely Mrs Mack.

The fire must have burned low and nana got up to put some coal on. I looked over to Mrs Mack who smiled at me and I began to weep. She got up quickly and came over to the sofa. She started rubbing my arm, saying: "Whatever's the matter, pet?" "I don't know," I replied. "I'm just sad, I think." Nana came through from the kitchen with the coal scuttle and asked what was wrong, too. "I'm just being silly, I think, Nana," I lied. "Well, stop being silly," she said, rubbing my knee vigorously. "Your tear ducts are too near your bladder!" she exclaimed, and we all started to laugh. Nana turned to Mrs Mack and said: "Don't worry about Julie. She just gets like this sometimes."

When Mrs Mack left for home, nana sat next to me and said: "Come on, out with it. What brought that on? What made you cry?" It was no good lying to nana, so I told her. "Oh nana. Mrs Mack's son is going to be killed in a car accident soon and there's nothing anyone can do about it!" "Oh dear," nana said, then thought for a while, before saying: "I think that's best kept between us. If nothing can be done about it, then it doesn't serve anyone to know about it." And that was it. The next year, Mrs Mack's son lost his life in a car accident. It wasn't his fault; he was a passenger in a car that was hit head on. He died instantly. When it happened, my nana was an amazing friend to Mrs Mack, and the only reference nana ever made to my premonition was to say that you can't change life's design I didn't really understand the meaning of the statement, but felt a calm acceptance accompany it.

The second thing to happen was to nana's old dog Rex. Rex was an Alsatian-Labrador cross. He was a good dog who was quite anti-social, really. He didn't much like patting, stroking, or fuss. He liked eating and sleeping, usually under nana's table, just in case there were any scraps passed under the table to supplement his diet. One particular day, I was playing in the crystal palace (nana's disused greenhouse) when Rex wandered in. This was unusual. He seldom sought company, so I was quite surprised to see him. Norman was with me that day and he told me that Rex had come to say goodbye. "Why, where's he going?" I asked. "Oh, to a much better place," Norman said, and I guessed that Rex was going to heaven. "He's not poorly," I reasoned with

Norman, who told me that it was Rex's time to go. Rex stood quite still while I put my arms around his neck and cuddled him. And as I did, I had an idea. Rex's only joy in life was food, and he especially liked sweet things. I decided that he should have something special before he went. I went into nana's pantry in the kitchen and uncovered the Bramble pie that she had baked earlier that morning for our tea. Nana was asleep in the chair in the front room, so I took a knife and carefully cut a section of pie from the plate, put in on a smaller plate, and very quietly carried it into the kitchen. I sprinkled some sugar on it and poured some cold milk on top of it, just like I'd seen nana do. I then took the plate into the crystal palace, where Rex was waiting expectantly for me, and I put down the pie in front of him. At first, he looked at the pie sniffed it, and then looked at me as if he didn't dare to believe it was for him. I said: "Go on, boy," and gestured for him to take it, which he did. He devoured it at speed and then proceeded to lick all the crumbs and milk off the plate, leaving a spotless tea plate with all the evidence removed. He licked his lips appreciatively and nudged my hand as a means of thanking me. I patted his head and then he left. He walked down nana's path, jumped the gate, and was gone.

The minute he was out of sight I began to panic. Oh God! How was I going to explain the missing piece of pie to nana? She would be really cross. I felt sick with nerves. I just hadn't considered the consequences of my actions. My only thought was of Rex and wanting him to have something lovely before he left. As the day went on, I felt more and more anxious. Harold came home, as usual, around five o'clock and went into the bathroom to get washed. Nana stood up and announced that she would put the tea on the table. We were having braised steak and onions. It was already stewing away in the oven, and the turnip and potato were in their pans. She put out our dinner and the three of us sat down to eat. I was dreading finishing my dinner, knowing that when we finished, she would be going to fetch our pudding – the bramble pie. Harold stopped eating, looked under the table and said: "Where's the dog, mum?" "I don't know," said nana. "He's usually in by now. It's not like him to be missing at tea-time." I took a sharp intake of breath and began to choke. Harold got up quickly and started to pat my back, while nana ran into the kitchen to fetch me a drink of water. I was coughing and wheezing, finding it very hard to breathe. Nana took over from Harold rubbing my back, quite roughly, saying: "Come on, pet, breathe, calm down – just breathe." It was probably only minutes later, but it seemed like half an hour before my breathing returned to normal. The whole episode had made nana's legs turn to jelly, she said, and she left me at the table and went to sit in her chair. I remained sitting there, just sipping my water. What a drama! After a little while, nana sighed and started to get up off her chair. "What do you want, mum?" Harold asked her, which seemed to stop her in her tracks. "I'll just get your pie for afters," nana said. "You just sit there and pull yourself together. I'll get my own pie," he said. "Get our Julie's, too," she said, as she leaned back into her chair. "I'll do it!" I sprung from my chair before either of them could protest, adding: "I'm okay now. I'm fine!" Nana didn't fancy any pie. I cut a smaller than usual piece for Harold and an even smaller piece for myself, added the sugar and milk, then carried the bowls into the lounge, hoping nana wouldn't see the portion sizes. We ate our dessert in silence. It gave me time to thank God that nana would never know about the pie I'd given to Rex who failed to come home that evening, or any other evening after that. Harold walked around the estate calling his name but to no avail. I prayed that night that Rex had got to heaven safe and happy – with a tummy full of bramble pie!

The final remarkable event that year occurred when I went to nana's brother's house. Nana often spoke of her brother – my dad's uncle – Jack. I hadn't ever realized that he was alive, though. Her stories of him were when they were children. She loved Jack, and they had been quite close as children. One day, my dad came to nana's while I was staying there to say that he had received a telephone call from Uncle Jack's daughter, Myra, to say that her dad was really poorly and he had been asking for nana. Dad offered to take nana over to Middlesbrough where Jack lived. I had no idea where Middlesbrough was, or the fact that it was only a few miles away. Uncle Jack lived so near, yet nana never got to see him. She said that she would like to see him, and dad said he would take her the next day. The following day was Sunday, and dad arrived with mum to take nana to Jack's house. As I had been staying at nana's, I was allowed to go, too. It seemed to take forever to get to Jack's house, and nobody spoke much on the way. It was only ever me that broke the silence by asking questions; usually, "Are we there, yet?" We finally arrived outside a really nice house. Uncle Jack's house was truly lovely. Myra opened the door and let us all in, and once inside Auntie Ada, Jack's wife, greeted us all then made us some tea. The lounge was bright and airy, the carpets were really thick, and it was decorated beautifully. I loved the vibe in this house and hoped that we would stay for a good while. The grown-ups were speaking in low tones, and I couldn't hear what they were saying, but I guessed that Uncle Jack was really, really poorly and everyone looked very sad about it. Mum was frowning compassionately at Auntie Ada, who kept having a few tears. After we had our tea, which was in lovely china cups and saucers, Auntie Ada, Myra, nana and my mum all made their way upstairs. Apparently, Uncle Jack was so poorly that he just stayed in bed, and they had to go up in order to see him. Dad stayed downstairs with me. We each took a chocolate biscuit off the plate that was untouched by the others and sat in silence. The room was so quiet, the only noise was that of the clock ticking, and I looked at dad. "You alright, petal?" he whispered. "Yes thanks, dad" I replied quietly. I felt quite grown up and understood that to be quiet in times of sadness was respectful. I felt proud that I was acting like a grown-up.

We had been sitting for about ten minutes in silence when I nearly jumped out of my skin on hearing someone barking orders. "Left right, left right, halt, present arms." It was funny to hear, but shocking nonetheless. I then started to hear horse's hooves and I began to look around to see where I was hearing this from. I looked over and seemed to be able to see a parade ground playing out on the television, which was,

I may add, switched off. Dad asked what I was staring at, and I said: "Can you see it, dad? On the telly, those soldiers and horses and stuff." He shook his head. It was obvious he couldn't, and he asked me to explain what I could see. I told him that there were soldiers all lined up on some sort of parade ground, and men with bright red jackets on horses. I told dad how I could feel the atmosphere was exciting and that I expected that the Queen would arrive shortly. Dad just sat quietly while I relayed what I could see to him, making no comment at all. Then everything stopped just as soon as it started, and I was left staring at a blank television screen. I then heard footsteps as nana and the others came down the stairs. Nana had been crying and when she looked at dad she just shook her head. What she had encountered upstairs had obviously disturbed her. Myra made us all some more tea, and after drinking it, we made moves to go home. Goodbyes were said and we left in the car. Another quiet journey home ensued. Dad didn't mention to mum or nana anything about the vision I had had at Uncle Jack's house, and I sensed not to talk about it, either. We dropped nana off at home, and I collected my things before returning back home with dad and mum. I hugged nana hard before I left. I sensed that she needed it.

Once we were back in the car, dad told me to tell mum what had happened at Uncle Jack's. So I did. She kept quiet while I was telling her about the soldiers, the horses, and the television. When I finished, she looked at dad, who shrugged. She then asked me: "Julie, has nana talked much about Uncle Jack to you?" "Yes. About when they were children," I replied honestly. "She didn't tell you about what his job was then?" mum asked. "No, not at all, mum," I said. Dad then told me that when Uncle Jack had been young he had been in the army. He was a regimental sergeant major and a brilliant horseman. He had served in the Queen's Guards and had had a wonderful career. "Oh, right!" I replied, quite uninterested in the knowledge. I still didn't really understand why I had seen what I had earlier in Jack's house. Later that night, at bedtime when Norman came to check on me, I asked him what the vision was all about. He explained that while we were in Jack's house that afternoon, Jack was dying and, that as he was dying, he was watching his past life being played out in front of him. He went on to tell me that I had been allowed to watch, with Jack, as he celebrated the grand events of his life and some of his happiest times. I told Norman that I thought Uncle Jack must have really had a nice life and that, in my opinion, he would have enjoyed his life very much. Norman agreed. Uncle Jack died that night. His own biography reel had run to its end. I felt sure that he would have died happily, knowing that he had led a full and happy life. I hoped that everyone that I loved would live a full and happy life; after all, Norman reckoned that that was the only way a life should be lived.

17

BIBLES, BIBLES EVERYWHERE!

In October 1972, we moved house yet again. Dad was no longer working for Sparks bakery, so we weren't allowed to remain in the flat that belonged to them. This was, I thought, the end of my world. I was happy at school and had some lovely friends, who I didn't want to move away from. Dad and mum tried all ways to bring me around to their way of thinking, but I would not be moved. My protests were futile, and we were going. Mum told me how great it would be living nearer her sisters, my aunts, and my cousins. She said how nice our new house was and that it had a lovely big garden to play in. This was rich! Both dad and her hated gardening – it would look like a wilderness in no time at all! A fact that seemed to elude them. When I expressed my concerns about moving to a new school, I was told that my new school would be marvellous, and that it was the school where mum herself had attended as a child. This school was also only 200 yards from our new house, apparently. Nothing my parents said made me feel any better, and I seemed to sulk for weeks. Norman visited me continuously and even he seemed to be on their side, saying things like: "View this as a new opportunity for learning" and "View it as a new chapter". I didn't want a new chapter, I moaned – I was quite happy with the existing one! The fact that Norton was in close proximity to Billingham mattered not. After all, I couldn't drive, could I?

The day of the move came, and Mark, Alison, Andrew, and I were dropped off at nana's early one Saturday morning, so that mum and dad could get everything sorted. I continuously moaned to nana during the day about how unhappy I was at leaving Norton. "Well, best just get on with it," she said, which made me feel as though even she was part of the moving conspiracy. I settled down to the inevitability of it all after Nana promised me that, if I became very unhappy at Billingham, she would allow me to come and live with her. Maybe things weren't so bad after all. Godforsaken Billingham. I just knew I would hate it! Dad and mum came and collected us around six o'clock and seemed really excited about showing us our new bedrooms. I was remaining awkward.

To be fair, the house was really nice. The wallpaper was quite old fashioned; apparently, the previous tenants – a Mr and Mrs Harrison - were old. Nevertheless, it was a cosy house and immaculate. Mum, as usual, had made it homely and appealing all in one day, and when we arrived there and dad opened the front door, we all wandered around the house, the other three going from room to room like excited puppies exploring new territory. Just through the front door, the stairs were straight ahead with a door to a front room either side of the stairs. At the top of the stairs was a large landing leading to three bedrooms and a bathroom. On one side of the stairs was dad and mum's room, and at the other side was the bedroom I was to share with Alison.

Mark and Andrew were to have the much smaller, back bedroom. They didn't seem to mind the lack of space; they were just thrilled at the new bunk beds dad had put up for them. Mum had made my bedroom especially lovely. It was a large bright bedroom that looked out onto the front garden. She had put twin beds in there: one under the window, the other against a wall. We each had a small set of drawers at the end of our bed and mum's own dressing table had been put between our beds, for us to share. I immediately liked this room and commandeered the bed under the window. I often liked to look at the moon and stargaze, so it was perfect for me. I had packed my own personal belongings into a box and taped it up, and it was left for me to open at the foot of my bed. I took out my jewellery box and placed it on my side of our dressing table. The dressing table had a large mirror in the middle and a box drawer either side. Although Alison was too young to own anything valuable, I was quite magnanimous and told her that the drawer at her side was especially for her. I put my Bible in my drawer. (Nana had bought it for my ninth birthday, and I treated it with reverence, just like she did with hers.) I had tried reading it a few times, but couldn't really understand what it was all about. But that did not alter the fact that it was a most prized possession.

Auntie May had bought me a lovely pink brush, comb and mirror set, and I placed it on the middle section of the dressing table and decided that I would brush my hair a hundred times each night in front of the mirror. This, incidentally, never happened! I was always too scared to look into the mirror for any length of time. At the bottom of my personal box were some small ornaments that I had carefully wrapped in newspaper; little animals I had bought when we had gone on holiday to Whitby the year before. I decided that they would look nice on the window sill, so I started to arrange them, making sure that the same distance was between each of the four ornaments. While I was doing this, I noticed a small black book in the corner of the window sill. I picked it up and noticed how cold it was. This small black book was old, no bigger than dad's cigarette packet, and was titled *Common Prayer Book*. The pages were like those in my Bible, fine paper with really small writing on them, on every page a different psalm or prayer. I ran to find mum to ask if I could keep this little book. She was downstairs in the kitchen with dad, waiting for the kettle to boil. My older cousin, Maurice, had just plumbed the gas cooker in and this was their first cup of tea since breakfast. Dad was busy putting things away in the pantry in the kitchen. "Mum?" I said questioningly. "I found this little book on the window sill in my bedroom, so can I keep it?" Dad came out of the pantry on hearing me, took the book off me and started turning it over in his hands. He then said to mum: "Another one." "Another one, what?" I asked. "Oh, nothing," mum replied. She then looked at dad and shrugged. "Can I then? Have it I mean, to keep." "Yes, I think so," she said, and dad gave it back to me. "Thanks, I'll put it with my Bible," I announced. "It feels really cold," I said. "You would think it had been kept in a fridge." They both just looked at me and said nothing. Then I saw mum visibly shake herself and suggest to dad that he go to the chip shop for supper.

It was by now about eight o'clock, and although us kids had already eaten at nana's, mum and dad hadn't. Great! This was a bonus - chippy for supper! Dad got his car keys, put on his coat, and mum gave him some money. When he left, I ran up and put the little black book in the same drawer as my Bible, feeling quite pleased with my find. I then went back downstairs to help mum. I buttered some bread and got the tray ready with salt and vinegar, sauce and pickled onions, and took it into the lounge as per mum's request. This Billingham house didn't have a dining room; just two front rooms, one of which mum intended to save for best. So we were allowed to eat our meals on our knees, whilst watching the television – another good point about this house. Perhaps I was changing my mind about Billingham, after all. I was certainly warming to this new place. Dad returned shortly and called the kids to come and enjoy their bags of chips. We all sat together, the first night in our new house, and everyone seemed really happy. The fire was on and everyone seemed happy and content. So why was I so cold?

We went to bed later than usual that evening, and dad and mum came into our bedrooms to tuck us in and check that we were all okay. I had a really fitful night's sleep that night and was troubled by vivid dreams of walking through strange rooms, encountering strange people – none of whom were remotely familiar to me. I woke up early the next morning and it was apparent that I was the only one in the family who had. The house seemed so quiet and I felt like I had laid there for ages, my blankets pulled up under my chin, before anyone else stirred. Dad was the first to get up. I heard him cross the landing and go into the bathroom, closely followed by mum, then her quick little steps downstairs and into the lounge. I just lay there listening to the unfamiliar sounds of this house: the sound of the lounge door as it opened, the noise the tank made when the water was running, the loud clicking of the ignition as someone struggled to light the gas fire. Another major bonus this house offered was the gas fire. Instant heat was bliss for me. No more waiting with a blanket around me till one of my parents lit the coal fire.

I put my dressing gown on and went downstairs. Mum was in the kitchen, grilling toast and making tea, and dad was sitting in a chair near the fire filling a form in. He remarked upon how early I was up for a Sunday and asked if I was alright. "I'm just so cold," I said forlornly. "This house is freezing." Dad got up and said: "Here chick, sit in this chair. I've warmed the seat for you." I did and he took of his cardigan and covered my legs with it. At last I felt warm. He went through to the kitchen to help mum, and they both appeared minutes later with tea and toast for all three of us. Mum and dad sat together on the couch, and we all ate in silence. When we had finished, dad said: "I really like it here, Ena." "Me too," she said. "I'll soon have it looking more like a home." "You have done a great job already," he enthused, and then they both laughed at what a day they had had yesterday and how glad they were that the worst of the move was over.

I sat with my cup in my hand, and they carried on with their conversation, forgetting that I was there I suppose. My interest was taken with a huge built-in cupboard that stood on the floor at the end of the lounge, below the window. This cupboard was put in when the house was built and it stood between the coalhouse, which took up one corner of the room, and the pantry in the kitchen, which was in the other. The cupboard was painted white and it had an old brass catch that kept it shut. I was aware still of dad and mum's mutual praise of the new house, but this cupboard was a far more interesting focus. I was transfixed looking at it and jumped slightly when all of a sudden the door of it sprung open. It opened with such a force that dad and mum jumped, too. Dad looked at mum, then got up and closed the door. "What's in there?" I asked. "Oh, nothing important," mum said. "Just boxes that I haven't had chance to sort out yet." "Oh, right," I said, and made a mental note to investigate further later.

Not long after, Mark, Alison, and Andrew trouped down the stairs like the three bears. Mum made fresh tea and toast, and we all sat around the fire while they ate their breakfast. That day was a flurry of activity, and we were all assigned jobs in our new house. We didn't get together again till lunchtime to eat our sandwiches and biscuits, then it was back to work. After tea, mum announced that she was going to clean the bathroom next, so that we could all have baths before our big day tomorrow at our new school. Once she had cleaned it to her standard, she called Alison and Andrew for their baths. Mark and I were old enough to go in the bath by ourselves, and I always insisted on going in last so that I could stay up later than the others, or at least until my hair was dry. After we were all washed and dried, we sat together once again on the couch. Dad had pulled it up in front of the fire and made us jam sandwiches and tea for supper. The whole vibe was one of contentment. So why was I still not sure about this house?

At eight o'clock, dad declared it was bedtime for the little ones, and he went with mum to tuck them in and settle them for sleep. I took this opportunity to look inside the mysterious cupboard; after all, nobody had said that I wasn't allowed to. I gently opened the brass clasp and looked inside. There were three large shelves inside, running the full width of the cupboard; one about six inches from the top, the next about 12 inches below that, and then a large shelf under that. The shelves all had something on them – boxes, as mum had said, that hadn't been sorted out yet. I recognized most of the boxes contained photographs, documents, letters, and other things that had been in mum's wardrobe in the flat at Norton. The only box I didn't recognize was on the bottom shelf in the corner. It was a really old box and I decided to investigate further. It was heavy, but I still managed to lift it out quite easily, making sure that I didn't get my clean nightdress dirty.

The box smelled dusty, and as I opened the lid, I was quite disappointed to find that the only contents were old books. Each one of these books had a brown, black, or navy cover, and upon closer investigation, I saw that they were either Bibles or prayer books like the one I had found on my window sill. I was lost in the mystery of these old books, so failed to hear dad and mum come into the room. "Julie, what are you doing?" Mum startled me. "Nothing," I said. "I just wanted to see what was in the cupboard." "Well, that's enough now. You'll get filthy. Leave them." She motioned to the books and dad came over and started putting them back into their box. Once he had done that, he tried to put the box back into the cupboard. It wouldn't fit! It really wouldn't go back into the space that I had taken it from. He huffed and puffed and scratched his chin, trying to figure out why it wouldn't go. Dad asked me if it had been difficult to get the box out of the cupboard to begin with. "No, not at all Dad. It came out easily," I said. "Well that's a mystery and a half!" he exclaimed. "Oh, just leave it, Bill," Mum said. "I'll put it away after." Dad closed the cupboard doors and I asked mum who the books belonged to. "I don't know," she replied, "I noticed when we moved in yesterday that there on each window sill was either a Bible or a prayer book," she said looking perplexed. "Is that a good or a bad thing?" I questioned. "Oh, I'm sure it's a good thing," she said. "Whoever lived here before us was obviously very religious." Mm. I wasn't so sure. I went to bed that evening wondering about the books, the box, the cupboard, and the house. I had another restless night and dreamt that I was in a railway station being passed by lots of people who knew me, yet I didn't know them.

I was quite surprised the next morning when dad was still at home when we got up. He usually left early for work. He was, by now, a lorry driver for a local door manufacturer, and was much happier in his work. Mum explained that he had taken the day off to sort things out and help her with the running about she needed to do. But that first he was going to come with us to our new school. We had breakfast, got dressed, and then got our coats ready to walk the short journey down the road to our new school. The rug rats seemed quite unperturbed by this, but I was terrified. I wasn't ready to meet new friends, new teachers, or new anything for that matter. I considered feigning a poorly tummy, but figured that dad and mum would know that I was pretending, and that could get me in trouble. Dad was helping me on with my coat, telling me that being the eldest I should set a good example and go into school with a nice happy smiley face. I didn't feel much like smiling. I was yawning continuously, which prompted him to ask if I'd slept okay. "No, dad, I didn't," I said. "I hardly slept a wink. I had bad dreams and I'm tired," hoping that he would let me stay off school. He hugged me and then asked: "Did you get up and come down during the night?" "No," I replied. "Are you sure? It doesn't matter if you did, just tell me the truth." "I am telling the truth, dad," I said indignantly. "I didn't get up at all." "Okay, that's okay," he said. "Why did you think I got up?" I asked. "Oh, no reason," he lied, and off we went to school.

My first day at Billingham South School was fine. I sat next to a lovely girl called Deborah, and everyone seemed friendly and genuinely interested in me. My teacher, Miss Morgan, was a lot older than my previous teacher, and although she didn't smile much, I still liked her. The day seemed to pass really quickly. At 3:30 P.M., mum met me outside of my classroom. She had already collected Mark, Alison, and Andrew, and was glad to hear that my first day had gone so well. We walked the short distance home, and I was a little disappointed to find that dad wasn't home. Apparently, he had gone to hand in the keys to the flat. All day I had pondered about why he thought that I might have got up and gone downstairs. Once home, mum took her coat off and began to peel potatoes for tea. The kids were watching the television, and I decided to investigate the big cupboard again. I gently opened the clasp and, low and behold, the old box of Bibles was back in its original place. Mum came into the lounge wiping her hands on her apron to ask me to help her in the kitchen, and closed the cupboard doors. When I was in the kitchen, buttering the bread, she asked me: "How did you get that old box back into the cupboard?" "What?" I tried to keep from sounding surprised. "I said to your dad," she continued, "our Julie must have got up through the night to have another look in that box and then managed to put it back where it came from." "Oh, yes," I muttered quietly. So that was it! Someone had managed to put the box back in its original place. Well it was obvious that it wasn't dad or mum. And it certainly wasn't me. So who on Earth had done it? I hoped that she didn't question me any further about it. She didn't. Later that day, when dad came in, he too seemed to have forgotten all about the cupboard incident, and I was glad not to be questioned about it. I needed time to think about all this. That incident was the first indicator that that house was like no other house we had ever lived in before.

As weeks went by, I came to accept certain differences, apart from the obvious ones, that a house move often brings. The first noticeable difference was that Norman didn't seem to be so accessible anymore. I also realized that this house was very busy. It had its own energy field, and the numerous spirits I encountered there weren't always so friendly. The other definite difference was that the happenings in the house weren't always just exclusive to me.

18

MEET THE HARRISONS

At the age of 11, I don't think I gave too much thought to the differences between myself and my siblings. I never stopped to contemplate the whys and wherefores of my ability to hear, see, and feel what they didn't. I just accepted how things were, and that the strange things that occurred around me were exclusive to me. You will imagine my surprise when, shortly after moving into this house, peculiar things began to happen that were unexplainable to us all.

I had sensed that the house had a resident spirit before he ever appeared, and when he did he would often appear in a white mist. Quite ghostly. This spirit would wander from room to room, as though he was looking for something or someone. He was tall, smart, and quite serious looking. I didn't ever feel threatened by him, and he never tried to either frighten or befriend me. I most often saw him standing on the landing below the loft hatch. I instinctively felt that he had lived in our house before us. He often just stood and stared at us, watching as Mark, Alison, or Andrew passed by him. Whenever he was about to appear, this strange mist descended from the loft, then manifested into his form. It was as if he lived up there.

This house also had several other presences which didn't seem to visit as regular as this man – they just appeared now and then, usually only for short periods of time. Some were small, some tall, some whose energy felt good, some mysterious types of spirit that weren't always definable, and a male who visited that I didn't like at all. He seemed to have a dark aura and I felt quite threatened by him. Over the months that followed, I learned to differentiate between the spirit visitors that this house played host to. Norman explained that most of these spirits were earthbound and awaiting rescue. I didn't really understand what he meant, nor would he elaborate at that time. I was satisfied that Norman would always protect me, and he used to warn me to be careful or avoid certain areas of the house at times. He did say that this house had peculiar ley lines that meant there seemed to be an open doorway, a portal for spirits that had nothing to do with me or my gift of vision.

Needless to say, I constantly felt the cold in that house and often wore layers of clothes to keep myself warm. Often, when I was alone in my bedroom, the wardrobe doors would open on their own and my dressing table drawers would open and then shut. Some days, my bed would have an imprint on the candlewick, as though someone had been sitting on it. This house always had a musty smell that reminded me of old people, despite mum's attempts with air freshener.

I had decided, upon moving to Billingham, to keep to myself the thoughts and the things that I experienced that were sometimes unexplainable. After all, we were now in a new neighbourhood, and I had the perfect opportunity to reinvent myself.

Acting normal, despite my visions, became second nature to me. And if I ever was afraid in the house, then I would summon Norman, who would reassure me that all was well and that I was looked after. He suggested that if I ever got afraid, then I should sing; apparently, singing raises the vibration around you and attracts good things. I was no Lulu, but needless to say, I sang my head off most of the time. By Christmas of that year, just two months after moving in, we were all really settled in the house and especially in our new school. Some of our old friends forgotten, the road we lived in was large and there were kids of all ages to play with. Each of us had made friends quickly and easily. Mum and dad seemed settled, too. I think mum preferred being back in Billingham, the town where she had been born and where her three sisters still lived. Dad's work was steady, and life was looking good. I sensed that we would stay in this house for a long time.

I had noticed that mum never spoke much about her childhood and I surmised that having lost both of her parents, it was difficult for her. I hadn't developed much tact by that age and constantly asked questions about my grandma and granddad, feeling as though they were still part of our family even if they weren't around anymore. So at Christmastime, while I was helping her put up the tree and decorations, I asked if she had ever helped her mum to decorate the house when she was young. She told me how poor her parents had been, and that my grandma had made the house look lovely with the little she had, always managing to make things out of scraps of fabric, ribbon, and tissue paper, ensuring the house looked festive for my mum and her sisters. She went on to say with pride how her poor mother had made clothes for her girls, carefully stitching everything by hand, as she had no sewing machine. Mum laughed as she took a green garland out of our box of decorations, held it up and said: "My Mum would have hated this!" When I asked why, she went on to tell me about how superstitious grandma Ellen had been; insisting that her girls followed her rules of when they could trim their nails, what to do if they spilt salt, what they could and couldn't do on certain days of the week, and finally about her dislike of anything green. Mum explained that a lot of people of her mother's generation felt the same about the colour green. When I asked why, she didn't really know, but told me that if she or her sisters ever bought anything green, then they would have to sneak it into the house and make sure their mother didn't find out. "You don't mind green do you, mum?" I asked. "No, of course I don't," she laughed. "It's one of my favourite colours." Just a week later, it became apparent that someone in our house shared grandma Ellen's dislike of green.

That Christmas, mum had bought my little brother Andrew two t-shirts, both identical in style and pattern: one red and one green. He wore the red one on Christmas Day, but never got to wear the green one. It mysteriously disappeared before he had chance to wear it. My lovely cousin Lynn had sent me some clothes that she had grown out of. I loved Lynn's cast-offs even more than I loved getting new clothes, and amongst the things she sent was a lovely green jacket with a sheepskin collar. I hung it in my wardrobe with the intention of keeping it for when I went somewhere special. That, too, disappeared before I got chance to show it off. Dad and mum seldom went out, but once a year they would join Auntie May and Uncle Stan for a dinner dance at the local Catholic club. It was usually on St Patrick's Day, and they both loved going. Dad would buy mum a new dress for the occasion. She always had a lovely figure and, when she was ready, would float down the stairs like a princess going to the ball. Dad would always say: "Doesn't your mum look beautiful." And we would all nod our agreement. She was stunning!

Dad wasn't one for new clothes, really. He worked most of the time, and when he wasn't at work he would be working on his cars. So looking dapper wasn't really his priority. Mum liked him to look smart though, and that year she had bought him a lovely dark green suit from the nearly new shop in the village. He tried it on and it fit him perfectly. She got it dry cleaned for him, and it looked as good as new. The week before the dance he modelled it for us, making us all laugh as he strutted back and forth putting on a posh accent. Mum carefully put it back into the plastic bag it had left the cleaners in, and hung it in their wardrobe. On the evening of the dance, just as they were preparing to go, dad noticed that the breast pocket had been ripped. They both agreed that the rip hadn't been there the previous week when he'd tried it on. Mum quickly put a few stitches in to mend it for the evening, and they left, both perplexed as to how this could have happened. I reminded them that it was green and that strange things had happened to green clothing lately.

The dreams that I had in that house were always really vivid. So much so, that when I woke up each morning, I would still feel really tired. This sleep activity was wearing me out, and on weekends I would often sleep till after lunchtime, feeling exhausted from the nightmares that I had. A recurring dream bothered me: I would be up in the loft of our house and it would be crowded with people, none of whom I knew. These people were mournful and sad, crying because they were trapped up there. Those of them that weren't sad were angry and bitter, often snarling at me. I would always feel frustrated with them, pointing to the open loft door, telling them that they weren't trapped and that it was open for them to go downstairs. The reply was always the same: they needed to go, up not down, if they were to be free. I didn't really understand the loft energy thing. I knew there was something up there, because if I stood directly under the loft door, it made me feel really dizzy. One day, after a green blouse – a favourite of mum's – had disappeared, I told her that I thought that these green items of clothes may be up in the loft, and that Norman had said that it was mischievous spirits that were taking them. I suggested that she get dad to go up there to investigate, feeling sure that there was something up there that needed unlocking, or something that needed to be discovered.

When dad came home that evening, mum told him about the green blouse, and that I had thought that these mysterious thefts were naughty spirits who may have managed to store things in the loft. He looked at us both incredulously. "So, let me get this right," he said. "You two think that there is some sort of warehouse in the loft? You're as daft as each other," he laughed. We didn't. And mum told him that after he'd eaten tea, she would be grateful if he would humour us and have a look anyway. Dad hated heights, so he huffed and puffed about the daunting prospect, but knew better than to refuse mum. After eating his tea, which seemed to take him longer than usual, he got the step ladders and we both followed him up to the stairs, watching as he positioned them directly under the loft hatch. He was sighing and muttering under his breath about us and our stupid notions. We ignored him and waited expectantly as he tried several times to dislodge the loft door. "I tell you what, Ena," he said in an exasperated tone. "If we have ghosts in this house, then they're getting more meat than I am, because this door hasn't been opened for donkey's years." Eventually, after much huffing and puffing, he managed to punch it open, causing a downfall of fine, black dust to land on him. Mum and I quickly got out of the way. He was getting more irritated by the minute with this task. He took his torch from mum and went up on the step ladders until only his knees and feet were showing. "No, there's nothing up here apart from an old box. Are you two satisfied?" I wasn't. "What's in the box, dad?" I asked. "Probably just junk," he replied. "Fetch it down, then," mum added. After some more tutting and sighing, he climbed right up into the loft and appeared shortly after at the open hatch. He lowered an old, brown wooden box down to mum, warning her of how dusty and dirty it was. I couldn't wait to look into the box, convinced it would hold our missing items of green clothing.

It didn't! Inside, there were photographs and old love letters; the photos were of a young couple, both of them smartly dressed, perhaps in their twenties. One of the photographs had 1936 written on the reverse. There were other snaps of them taken separately, but all of them were just of these two people. The letters were addressed to Mrs Isabel Harrison at our address, and were from her husband Jack; letters written to his beloved wife while he was away fighting in the war. It was evident that Mr and Mrs Harrison were devoted to each other, and I realized that Jack Harrison was the man who I often spotted on the stairs; the quiet man, who always seemed to be looking for someone. The three of us looked through this box until dad decided that it was private and that perhaps we best put it away. He told mum that he would take it to the incinerator at work.

After dad's trip up into the loft that day, nothing else green ever went missing. But the presences and energies of the house became even more active. That night, I was woken by the sound of rustling at the side of my bed. The little square drawer of my dressing table flew open, and when I looked into it, my little Bible was open at Psalms No. 23. I grabbed my Bible from the drawer and held it close to my chest. Were the Harrisons trying to tell me something? Was this the reason that each room had had a Bible put on the windowsill when we first moved in? I didn't much care, my heart was beating so fast I could hear it in my head. The room had become so cold that I could see my breath in the air. I put my head under the bed covers and held my Bible to me and decided that from that night I would keep it under my pillow. Perhaps that was why my nana read the Bible each night? I made a mental note to ask her. Whatever the reason, though, I superstitiously felt safer with it close by me.

19

IS IT ME?

After that night, life seemed to return back to normal for a little while. The spirits I saw were few and far between, and my Bible, I believed, seemed to ward off the nightmares a little. The first winter in our new home was particularly harsh, and we had lots of snow in the January and February of that year. We kids thought that this was fantastic, and each day after school, we would dash home, rush our tea, and wrap up warm, hoping to be the first ones out in the road to enjoy the snow. Everyone seemed to come out and play that winter, and we spent the evenings making slides and having snowman-making competitions. Those with sledges would bring them out, and we would all take turns, riding on them, or pushing and pulling them. It was a magical time, and despite our varying ages, Mark, Alison, Andrew, and I all played happily together with our friends. We each of us dreaded the call for bedtime and would always ask for five more minutes which invariably became 15! We were worried that this magical winter playground that we had created would melt while we slept, and the first thing I did upon waking, was to look out of the bedroom window and screech with excitement when we'd had another flurry of snow.

Now that the spirit activity in the house had settled down, my sleep pattern became better, and I felt really glad that we had moved to Billingham. Dad was settled in his driving job on a permanent contract. Most of his deliveries were local, which meant he was home every night for tea. This was so much easier for mum, who busied her self each day with housework: washing and ironing most days, and picking up, cooking, and cleaning for us four. She always seemed to be ironing! I suppose with there being so many in the household that this was a never-ending task for her. I loved to watch her ironing. She always stood in the same place, positioning her ironing board at the rear of the lounge, so that she faced the front window and could keep an eye on what was happening out front. I seldom stopped to think about how much she did for us all those days, and on days when she looked tired, I would offer to iron the pillowcases, tea-towels, and handkerchiefs. One particular day in early spring, she positioned the usual mountain of ironing on the chair at the rear of the lounge and, as she often did before commencing the task in hand, put her favourite Jim Reeves LP on the radiogram. She would sometimes sing along to her favourite tracks as she ironed, lost in the world of love songs and laundry. *Distant Drums* was my least favourite song in the world and so I usually went up into my room when it was on. But on this particular day, I sat in dad's chair opposite her and read my latest copy of *Jackie* magazine. I loved this magazine! It had up-to-date posters of the latest pop groups, and interviews and fact sheets on them, too, plus lyrics of a top ten hit, and problem pages for teenagers. There was always a good short story, too. *Jackie* was targeted at teenagers, so I felt really hip and mature reading it, despite the fact that I was only 11. I bought it every week with my pocket money.

I always felt so relaxed when mum was ironing. The gentle whoosh of steam and the noise as the iron glided over the numerous garments. The lovely smell of newly washed laundry and the heat of the iron often made me sleepy. Mum seldom spoke when she ironed, she once said that it was the time when she did her best thinking and preferred to just listen to her music. Not long after she had started to iron, and Jim Reeves was warbling track number two, I became aware that she had suddenly stopped ironing. I looked up from my magazine and asked if she was okay. She was standing very still, like a statue, and at first she didn't answer me. "Mum," I said a little more urgently. "Are you alright?" She didn't move, but answered: "Julie, do you see anyone standing behind me?" "No, Mum," I answered honestly. "Come over here," she said. "Walk slowly and come over here." I did and stood in front of the ironing board facing her. "Is it me, or is someone breathing on the back of my neck?" she asked. Panic made me tune in, the speed of the energy shift making me a little dizzy and I didn't like what I saw. Standing behind her, to her left, was the dark presence that I often tried to avoid. He was a dark, misty figure and he was hovering over her left shoulder sneering. "Do you feel it more to the left?" I asked. "Only on the left," she replied. "Who is it?" "I don't know, mum," I said. "I don't like it!" she said, panic creeping into her voice. I was scared, too, and asked Norman what we should do. He told me to order this spirit to leave, telling me to say the words "Go in Peace". I began to chant "Go in peace, go in peace". It became a mantra that mum joined in with, and I watched as the energy of this spirit diminish, then leave. After it had gone, I hugged mum. Her legs were shaking. She unplugged the iron and sat down, and I made us both a cup of tea.

That afternoon, for the first time ever, mum and I had a long conversation about spirits and Norman and the things I saw and experienced. She asked me lots of questions, and I answered the best I could. She acknowledged Norman and asked me to ask him why she had felt this awful spirit when she wasn't that way herself. He explained that the energy of our house lent itself to the spirits who lived in it, and that due to the power of this spirit, anyone would have felt it. He also told me to tell her that perhaps her experience today was so that she could know what it felt like to be me sometimes. She seemed to accept this and said that she was sorry and that she would listen to me in future. Norman also said that the problems in the house may intensify around my adolescent years. I wasn't sure what that meant, but I knew enough to know that mum didn't respond well to bad news. I thought it best to keep that little snippet to myself.

When dad came home that evening, mum told him what had happened that afternoon. He seemed quite unperturbed by it, so I added my endorsement of the event. He grabbed the pair of us in a bear hug and told us that we were as daft as each other and that our imaginations had got the better of us. Mum seemed consoled by this. I wasn't. I knew better. Once again, things calmed down and our house seemed to normalize. The ironing incident wasn't mentioned again, but I noticed that mum never stood in that part of the lounge again to iron.

Later that spring, a series of events in the house made my parents question where to go for help. One morning, mum had gone up into the bathroom to find the bath full to its brim of water. There were no taps running and no plug in the bath. She screamed and the bath immediately started to empty. This happened several more times, despite dad's tightening of the taps. Another time, we all came home from school together, and as mum opened the front door, she froze when she saw that the landing window was wide open. It had never been opened before and, thinking that we had been burgled, she closed the door and we all walked with her to the phone box where she phoned dad's work. They sent him home immediately. When he arrived home, he ordered us to stay out front while he investigated. Once inside, he discovered that there was no sign of intruders or indeed any damage to the window. It was difficult to close the window, he remarked, and couldn't understand how it could have come open in the first place. The same thing happened a week later. This time, mum didn't bother getting dad home from work. When he came in and she told him, out of sheer exasperation, he hammered a two-inch nail through the window frame into the sill, remarking that it wouldn't come open again. It did! Two weeks later, we got home from school to find the window wide open. It looked eerie, the window swinging open, the nail still hammered into the frame, and the hole in the sill where the nail had been. We were all lost for words.

During the spring of that year, I had started going to church with some of my friends in our road. A beautiful church – St Cuthbert's, situated on Billingham Green – it dated back to the ninth century. Mum had been christened there, and when dad proposed to her, it was decided that they would marry there, too. St Cuthbert's was very different from the church I went to whenever I stayed at Auntie May's house. The church she went to was just at the end of her road – a lovely Catholic church called Holy Rosary. Each Sunday, Auntie May, Lynn, and me would go off to mass after breakfast. This was my first ever experience of religion, and I loved the drama and atmosphere of the service. I always left church feeling better than I did when I entered. I was completely awestruck the first time I set foot in St Cuthbert's; this beautiful old church had such good vibes, and I daydreamed about all the thousands of people who may have sought solace here over the hundreds of years that it had stood there. The service here on a Sunday was very similar to the mass at Holy Rosary, so I felt quite important being able to know the responses to the prayers without having to look at the order of service. I felt that I belonged there and I looked forward to Sundays, and got out of bed readily to get ready for the 11 A.M. service.

I still had regular visits from Norman and the other nice spirits he brought with him, but he agreed with my decision to keep his wisdom to myself in the hope that I wouldn't be thought of as different. Norman liked coming along to church and would often explain after the service the message the sermon was meant to give, or the reasoning behind certain aspects of the communion service. I would join the line of congregation as they went to the altar for their bread and wine, and would bow my head so that the vicar could put his hand on my head and bless me. I felt sure that I wanted to receive communion when I was old enough.

The vicar, Mr Brown, was a lovely, gentle man. He was tall, thin, in his late 50s, and he always had time for his flock. He had a special gift of making you feel special and was obviously adored by his congregation. After each Sunday morning communion service, tea and coffee were served in the church hall, opposite the church. Mrs Brown, the vicar's wife, would stand behind the hatch, handing out drinks and biscuits to those who wanted them. She was lovely, too; the perfect match for her husband, equally as kind, understanding, and compassionate. After a few weeks, I offered to help her in the kitchen and was delighted when I was allowed to work behind the hatch with her, plating up biscuits and washing the endless cups and saucers left behind after this get-together. Mrs Brown was always really appreciative of help, and those of us that helped her did so willingly.

Attending church each week became an important part of my life, and I soon became involved in the youth activities associated with it. Each week, on Thursdays, there was a youth club where you could play table tennis, darts, cards, or just socialize. The girls generally sat around listening to records, discussing the latest fashions. The highlight in the church's youth calendar was the disco on the last Friday of every month. Best clothes were donned, and we all had a fabulous time dancing to the latest chart releases. I volunteered for most of the committees the church had and was allowed to help run the tuck shop at the disco. I felt so proud behind the hatch, serving crisps, sweets, and various fizzy drinks to my peers. This was probably one of the happiest times of my young life, and I dreamed of marrying a vicar just so that I would always have an involvement in church life.

Strange things were still happening at home – but only to mum and me. I remember noticing that she no longer mentioned the weird movement of objects or electrical disturbances to dad anymore. Probably because he thought that whatever happened was "all in our heads." It became usual for the television to switch itself on or off, or lights to switch on. And when the records we played just stopped abruptly, mum and I would just exchange knowing glances. We always told each other what happened, though, and it was good that I no longer had to keep things of that nature to myself. Most of the weird happenings that took place, did so when there was just mum and I at home.

One day, as I was on my way home from school, I noticed that mum was talking to the old lady across the road from us. Her name was Mrs Allen, and she was a nice lady. She was always dressed in lovely clothes, and wore shoes and hats that matched her numerous colourful outfits. Her husband was always smart, too. He smiled a lot and often cracked a joke with whoever was playing out in the road. I had noticed Mrs Allen at church on a few occasions, and she always acknowledged me with a nod and a smile. I joined mum as she was talking to Mrs Allen, who asked how I was settling in at school and if I was enjoying church. I said yes to both questions. Mrs Allen remarked to mum how well behaved the four of us were, and I could see mum bustling with pride. She went on to ask if we had settled in the house alright. Mum replied that we were all enjoying living in such a nice neighbourhood and asked Mrs Allen how long she had lived in her house. "Oh, forty-odd years," she replied. Mum went on to ask her if she had known who had lived in our house before us. "Oh, yes," Mrs Allen enthused. "Mrs Harrison was a very good friend of mine – we always went to church together." "Did she ever mention any strange goings-on in her house?" mum asked tentatively, trying not to sound nosey. "No, I don't think so, dear," Mrs Allen replied, looking puzzled. "Why?" "Oh, nothing, really," mum shrugged, and then proceeded to tell her some of the bizarre events that took place there. Mrs Allen looked really interested and also a little thoughtful, obviously searching her memory for any parallel tales from Mrs Harrison. She then appeared to have had a slight recollection and said: "I do remember, though, that before Mrs Harrison got poorly and was still going to church, I would call for her. She was seldom ready and always had to go upstairs for her hat. On numerous occasions I would hear her talking," Mrs Allen continued. "And one day, my curiosity got the better of me. I asked her if I was mistaken or had I heard her talking to someone upstairs. She told me that it was Jack, her late husband, whom she had been talking to, and remarked that he was still there, still with her." Mrs Allen added that Jack had been dead for over ten years. She then went on to say that she hadn't liked to pry and that the subject hadn't ever been spoken about again. She said that the Harrisons had been devoted to each other and had kept their lives very private, preferring to spend their time just the two of them together. As we left Mrs Allen and walked over the road to our house, mum asked what I thought about that, and I just shrugged saying that it was a little odd.

That night at bedtime, I told Norman about the conversation that mum had had with Mrs Allen and asked for his thoughts on it. He explained that Mrs Harrison's belief that her husband was still with her, twinned with her reluctance to accept his death, had rendered Mr Harrison earthbound. He said that he thought that she probably was able to communicate with him and said that he thought it was sad that when it was her time to pass over, that her soul had probably progressed as it should have, and that her poor Jack was still here, both trapped and earthbound. This information made me feel sad and I asked Norman whether Jack Harrison's soul would ever be able to join his wife's. He said that it would if he was rescued and given energy that would enable him to be released. I didn't really understand what he meant and pressed him for more details. He told me to accept that when I was older and ready for that kind of instruction, I would receive it. I knew by his attitude that the subject was closed. It seemed that for the time being, Jack Harrison's soul had to live in our house, and we had to continue to live in a house awash with these different spirit energies. My only consolation was that mum was also subject to them, which proved, at least to me, that these happenings were not just my wild imaginings.

20

CHANGES

I was seldom afraid of the supernatural things that happened around me, feeling that I had Norman's protection. The Bible that nana had bought me continued to be a great source of comfort to me, too, especially since I had been going to church and knew the importance of this little book. The dark presence in our house that had breathed on mum's neck the day she was ironing was probably the only spirit that I felt wary of at that time. This unwelcome visitor was male, had a dark grey mist around him, and seemed hostile and angry whenever he came. An awful smell and a noticeable drop in temperature usually accompanied him. The odd thing about him, I noticed, was that he usually put in an appearance during the day. Most spirits prefer to visit at bedtime, a quiet time of reflection for us, and a time that they do not have to compete with television or the company of others to get noticed. This dark spirit, however, came during the day. And usually, as soon as he was near, I would be on edge, expecting something awful to happen.

I sensed, but didn't see, him one Sunday morning as I was getting ready to go to church. My mind that particular morning was full of things that I was going to talk to Vicar Brown about after the service. I had decided that I would like to be confirmed the following year in St Cuthbert's church. I felt the need to participate in the receiving of the bread and wine at the altar during the communion service, rather than just receive a blessing. It was August 1973, and I would be 12 years old in November; old enough to be considered a candidate. The classes were to begin in the next few months, and I hoped with all of my heart that there would be a place for me on them. I deemed myself ready for this re-baptism. I was mature for my age and I felt sufficiently grown up to understand the meaning of confirmation.

I was getting ready in my bedroom, standing as usual in front of my dressing table to dress. I had put on my new white blouse and had picked my favourite skirt to accompany it. The skirt was made of a silky fabric – it had soft blue and green colours on a white background and had a comfortable elasticized waistband. It was long and floaty, and made me feel very girly. I was reaching up to put my hair into a ponytail when I felt my lovely skirt being yanked down to my ankles. I quickly pulled it back up and sat on my bed feeling quite shaken. My hair had fallen back onto my shoulders, and I sat still for a while trying to work out what had happened. I reasoned that due to the length of the skirt that I had perhaps caught the hem with my shoe while I was doing my hair, thus pulling it down accidentally. The more I thought about it, the more I became convinced by my theory. I stood up, gave my head a shake, and resumed my position in front of the dressing table to once again do my hair.

I began to feel some coldness behind me and could smell the familiar stench of the dark spirit that scared me. The smell was a mixture of bad body odour and urine. However, when looking into the mirror, I couldn't see anything at all behind me. As I was brushing my hair, I felt some static around my body and stood rooted to the floor, watching in disbelief as my skirt started to slide over my hips and down my thighs to the floor, this time very slowly. I screamed and tried to run from my bedroom, but in my panic, the skirt that was now around my ankles tripped me up and I hit the floor with a thud, banging my chin. The fear I felt made me get up, far quicker than I went down, and I rushed out of the room and began my flight downstairs. Dad appeared at the bottom of the stairs, he had rushed out of the lounge when he had heard me scream and the thud. I rushed downstairs into his arms, babbling incoherently about what had just occurred. Mum followed soon after him and ushered me into our other front room, the one kept for visitors and privacy. I felt scared again once dad had left the room with mum's order to make me some tea. Dad's arms had felt big, strong, and protective, and I felt sure that mum couldn't protect me from whatever had just happened. He soon reappeared with my tea, explaining that the other kids were fine and on with their breakfasts in the other room, oblivious to what had happened. As I drank my hot, sweet tea, I recounted the whole story again – this time slowly, trying not to miss out anything. When I finished, mum looked to dad for one of the logical explanations that he always seemed to come up with. This time, he just shook his head and suggested that the three of us go up and take a look in my room.

I became frightened again and told him that I didn't want to go back upstairs. He assured me that I would be alright with him there, and mum reassured me that I really would be fine and that she would come, too. "Come on, I'll go first," dad said with enthusiasm. He marched up the stairs at a quick pace, followed by mum, then me, and was in my bedroom before we had chance to reach the top of the stairs. "It's okay. Come on in, there's nothing here!" he called out. Sure enough, everything looked pretty normal. The vibe in the room was as normal as it usually was, with no sign or feeling of anything malevolent. The only thing that was odd was that my skirt, which should have been on the floor where I'd scrambled out of it, was gone. "Where's my skirt?" I asked. "What do you mean?" mum said. I explained to her that the second time it had been pulled off me, I had darted from the room leaving it on the floor, and that now it wasn't there. "That's funny!" she said. I wasn't laughing, though, and she searched under my and Alison's beds to see if it was there. It wasn't! Dad asked me where I usually kept it. "In my wardrobe," I said, pointing to my wardrobe at the end of my bed. He opened the door, and I gasped as I saw, hanging on a hanger, the skirt that couldn't possibly be there. "That's it!" I said pointing to the skirt. "That's the skirt that was pulled off me."

Dad looked at mum and then at me, and shrugged his shoulders. I began to cry with frustration, feeling sure that dad didn't believe me. Mum hugged me, saying: "Don't cry, Julie. It's alright." Dad scratched his head and muttered that he didn't know what the hell was going on. Mum told him that she believed me, and that nothing that happened in this house surprised her anymore. Dad walked from the room and went downstairs, and mum stayed with me until I calmed down sufficiently to get dressed. I put on some jeans, not wanting to wear the skirt. I was disappointed that I had missed church but I didn't feel much like going now. I just felt tired all of a sudden and went downstairs with mum to join the others.

The episode had left me feeling drained and all day I reflected on what had happened. I felt really sorry for myself: victimized and alone, not really understanding why I had been targeted to experience the bizarre goings on, hating the fact that I had been made, once again, to feel different. My friends called round after church to see why I hadn't gone, and I lied and told them that I was feeling unwell and that I would be staying in for the rest of the day. They were disappointed but left the doorstep wishing me a speedy recovery, in the hope I would be fine to play out the next day. I didn't want to talk about that morning to anyone – not even mum. I felt isolated and decided to be on my own for a while. I sat alone in the front lounge. Both mum and dad kept popping in to ask if I was okay. That evening, I went up to bed at the same time as Alison, worried that something would happen to her. Of course it didn't, and I fell into a deep, restful sleep.

The following day was sunny and bright and I woke up early. The previous day's events seemed a million miles away and I got up and had a noisy breakfast with Mark, Alison, and Andrew. They were all very animated, excited at the thought of yet another Monday off school and the chance to play out with their friends. I went upstairs when Alison did, to wash and get dressed. I kept my dressing gown on so that it covered me until I put my trousers on. I felt vulnerable and worried about the possibility that someone might be watching me, waiting to strike. From that day, I have always dressed quickly, unable to wander around in a state of undress, keeping my robe around me until I have put either my skirt or trousers on.

This was my very first personal attack and it completely changed me. Just before that Sunday morning, I had become aware of slight changes in my body; that puberty had started to fashion. But my mindset was still very childlike, and I was in no hurry to grow up. I had never felt that I needed to protect my body, always safe in the knowledge that dad and mum would keep me from personal harm. Norman explained that I was going into a transitional period in my life and that not only my body, but my mind also, would develop. He said that my ability, this so called 'gift', would get stronger, but that in doing so, I would need to protect myself. I told him that I didn't want to change and I was quite happy to stay as I was. He regretted that this was not an option for me. He reassured me that I would always have his spiritual guidance and protection through this phase of change, and placated me with the promise of great spiritual teachings and rewards that would follow this transition, telling me that it would be worth it. I wasn't so sure, feeling afraid of the future and very vulnerable, dreading to think what was in store. I so wished that I hadn't been singled out for this gift that felt more like a curse in those days. He reminded me that I didn't have much choice in the matter and that I would come through and be able to use my experiences to help others.

I can completely empathize with psychically inclined adolescents, some of whom don't experience anything at all until they hit puberty. Those kids who have had previous episodes seem to have more very profound visitations or happenings at this age in their young lives, when they could well do without it. It is my belief that we are targeted at this age because we are more sensitive or vulnerable to experience in these years of development and change. Lots of paranormal activities and haunting occur in houses as children enter puberty. Perhaps the dilemmas that we experience in our early teens make us an easy target for earthbound, mischievous spirits. Whatever the reason, I felt sure that the skirt incident was to be the first of many that would happen to me, and, of course, I was right!

21

CHURCH BLESSINGS

The following week, I made it to church without any dramas. The house settled down once more, and I knew that there would be another lull before it started up again. It was inevitable. After the 11 A.M. communion service, I went, as usual, to the church hall and helped Mrs Brown with the washing-up in the kitchen. I had decided to ask the vicar about the forthcoming confirmation classes and was feeling a little nervous about doing so. As soon as everyone had left, he came to join his wife and me in the kitchen as usual, always thanking us for a job well done. I blushed terribly as I asked him if I might have a word with him about something. He, of course, said yes and instructed me to follow him back into the church hall, where he pulled up two chairs and invited me to sit with him. It seemed really strange to be sitting, just the two of us, in this large hall and I noticed that when I started to speak that my voice had a slight echo. I stuttered a little and, once again, felt my cheeks go pink. But I managed to blurt out my request to join the forthcoming confirmation classes. Vicar Brown smiled kindly and asked me if I felt ready for this next step into the church. "Oh, yes!" I enthused and told him how much I loved coming to church, and wanted to fully take part in the service by taking Holy Communion. He told me that, in that case, he was more than happy to add me to his list. He explained a little about the importance of the classes to prepare us for this commitment to Christianity. I nodded solemnly and could barely contain my joy. He went on to ask what my parents thought about my desire to be confirmed and – can you believe it? – I lied! Oh my God! I opened my mouth and lied to a man of the church – nana would say that was sacrilegious. I spluttered: "Oh, they're both really glad that I want to." In truth, I didn't know what they thought. I had briefly mentioned over tea one night that I was thinking about starting confirmation classes, but I couldn't remember what they had said. More than likely, like so many other things that were discussed at the table, it wouldn't have been paid attention to or commented on. I sincerely hoped that my pink cheeks wouldn't give me away and I made a quick mental note to pray for forgiveness later on. I felt sure that I could square it with God and Norman. We walked back into the kitchen and the lovely Vicar told his wife that I would be taking confirmation classes with him, later on in the year. Mrs Brown said that she was sure that I would make a good candidate. Phew! That was close. And just when I thought I was out of the woods, Vicar Brown told me that he would like to come to my house and speak to my parents about it. He explained how he hadn't seen them at church yet, and that it would be a nice way of meeting them. Oh Hell! This was payback time for lying, I thought. I muttered that I would tell them that, and he took out the latest church magazine from the papers he was holding, and jotted his telephone number on the front of it, asking me to tell them to ring him and he would call round at their convenience. Well, this was not convenient for me! Nevertheless, I thanked him and told him that I would pass on the message.

I walked home slowly that day, my head like a toy box, cluttered with things that I would need to get straight before I told mum and dad about the vicar's intended visit. I knew that I would have to pass on his request and thought that, first of all, I would tell them that I had mentioned previously about the classes and that they can't have been listening. That bit was easy; my dilemma was what if they told the vicar about my strange ways or how my childhood had been frequented with sightings of (invisible to most) spirits. I feared that if he knew about my earlier life, that he would forbid me from going to his church, and that I was certain to be excluded from confirmation classes. Another concern was that what if something strange happened in our house while he was visiting. I wondered if these mischievous spirits that lived with us would target him. I felt in a hopeless situation, really unsure as to what to do for the best.

A few days later, these things were still troubling me, and I still hadn't mentioned to dad and mum about either my intention to be confirmed, or the vicar's request for them to telephone him. I knew that he would ask me after church on Sunday whether I had passed on his message, and I also knew that I would feel really bad if I had to lie once again. So on Friday, as we were all seated at the table eating our tea, I casually asked them both if they remembered me mentioning about the upcoming confirmation classes at church. They looked at each other before dad said: "No, I don't think so, pet." "Oh, I did – ages ago," I continued. "Anyway, the classes are starting in November, and I'm allowed to join them, if it's okay with you two." "Well, I think that would be alright, don't you, Ena?" Dad looked to mum. "Yes, that would be lovely, Julie," she added. "The thing is," I continued, "Vicar Brown needs to speak to you both to make sure that you agree with it, and he has asked me if I would get you to telephone him so that he can arrange to come and meet you both." I said this as nonchalantly as I could muster. "Right," said dad. "I think we can manage that, don't you, mum?" "Sure," she replied, and I passed her the church magazine with the vicar's number on it. "I'll give him a bell after I've cleared this lot," she said, as she started to clear the table.

Sure enough, as soon as all the dishes were washed, dried and put away, mum put on her best posh voice and rang the vicarage. Vicar Brown answered and, after a brief exchange, they agreed that he would come over the following Friday at 6:30. When she put the phone down, she remarked to dad that the vicar seemed like a nice man, and dad looked up from his paper and said that he would look forward to meeting him, then. So that was it. The meeting was arranged and there wasn't much I could do about it. Church the following Sunday was as good as ever and whilst praying, I asked that everything would go well when the vicar came , promising to be a good Christian and apologizing for telling fibs, pledging never to lie again.

The following week passed really quickly, and I became anxious as Friday approached. The night before the scheduled visit I couldn't stop worrying and decided to ask mum and dad if I could talk to them about something. They, of course, agreed and as soon as the other kids were in bed, the television was put off, and dad and mum sat together on the couch, waiting expectantly for me to talk. I sat in dad's chair, wringing my hands in my lap, not knowing where to start. They waited patiently for me to begin and when I did, mum jumped when I started to talk. "You know before we moved here?" I began. They both nodded. "Well, can you remember how I used to see and hear things that nobody else could?" They both nodded again, but kept quiet. "Well, I don't anymore. I'm normal now!" "Oh, I see." Dad was the first to speak. "And what about Norman – do you not see him anymore?" "Oh, I haven't heard from him in ages," I lied, both my fingers crossed in my lap. "Why are you telling us this now, Julie?" mum asked, looking puzzled. "Oh, no reason, really; it's just that when Vicar Brown comes tomorrow, I don't think there's any point in mentioning what I used to be like, because I'm not like that anymore. I'm normal." "Ah," dad said, the penny seeming to have dropped with him. "I take it that the vicar doesn't know about your visions or Norman?" "No!" I said a little too quickly. "It must have been moving here that changed me," I reasoned, sounding more convincing than I felt. "I would really rather just forget all that stuff and be normal now." "That's the fourth time in five minutes you have told us you're normal," mum observed. "Well, I am!" I said defensively, starting to get upset. "Alright, alright – that's alright," dad said. "So you don't want us to mention anything that happened to you before we came here, is that right?" "No, dad, I don't," I said. "I just want to forget about it all." "That's fine then, isn't it Ena?" He looked to mum for agreement. "Yes, of course" she added. "There's no need for anyone to know anything. It's nobody's business." "Thanks," I sniffed. "That's all it was."

Dad went on to ask if there was anything else on my mind or troubling me, and I assured him that I was fine. "Right, well, you get yourself off up to bed and don't worry about the vicar coming tomorrow." I kissed them both and went up to bed feeling that my initial dilemma may have been solved, but racked with guilt over my denial of Norman. That night I prayed that the visit would go well and that somehow Norman would both understand and forgive me.

At 6:30 prompt the next evening, Vicar Brown rang our doorbell. Dad went to the door and invited him into the lounge, where he introduced him to mum and then Mark, Alison, and Andrew. Once pleasantries had been exchanged, mum invited him through to the sitting room. This separate room was kept immaculate and was reserved for private talks, doctors' visits, and posh guests. Once dad and Vicar Brown were seated, she asked me to help her make some tea. Reluctant though I was to leave dad alone with the vicar in case he dropped me in it, I followed mum through to the kitchen. Here she put four cups and saucers, a matching sugar bowl, and milk jug on a tray with a plate of biscuits. I couldn't ever remember her using this tea-set. Once the kettle had boiled, she poured the water into a matching china teapot, very different from the steel one we always used. I carried the tray with the cups and saucers on through to the sitting room, while she followed with the freshly brewed tea. I prayed that dad wouldn't dunk his biscuits in his tea tonight, something that he did every day, and luckily my prayers were answered. He obviously struggled with his big hands to hold this china cup with finesse, but managed nevertheless.

The vicar asked how dad and mum were settling into the neighbourhood, and after a brief chat the conversation turned to the forthcoming confirmation classes and my intention to join. Dad and mum kept their word and didn't once allude to my psychic ability. I felt almost normal and was sure that this meeting was going well, and that nothing would stand in my way of being confirmed now. I was really enjoying the conversation until Vicar Brown mentioned that he had known Mrs Harrison, the former tenant of our house. I felt slightly uneasy as he continued on about her, telling us what a lovely lady she was and how she had been a valued member of his congregation. Mum mentioned that she had spoken about her to Mrs Allen over the road; Mrs Allen was also well thought of by Vicar Brown. For some reason, I began to feel nervous, perhaps because I wasn't comfortable about where this conversation was going. Vicar Brown remarked about how devastated Mrs Harrison had been when she had lost her husband and confided that she had found it very difficult to come to terms with his death. Dad chirped up with "they looked like a nice couple." "Oh did you know them, Mr Savage?" the vicar enquired. "No," said Dad, "but when mum and Julie made me go in the loft when things were going missing. We found a box of photographs and letters that belonged to the Harrisons and they looked really nice." "Did you find the things that were missing, too?" asked the vicar. "No, no we didn't, it's just another mystery about this house." The Vicar looked at dad with a puzzled look on his face, and by now dad was in full flow and told him about all the odd things that had happened in the house since we had moved in: the bath filling up with water, the missing clothes, the landing window, and, latterly my skirt being yanked down. I was completely mortified. My heart was beating so fast I felt sure I was going to faint. I mentally willed dad to shut up, but oh no, he recounted everything that had ever happened in the house, even the things that he had discounted and told mum and me that it was in our imagination. When he was finished, Vicar Brown said one word – "Golly!" Golly alright, I thought. Bloody golly hell!

That's what it was like living in this house, irrespective of the Bibles and prayer books that had been left in it. The vicar was genuinely concerned and asked mum how she was coping with all of these happenings. "Oh, I'm fine really. I just love the house and the children are settled in school, and the neighbours are lovely." After they discussed the house for another torturous few minutes, the vicar announced that he thought that we should all pray. So we closed our eyes and said the Lord's Prayer, then he asked for a blessing on our house and for those of us living in it, and went on to ask for us to be looked over and protected. After our prayers, he stayed for a few more minutes before announcing that he would have to leave as he had another appointment that evening. He reminded mum and dad that it was family service at church the following Sunday, and that they would be more than welcome to pop along and join in. Dad actually said that yes, he would love to attend. Golly, golly, gosh! One prayer and my father was hooked on religion!

It was settled - mum and dad were to join me at church on Sunday and were bringing with them the little Savages, too. Dad and mum saw the vicar to the front door, and when he'd left, they cooed to each other about what a nice man he was. We all went back into the sitting room, and mum remarked: "Do you know, Bill, it seems different in this house now; calmer almost." "Yes, you're right, pet," he agreed. "It must have been those prayers. Maybe everything will settle down now." At that, I heard someone laughing, almost hysterically, and I knew that it would take more than one prayer to sort our house out.

We went as a family to church on Sunday, and every Sunday after that. Mum and dad made some new friends in the congregation and were soon invited to join the confirmation classes. They declined the vicar's offer, explaining that it was too difficult to leave Mark, Alison, and Andrew – they didn't have a babysitter. So the vicar actually offered to coach them at home. They were delighted, and each Tuesday evening he would come to ours and spend time in the posh sitting room talking religion with them. This was a nightmare for me, and I felt myself constantly reminding them of how normal I was now, and not to mention my past. Dad told me not to worry about it and to trust that he wouldn't slip up and say something. I also decided that if anything happened to me in our house from now on, that I would keep it to myself, hoping that mum wouldn't get targeted anymore.

22

FOREBODING FEELINGS

In the autumn of 1973, prior to confirmation classes, I had a deep feeling of melancholy. The weather was atrocious; damp, grey days that I blamed for my feelings of misery. I always hated the rain and seem to have always been affected by the weather, so I accepted that this was why I couldn't shake the feeling of sadness that I woke up with most mornings. Even the forthcoming classes that I had really looked forward to earlier in the year didn't seem to cheer me at all. The first class was to be on the Sunday before my twelfth birthday. I had never really enjoyed my birthdays in the past; sad things seemed to happen on or around them, so I wondered if perhaps this little dark cloud that I felt was hanging over me could be for that reason also. Spirit activity was starting to happen again at home; just small things: lights would go out, objects would move or vanish for a few hours, and the smells and coldness returned more frequently. For several successive nights prior to sleep, I would be visited by the man with the dark energy who had pulled my skirt. The rancid smell of him would be evident before he came, and he would sneer and tell me that I wouldn't be able to make my confirmation classes and that he would stop me going. Norman would ask me not to take any notice of him and to accept that his trapped soul was miserable with the sins he had committed on Earth, and to try and pray for him. Pray for him?! I hated him with a passion and couldn't find any compassion in my young soul to pray for someone so horrible.

At the beginning of November, my friend Liz, who lived opposite us, invited me to go babysitting with her one evening after school. Liz was a year older than me, and each morning we would walk to the bus stop together, to catch the school bus. Liz went to a different school to me, but both schools were on the same campus, so we always travelled together. She was the youngest in her family and often looked after her young niece so that her sister, Yvonne, and her husband could go to the cinema. I jumped at the chance to go babysitting with Liz. I loved children, and the plan was to go to Yvonne's straight from school, where we would have our tea before looking after Liz's adorable little niece. It was also arranged that Yvonne's husband would drop us off at home around 9:30 when they got in. Dad and mum were fine with this arrangement. They knew the family and agreed that I would be good company for Liz. The week prior to babysitting, Liz told me how much fun we would have going to Yvonne's. Her older sister had all the latest records and a modern stereo system that we could play them on, her house was modern and a pleasure to spend time, in apparently. And she always left lots of sweets, crisps, and lemonade, if we wanted any. I felt very grown up at the thought of being a responsible babysitter, even if I was only company for Liz.

Finally, the long-awaited Friday we were to babysit arrived, and along with it two major disasters. The first was on the Friday morning when I called for Liz to go to school. Liz's mum answered the door and told me that Liz had been poorly through the night and was not going to school. She must have seen the look of disappointment in my face when I asked if our babysitting had been cancelled. But she quickly reassured me that, no, she felt sure that after some more sleep, Liz would be fine and fit enough to go. She went on to say that, if I still wanted to go to Yvonne's, I was to get off the bus at the town centre as arranged, the only difference being that Liz would see me at her sister's house rather than travel with me. I had passed Yvonne's house several times and knew exactly where it was – just a short walk from the town centre. My mood immediately lifted, and I thanked Mrs Gray – Liz's mum – and told her that I would probably arrive at Yvonne's around 4 P.M. and asked her to tell Liz that I hoped she was soon feeling better. I hurried to the bus stop, determined that the grey drizzle wouldn't affect me that day.

The other upsetting thing that had happened that morning was that, as I had been getting ready for school, I couldn't find my coat. I looked in the cupboard under the stairs where I had left it, and where it was kept when I wasn't wearing it, and it had gone. Mornings were always hectic in our house. Mum would rush about making sure that we were washed, dressed appropriately for school, and that we had eaten our breakfast. With four of us to oversee, it can't have been easy, and I imagine she would have breathed a sigh of relief when we were all safely delivered to school. I eventually tracked her down; she was upstairs gathering dirty laundry together – something she did daily. On finding her in the boys' bedroom, I asked her if she knew where my school coat was. "Oh, Julie, I washed it last night and it's still damp. You'll have to wear another coat," she answered. "I don't have another coat, mum," I whined. "Yes, you do. You have that red cape," she said. "I'm not wearing *that*," I said venomously. "It's ancient. I hate it!" "You will have to; just for today," she said. "I can't do anything about your other coat; it's as damp as the weather, and I will try and get it dry for you in front of the fire today." Huh! If she thought that was going to placate me, she had another think coming.

I hated that cape with a vengeance and would do anything not to wear it. I stomped off into my bedroom, determined to find something else to put on. After frantically searching through my wardrobe to no avail, I realized that apart from the 'cape of fear', I had nothing other than a summer anorak to wear. I had no option. The disgusting red cape hung there at the back of the wardrobe like a bullfighter's cape. Mum shouted upstairs for me to get a move on or I would miss my bus, and I knew that if I missed the bus that I would be at least half an hour waiting for the next bus and would be far too embarrassed to arrive at school that late. So I dragged it off its hanger and trailed it across the bedroom floor, before reluctantly putting it around my shoulders. The same old feelings of anxiety came as I fastened it up, and I wished hard that this would be the last time that I would ever have to wear it. I made a point of looking miserable as I said goodbye to mum, hoping that she would know how disgruntled I felt. As I stepped out into another rainy day, I felt as I had years earlier whenever I had worn the cape; that something awful would happen to me while I wore it. I felt very sorry for myself that Friday morning.

The rain persisted all day, and my mood plummeted even further. The stupid red cape was also adding to my feelings of doom. I felt very self conscious in this childish garment, and between lessons I carried it over my arm rather than wearing it and attract attention to myself. After all, who at my age would be seen dead in such a garment?! I was worried that I would be ridiculed and referred to as Red Riding Hood. By lunchtime, I was sick of my own feelings of sadness and tried to cheer myself with thoughts that in just a few hours I would be at Yvonne's with Liz, and would feel much better. After school, I rushed to get the bus that would take me to the town centre and, once on it, I felt a little brighter.

It was still raining, but at least I had got through my school day without mention of the cape. The journey only took ten minutes, and I fastened my cape before getting off the bus. The rain was coming down harder now, and it was dark, and I was thankful for the hood. I walked through the town centre and felt as though I needed to rush to get to Yvonne's. I had heard some ladies on the bus talking about the probability of thunder and I was scared of lightning, so didn't want to get caught in it. I was still rushing as I got to the crossroads just 30 metres from Yvonne's house and, with other things on my mind, walked into the road without looking.

I was struck by a car and everything seemed to happen in slow motion. I hit the bonnet of the car and was tossed into the air, before I landed some distance away. I couldn't feel anything: no pain, no alarm, just incredulity that this was happening to me. I was aware, after the initial silence, of a man – the driver, I think, repeatedly saying: "Oh my God! I didn't see her," and then a ladies voice saying: "I'm a nurse. Phone for an ambulance; I'll stay with her." Someone asked my name and where I lived, and I managed to tell them that I was due at Yvonne's house, and gave her address, too. Yvonne arrived just as the ambulance did. She looked terrified and told me not to worry, that she would let my mum know what had happened, and that I would be alright. The ambulance man was lovely; he asked if I could feel anything, and when I said no, he asked me if I could wiggle my toes. I tried to, but I don't think I managed. He managed to put my head in a type of brace and then put an inflatable sheet under me. He pumped some air into the sheet, and he and his driver carefully put me into the ambulance.

Lots of unfamiliar faces seemed to have come to see what was happening, and I remember hoping that nobody I knew could see me in this awful red cape. Norman appeared in the ambulance when the sirens started. This had alarmed me, and I felt so glad that he was there beside me. His presence, as usual, was reassuring. I kept saying to him: "I'm sorry, I'm sorry," and wasn't aware that I was voicing this out loud until the ambulance man said: "Don't worry, honey, we'll soon have you there." I think I fell into a little sleep after that. Shortly after, I arrived at hospital, was transferred onto a trolley, and wheeled down to the accident and emergency department.

A nurse came into the cubicle I was in and asked me some questions, then told me that I would be going to the x-ray department before seeing the doctor. She was small and dark, and had a nice, kind face. She kept asking me if I felt any pain; the answer always being the same: "No, I'm just numb." She reassured me that I would be okay and that they would soon have me fixed. This whole situation felt like it was happening to someone other than me and that I was just an observer. Norman stayed by my side the whole of the time and, once in the x-ray department, I asked him why I didn't feel any pain. He told me that I was receiving divine healing and to trust that this numbness was preferable to the pain that would surely follow. This made me frightened, but he reassured me that time would see me back to normal. Once the x-rays were completed, I was wheeled back to the accident and emergency department, where I was to be examined further. They didn't want to move me and so, much to my delight took some huge scissors and began to cut away at my clothes – including the cape.

Apparently, the doctor and nurses were waiting for a spinal doctor to view my x-rays and, until he could come, I was to be kept in the same position. The nurse asked if I could feel her tickling my feet, and I said no, that I couldn't feel anything. I was lying in my vest and pants with a blanket over me when mum arrived. Mr Paxton – a neighbour had kindly driven her to the hospital when the police had called to inform her about my accident. Mrs Paxton was looking after my siblings while mum was here, and dad was on his way, coming straight from work. Poor mum looked frantic with worry and rushed into the cubicle towards me. The nurse that was looking after me asked her not to cuddle me, explaining that I shouldn't be moved until my x-rays had been checked, and that it was possible that I had a spinal injury due to my inability to feel anything.

Mum began to cry and Norman told me to tell her that I would be alright. "Don't worry, mum, I didn't break my back," I said. "I'll be fine." This seemed to make her cry even more. She kept telling me how brave I was for not crying and she sat on a chair at the side of the trolley I was laid on, and held my hand. Ten minutes later, dad arrived. He rushed into the room still in his blue overalls from work and, as he did, Norman told me that it was time for him to leave and that I had five more minutes. I didn't exactly know what he meant; even so, I looked at the big clock in the room. It said 5:20, and I felt that I was counting down to something. Mum explained to dad what the nurse had told her so far. He just kept rubbing his forehead, saying how he couldn't believe what had happened.

At 5:25, two things happened: the spinal doctor appeared from behind the curtains to my cubicle and my pain came with him – excruciatingly, burning pain that seemed to sear through my feet, up through my legs and into my back, arms and head. Every part of my body hurt and, as I screamed out in pain, the doctor ordered that I be given an injection and then told my parents that this was good. Good! It was horrendous; I had never felt anything like it and felt sure I would faint with the pain. He explained to dad and mum that it was feared initially that my paralysis would be permanent. He then went on to explain that sometimes the body goes into shock and along with it comes this temporary paralysis. He had also checked my spinal x-rays, which were fine. I had broken my toe and fractured my ankle, sprained my wrist, and the worst damage was to my knees. The gravel from the road was imbedded into my knees, and one of them had dislocated. But, apart from that, I was lucky. I didn't feel lucky as my knees were cleaned and some gravel was removed from them with tweezers, or the least bit fortunate when I was strapped up with more bandages than I had ever seen in my life. My knee was put back into place and I had stitches in my foot. The bandages around my knees were so thick that I couldn't put my legs together, and my parents were told that it might be a few days before I could walk on them. I was allowed home later that evening, and dad had to carry me to the car, my legs outstretched in front of me. I was wearing his work's overcoat with mum's cardigan underneath it. Even so, I felt more comfortable dressed like this than I ever had in that dreadful red cape that was now hopefully in the hospital incinerator.

The district nurse came to our house most days for the following three weeks to dress my knees, which became very infected and I missed a month at school. I was sent lots of cards from my friends there, though, and my tutor came to see me. I also missed my first three confirmation classes, but was still allowed to attend the course. Vicar Brown brought me books and told me what I needed to read, and when he came to give mum and dad their instruction, he gave me some, too.

Surprisingly my twelfth birthday on November 25th 1973 was quite enjoyable. I had loads more fuss than I had had since my siblings had come along, which was nice. Norman visited every day and gave me hours of blissful healing. I loved him even more and decided that I would never again deny him, even if I did keep his visits to myself. He brought such lovely things into my life: understanding, support, friendship, and a wealth of knowledge that I could never have learned from books.

The house once again returned to normal and was quiet the whole time that I was recovering. Vicar Brown's prayers each week must have helped. He would pray with mum and dad after their confirmation meetings. My folks were convinced that this was the solution. I, of course, knew better. I felt that the solution to quietening this house for good would lay with someone else, and I also felt that we would be provided with the way soon. The rest of the winter passed uneventfully, and in the spring of 1974 dad, mum and I were confirmed at St Cuthbert's Church by the Bishop of Whitby.

JULIE SAVAGE

23

DAD STARTS BELIEVING

Over the next year, I started to realize that there seemed to be a pattern emerging to the ghostly visits and strange occurrences in the house. I could never pre-empt whether a visit would be from a good or bad spirit, or whether it would feel malevolent or just plain mischievous. But what I did come to see was that all the profound happenings occurred around either Easter, Christmas time, or on a family birthday.

I continued to go to church each Sunday, enjoying the service even more since my confirmation. I now felt that I could fully take part in the communion. I had joined the Church Youth Committee and loved being part of the team that organized discos, rambles, and concerts. My social life was great and I felt very fortunate to have made some great friends since moving to Billingham. I felt that I belonged there and was proud to live in such a good place. In the town centre there was a large leisure complex called the Forum. There, you could swim, play sport, take dance and gym classes, go to the cinema, or ice skate. There were several bars and cafes inside the complex, and it was a popular place for children and grown ups, too. People travelled from neighbouring towns to go to the many theatre productions that the Forum held, and it was open every day and most evenings.

I loved going to the Forum and was especially keen to go ice skating. My cousin Lynn had been to ice skating lessons there a few years previous and she handed down her white ice boots to me when I was 13 years old. By this time, Lynn was nearly 17 and working as an office junior for ICI – the huge chemical firm in our town. I was delighted with the boots; they were fantastic, and I couldn't wait to wear them. Most of the kids who visited the Forum's ice rink hired the boots from the hire shop there. These boots were royal blue and not very stylish and it was deemed really cool to own your own white boots. Dad whitened them for me and said that he thought I was old enough and sensible enough to be allowed to go to the Saturday afternoon ice-skating sessions with my pals.

I had a wonderful time there. Although ice- skating was far harder than it looked, I loved it and persevered and managed to stay upright for a whole half-hour before the session ended. The three friends that I went with were really good fun and we skated around the rink, hand-in-hand, forming a little chain, singing along to the latest chart music that the ice-DJ was playing, and laughing at the slips and slides we caused each other in our efforts to stay up. I couldn't ever remember having so much fun and was disappointed when the two-hour session ended, and we had to leave the ice rink. We put our shoes on and got ourselves crisps and lemonade from the café, before catching the bus home.

I felt totally invigorated by the experience of skating and talked about nothing else for the rest of the day. As soon as I got home, I asked mum if I could go again the following week, and she said that I could if I was good and helped out a little with the chores. Saturday afternoons became the highlight of my week, and I counted down the days until it was time to go again. Life was really good, and I woke up happy most days. I loved school, and we were about to choose the subjects that we wanted to study to O-level standard. The school held a special parents' evening, and dad and mum went. They were really proud to be told that I was expected to do well in my chosen subjects, and that I was in the top set for Maths and English. When they came home that night with my yearly report, they both told me how proud that they were that I had worked so hard in my lessons, and dad reminded me how important education was. I wasn't so sure he was right, but I did enjoy my school days and found tests more exciting than daunting.

Norman helped me with my schooling and would often be around when I did my homework. He seldom answered the questions for me, but he was really good at explaining things in a way that I could understand – something I couldn't always say about my teachers. I felt lucky having his guidance and help. Recently, he had started to explain about psychology and would explain to me why people acted or reacted in certain ways, telling me that it was always good to see things from another perspective.

I had gathered that I was growing up, and although I still felt childlike in my head, I realized that my body was changing drastically. I became shy and self-conscious of my body, insisting on locking the bathroom door when I was bathing and waiting until Alison left our bedroom before getting undressed or dressed. I wasn't really pleased with this ever-changing shape of mine and realized what a nuisance breasts were. I prayed each night that they wouldn't grow any more – to no avail. Swimming and gym lessons at school were a pain. Communal showers in the girls changing rooms meant that we had no privacy and everyone could see what each other had. Some of my peers had far smaller chests than me, and my ever-increasing boobs were a constant source of embarrassment. We all had to wear a regulation black swimming costume at our school, and mine was getting tighter by the week. One day, I spent longer than I should have in the changing rooms trying to rearrange myself and my swimming costume so that I was as covered as I could be. This was a huge mistake! My dilly-dallying meant that, when I walked through to the pool area, the whole class were already assembled there, lined up at the side of the pool. I tried to creep unnoticed to the end of the line while the teacher was asking if anybody required any floats. A horrible boy in my class called out: "Julie Savage doesn't need any, sir. She's got her own!" Everyone started to laugh, and I felt the flush of embarrassment from my toes to my head, making my cheeks go bright red. I was fuming and I gave him one of my withering looks. The joke was on him when, seconds later, he slipped and almost flew into the pool like a torpedo. He came to the surface coughing and spluttering, whingeing that somebody had pushed him. "Don't be stupid, boy," the teacher scoffed. "Nobody pushed you." I could see that I would have to invent a verruca for the rest of the term to save embarrassment.

In the spring of 1975, mum decorated the lounge in time for Easter. She had decided, with the help of a neighbour, to do her bit for Women's Lib and build a stone fireplace. It looked fabulous, and even Dad was impressed. He did his bit by panelling the wall over the chimney breast with some sheets of light wood, which he then varnished. This completed the look, and mum bought some new pictures and horse brasses to adorn the feature wall. She loved pictures and had them on most of the walls in the lounge. She was a true home-maker and would often change the furniture around to make rooms look different. That year, my parents had saved up enough to afford a new carpet and three-piece suite. The suite was lovely; cream PVC with bright orange cushions – our new lounge looked lovely.

After church on Easter Sunday, we went to visit nana. Mum had bought us all new clothes for Easter, and we had a lovely day. That night, we all sat together in our newly decorated lounge and watched a film while we ate our chocolate eggs. I was always the last of the kids to go to bed, which was only fair as I was the eldest. Most weekends, I was allowed to stay up until ten o'clock. Dad or mum would tell me when it was time for bed, and this particular night I was tired and ready to go up without a protest. I wished them both goodnight and, as I was walking up the stairs, I noticed that it seemed a little misty on the landing. About three stairs from the top, I felt a whoosh of cold air fly past me with such a force that I fell against the wall. I then heard a series of bumps and bangs coming from the lounge. Mum screamed; dad shouted. Then silence. Time seemed to stand still for the next few minutes while I stood on the stairs deciding what to do. I turned and made my way back downstairs and, as I did, I realized that dad and mum were moving around. As I opened the lounge door, they both stood still like statues, as if they expected someone other than me to walk through the door. "What's happened? What was all that banging?" I asked, and then looked around at the chaos. Every picture, horse brass, or plaque that had been on the wall was on the floor. None of them were broken, and all the previously adorned walls were bare. There must have been around 20 or more pictures on the floor – scattered and strewn about. Mum and dad, by this time, hadn't answered me, so I added: "Do you think there's been an earthquake or something?" "No, no I don't think so," dad said. He looked pretty shaken, and then he looked around the room before remarking to mum that every hook or tack that had held the pictures was still in the wall. This was the first time that he had witnessed first-hand the strange things that could happen in our house, and he looked unusually ruffled by the experience.

The next day, Easter Monday, we all went to Whitby in dad's car. We all loved Whitby, a beautiful old sea port steeped in history. As we walked along by the beautiful harbour, dad asked me if I knew why the pictures had fallen from the walls the previous night. "No," I answered truthfully. I could tell that it had bothered him when he remarked absentmindedly that it was beyond him, too. Over the following few months, dad would tell the story of the falling pictures to family and friends. Each time he told the story it got more and more humorous. It was almost as if he wanted to treat the matter light-heartedly, so that it didn't seem frightening. He didn't laugh at Christmas time that year, however, when he experienced another ghostly event – something which had, up until that time, only ever happened to mum or me.

It was Boxing Day, and I was thrilled to be allowed to go to the Forum ice rink for the evening session. Older teenagers went on an evening, and it was the in place for anybody who wanted to be thought of as hip and trendy. The session started at seven o'clock and didn't finish until 9:30, which meant that I wouldn't be home until ten o'clock. My friends all lived close by, so we were all allowed to go after being lectured about the dangers of missing the bus, *et cetera, et cetera*.

Mum's friend Pat, who lived at the end of our road, used to foster children and on this particular evening she rang to say that she had just been given a tiny Chinese baby to look after for a few weeks. The child's mother was ill, and she was going to take care of the baby until its mother was well enough to leave hospital. She invited Mum down to see the baby, and mum asked if she could bring Alison and Andrew with her. Pat said yes of course she could, and the three of them left our house just after I left for the ice rink. Mark was going to stay in with dad to watch *The Guns of Navarone*. It was a cold night, so dad pulled the couch up in front of the fire so that the two of them could lounge and watch the film in comfort. Apparently, mum was really enjoying her evening at Pat's and forgot the time, so when I returned home from the Forum at around 10 P.M., she was still at Pat's house. When I walked into the lounge, it was empty – this was unusual, there was always someone home, and I called out upstairs to see where everybody was. I heard dad shout from the kitchen that he was in there. When I went into the kitchen it was freezing, and both dad and Mark were standing, having a cup of tea. "What are you doing out here?" I asked. "It's freezing out here, why aren't you in front of the fire?" Dad looked at Mark, who didn't say anything, and then looked at me, and said: "We're staying out here until your mum gets in." "Why?" I asked, sensing something was amiss. At that, the front door opened, and mum, Alison, and Andrew came in. I walked into the lounge to greet them all, but dad and Mark didn't follow me. This was strange. "Where are your dad and Mark?" mum asked. "In the kitchen; they won't come out," I added dramatically. She frowned and then walked into the kitchen, closely followed by us three.

"What's wrong?" mum asked, looking from dad to Mark, who once again looked at each other. Dad started to gabble the story of how he and Mark had been watching the film and, during the commercial break, Mark had decided to have some breakfast cereal – something he often ate for supper. When he had finished with his bowl, he had put it on the fire hearth at the side of the fire, with the spoon resting in the bowl. It had stayed there a while they continued to watch the movie, Mark not wanting to miss any of the film. Some 20 minutes later, they had watched incredulously as the bowl had started to rise from the fireplace with the spoon still in it. It rose about two feet into the air, stayed there for a few seconds, then floated back down to where it had been. They had both witnessed this, were paralysed by fear, and had been unable to do anything about it. When the bowl landed on the hearth, it did so with a clatter, and at this point dad and Mark jumped up into each other's arms and then fled into the kitchen, where they had stayed until we came home.

It was obvious that this had really happened; Dad kept seeking Mark's confirmation of events as he was relaying the story. They were both visibly shaken by what had happened. Mum looked at me. I shrugged. She turned back to dad and said: "Well, at least now you might believe what Julie and I have been telling you since we moved here!"

We all went upstairs to bed at the same time that evening, and as I lay in my bed, Norman came and I asked him what he made of the rising bowl. He said that it was a mischievous child spirit that had lifted the bowl, and that this little boy had done so with the intention to shock or perhaps scare dad and Mark. I thought this explanation was really funny and was not at all frightened by it; in fact, part of me was glad that they had witnessed it. Before sleep came that evening, I could hear dad talking to Mum in bed. He was obviously still shaken by the incident, and perhaps scared that she would fall asleep before him. I wondered just how funny he would make this story sound!

24

NO SMOKE WITHOUT FIRE

After Christmas, things calmed down again and life – and our house – settled back into normality. Apart from a few objects moving around at Easter time, which by now were considered usual, there wasn't anything untoward happening. I was still enjoying my Sundays at church and was thrilled to be asked to help out at Sunday school. I adored children and was blessed with the baby class – two to 5-year-olds, who considered Sunday school fun, almost an extension of nursery. We had lots of fun and I loved my little charges.

My best friend Deborah – Deb – lived next door but one and we spent lots of time together. I loved Deb and she's still a dear friend, even though we don't see much of each other anymore. Deb was the only child of Brian and Norma. Brian worked as a driver for a local cement firm and Norma had a really good job as a secretary for a manager at ICI. Brian was also a concert chairman at the local social club, which meant that each night Norma and Brian would leave the house at around 6:45 to go to the club. This left Deb and I alone in their house, which was great: we could watch what we wanted on the television, eat and drink to our hearts desire, and get up to mischief – which we did quite often.

Norma and Brian both smoked, and one day, in her infinite wisdom, Deb decided that we should do the same. So as they were getting ready to go to the club, she stole two cigarettes from Brian's packet and two from Norma's. When I arrived at hers around seven o'clock, she declared that this was the night that we would try smoking! Deb was hilarious. She always had a fantastic sense of humour and acted much older than her 13 years. She had laid the four cigarettes out like little soldiers on the coffee table with a box of matches at the side of them. We sat and stared at them for a few minutes in silence, broken by Deb reflecting that she'd heard her mum say that a cigarette always tasted better after a meal. I joined her as she walked through to the kitchen to look in the pantry, and decide which food would better prepare out palettes for this nicotine intake. We agreed to have jam sandwiches and a cup of coffee each – sophisticated or what?! We sat eating and drinking in silence – very unusual for Deb and me. I felt really nervous about what we were going to do. Norman's voice came into my head, saying: "Don't smoke, Julie – it's not good for you." He sounded like a boring adult, a spoil sport, and I think he sensed that this time I would disobey him. He repeated his request, but I neither answered nor acknowledged him. He shook his head, then left. I felt a little strange, this was the first time I had ever disregarded his advice. I was shaken from my reverie by Deb asking: "Are you ready, then?" "I don't know – what do you think?" I answered. "Two fags aren't gonna kill us," she reasoned. "I know, but my dad might, if he finds out!" I replied. "How's he gonna find out?" she said, making me feel like a stick in the mud. Deb had gone to the trouble of stealing the cigarettes and she assured me that nobody could see through the net curtains. So what was the point of worrying about getting found out? There was no way we would. "Okay," I said resolutely. "Let's do it!"

Deb struck a match and held it to her cigarette. She began to suck, and her cigarette lit. She then blew smoke from her mouth and said: "Nectar!" She told me how wonderful it tasted and encouraged me to light up. I did. My hands were shaking as I tried to strike the match, and it snapped in half. I got out another match, the cigarette still dangling from my lips and somehow managed to light it. "Wha' da' ya' think?" she asked, smiling at me "Mm. Nice," I said, lying. It tasted vile, my head was dizzy, and the taste of the smoke in my mouth was making me feel nauseous. "God you look dead grown up," she said. "So do you, Deb," I said convincingly, dreading taking another puff of this horrible weed. She inhaled another lungful of smoke and gestured for me to do the same. "Enjoy it! They don't last very long!" Thank God for that was all that I could think, but did as she instructed. What was the point of smoking I thought, and why did so many people suffer this to try it? But I persevered and managed to finish it without throwing up.

When the cigarettes were finished, we congratulated each other on making the transition to adulthood. Deb had already formulated a plan to steal her parents' cigarettes on a regular basis to keep us supplied. It was approaching the end of the summer, and the nights were getting colder and darker by the day. People were already talking about plans for Christmas, and Deb told me how Norma and Brian had already begun buying stocks of alcohol for the mammoth New Year's party that they held each year. Their house was identical in size and shape to ours and they used their spare front room for visitors – just like we did. After our first cigarette, Deb declared that we should have a drink with our next one and told me to accompany her into their unused, posh front room.

There wasn't much furniture in this room, just a couch, a chair and an old wooden sideboard. The sideboard was made out of dark wood and had three drawers in the middle of two identical cabinets. She opened one of the cabinets to reveal a selection of glasses, then the other one – which was full of bottles. There was stuff there that I hadn't ever seen before, and Deb began to get each bottle out and put it on the top of the sideboard, naming each type of alcohol as she lined the bottles up like infantry: gin, Bacardi, vodka, rum, whisky, brandy, Martini, Campari, port, and sherry. She then brought out two packs of bottles, four in each pack of Cherry B and Babysham. "What da ya fancy?" she asked, when she'd finished emptying the cabinet. "I don't know," I stuttered. I'd only ever tasted shandy at nana's and I didn't much like that. "Have anything you want," she said, as she swept her arm in the air above the sideboard, sounding like a benevolent hostess. "What are you gonna have?" I asked. "Vodka," she said with confidence, as though she ordered it on a regular basis. "I might have a few vodkas, and then I can top the bottle up with tap water. Mum will never know." She had obviously thought about it beforehand. I was taken aback by the prospect of a drink and took my time before deciding that I liked the look of the small bottles, and opted for a Cherry B; after all, I had already crossed the line of mischief by smoking, what harm would a drink do?

"No worries," Deb said, and looked hilarious as she opened the vodka bottle, prised the top off the Cherry B bottle with her teeth, and all of this while her cigarette was tucked behind her right ear. She selected what she considered to be suitable glasses and poured both the Cherry B and a handsome measure of vodka into two identical crystal tumblers. I followed her from the room as she carried the drinks into the kitchen, where she added some lemonade and ice to hers and a glacé cherry to mine. We went back into the lounge and took up our usual seats in front of the coffee table, and before drinking Deb put off the television and put her Cliff Richard LP on the record player. She then handed me my first grown up alcoholic drink and held her own in the air saying "Cheers!" as though she had done this many times before.

I really enjoyed the sweet taste of the Cherry B, and Deb looked to be enjoying her vodka immensely. She went through to the kitchen and reappeared with a large bag of salted peanuts, which we tucked into with gusto. We sat there eating, drinking, and singing along to Cliff. We were having a wonderful time. Deb decided that we should share the remaining two cigarettes, lighting just one at a time; after all, they were all we had, and that was fine by me. She removed the cigarette from behind her ear and lit it up like a professional smoker, savouring the first intake of nicotine. She then handed it to me, and we took turns puffing our way through this penultimate cigarette. This second one didn't seem to taste as bad as the first; perhaps the taste of the Cherry B was making it taste better.

We were getting through our drinks at quite a pace, probably due to the saltiness of the peanuts we were eating. Deb offered, and I gratefully accepted, another drink, and we went through to the room to replenish our glasses. I worried that the disappearance of two bottles of Cherry B would be noticed easily, and Deb allayed my fears by saying: "Don't worry, I bet Norma doesn't even notice them missing. They were tucked away at the back of the cabinet, and she's probably even forgotten she's bought them. Trust me" she added, and I did. Deb poured herself another glass of vodka before filling up the bottle with cold tap water.

The effects of the alcohol were starting to work, and we giggled about how mischievous we had been. We put back the alcohol in the drinks cabinet and when we had finished our drinks, we rinsed our glasses and put them back, too. My head felt light and I felt carefree and happy. I wished that I could have kept feeling like that. "Let's have our last cigarette," I said to Deb. "Okay," she said. "When this one is gone, I could look upstairs to see if I can find the odd half ciggy floating about." This time I lit up first and was actually starting to enjoy this whole smoking malarkey. We had eaten, drunk, smoked, sung, and laughed, and promised ourselves that we would do this again – soon!

At around 10 P.M., we opened Deb's back door and went out into the garden to dispose of the empty Cherry B bottles. Our back gardens backed onto a large field that we kids would play on – weather permitting – and Deb unceremoniously threw them over the fence. We heard them land in the long grass. It was a lovely evening, the sky was clear and the stars were really bright that night. It was a full moon. I loved the Moon and was always transfixed by its beauty. Often, I would sit on my bedroom windowsill just looking skywards, staring at it, feeling as though I was being energized by it. If I stayed at nana's house when a full moon was in the sky, we would go out into the garden and I would stand with her, watching as she held her arms out and up towards the sky. I often copied her not knowing why, but realizing that I felt good afterwards – charged somehow.

As I stood in Deb's garden, while she got rid of our evidence, the fresh air made my head feel a little spinny. But I looked heavenwards and held my arms out like I'd seen nana do. What happened next went unexplained for some years, but as I looked up into the sky, I became aware of a smell of smoke – fire smoke rather than cigarette smoke. Keeping my head up, I felt as though I was avoiding a fire that was at my feet. I couldn't move and knew that it was me, but not as I am now. I felt a wonderful warm feeling as the smoke from this fire rose up to my face, and I seemed to take deep breaths of it before I experienced the sensation of falling deep into a whirlwind kind of space that made me feel warm. I let out a gasp when Deb, who had been standing close by, nudged me and asked: "You okay?" Her arms were also held up to the Moon and she whispered: "What are we doing?" "Embracing the power of the Moon," I replied. "Oh, right," she whispered. "I know where there are two more ciggies," she added conspiratorially. "Great!" I whispered, before letting my arms drop by my side.

I followed her back inside, and we took our seats and smoked our fifth cigarette of the evening. I felt really close to Deb, as though by sharing these new experiences our friendship had been sealed. I felt the need to talk and I sensed that I could trust her. "I think I'm a witch," I uttered, as calmly as I could. "Oh, right," she answered. "What makes you think that?" I told her of some of my childhood experiences and about what had just happened in the garden; also about how the Moon made me feel. "Do you think you're a good one or a bad one?" She sounded like a counsellor. "A good one, of course," I replied. "Oh, right," was her predictable reply. I realized that as I was telling Deb my thoughts, that I was revealing things to myself, too. I had honestly never contemplated the fact before that night. I had always been interested in the myth and magic of the craft, but I didn't know why and I hadn't ever felt like I just had in Deb's garden. I wondered if it was the alcohol or smoking that had made me feel a bit strange. "Don't tell anyone what I've just told you," I asked Deb, and she reassured me that she wouldn't. Not ever. "It's been a great night, and I'm glad we're best friends," she said sincerely. "Me too," I said. And felt it.

For her final trick, she produced a packet of extra strong mints and declared that they would hide all evidence of smoke or drink. We sucked on them fervently, before breathing on each other, and deeming that all that could be detected was the smell of peppermint. I thought it best to go home before Brian and Norma got home, and Deb said that she would go straight to bed so as not to see them, too. As I walked the short distance home, I felt as though something had changed in me that evening. I felt different in so many ways. My head was full of questions about this recent self-discovery, and I was sure that if nana couldn't help me with this, then Norman would. I realized that a lot of things that I didn't know about myself were coming to light as I matured, and I awaited the next chapter of my life both with excitement and anticipation.

When I got home, mum and dad were watching a film on television. I stuck my head around the door, telling them that I was home, tired, and off to bed. "Okay, pet," dad answered and mum asked if I'd had a good night at Deborah's. "Oh, just the usual, mum," I lied, and made my way upstairs. As I was getting washed in the bathroom, I looked long and hard in the mirror, looking at my face for evidence of this change. There wasn't any, but I knew that that night had been the start of something. I was quite surprised when Norman showed up before I went to sleep. I had felt sure that he would be angry with me for disobeying him, and perhaps desert me in view of this recent insubordination and reluctance to take his advice. He was fine. So why did I feel a little anxious when he told me that from that day, I would be wholly responsible for my actions?

25

GINA

The next morning, I felt really rough – my head was aching and my mouth felt peculiar; furry, in fact. When I breathed into my hand, the smell of my breath was awful. I got up immediately and brushed my teeth rigorously. I was aware, as I went down for breakfast, that someone might detect this awful breath smell, so I sat apart from the others. After breakfast, I brushed my teeth again, got dressed, and went along for Deb. She was upstairs in her room getting ready, and Norma invited me to go up and see her. I really liked Norma – she was an older version of Deb; she had a brilliant sense of humour, too, and always asked after my family. That day was no exception, and I found myself holding my breath as I answered her, fearful that my halitosis would give me away. Deb was soon ready and she grabbed a packet of biscuits (her breakfast) on her way out of the house.

We had walked about 50 yards away from Deb's house in silence, before Deb looked at me and asked: "How do you feel, Jue?" "Okay, I think," I said. "My mouth tasted awful when I woke up, my breath was really smelly, and my head ached a little. But I'm fine now, thanks. What about you?" "Fine, I feel great – looking forward to another smoke, though." "Me too," I lied. "Have you got any money?" she asked. "Just my ice rink money for this afternoon," I said. "How about we skip the ice, get some cigarettes and a Chinese take-away instead, and stay in at mine tonight?" she said excitedly. "I didn't really want to, but I could tell she did. "Yeah, sounds good!" I said with an enthusiasm that I didn't really feel. "Great! That's settled then."

I had suspected for a while that Deb didn't really enjoy the ice rink the same way that I did. She was a little overweight, and we were at an age where our peers were quite cruel. Deb often had to suffer name-calling and barbed comments. She took insults on the chin, and her ability to retort with wit was amazing. I'm sure that, at times, she was more hurt than she let on, but she always managed to rise above the insults and come out of the situation having had the last laugh. People seldom insulted her more than once.

So it was decided that we would buy ciggies, have a Chinese meal, and spend the night at Debs watching television, and maybe listening to our records. I always hated lying, especially to dad and mum, so understandably began to worry about: a) what we would do when we were supposed to be at the ice rink that afternoon; b) what if our parents asked us if we had enjoyed the skating? and c) how we would be able to get the cigarettes – being far too young to buy them. "Easy!" Deb replied in her best reassuring tone, when I expressed my three concerns. "My mum and dad are at the club this afternoon, so we can stay in at ours. If nobody sees us, everyone will think that we're at the Ice anyway. We will just tell our folks what we always tell them – that the ice was great." She had also been thinking about how we would get the cigarettes and had formulated a plan. We had a regular ice-cream van that came around most nights and on afternoons at weekends. This van, as well as ice-cream, also sold sweets, crisps, and cigarettes. Deb said that it was a well-known fact that if the young lad was on the van, rather than his dad, then he would sell ciggies if you looked 14. "I look 14," Deb said confidently. "Yes, but what if one of our neighbours sees you buying the ciggies, and tells your Dad?" I asked. "I've thought of that, too – I'll buy them in another road. I know the route the van takes, so we could be round the block and out of sight when we get them." She seemed to have all angles covered. "Okay then," I said lamely. "If you're sure?"

Norma and Brian left for the club around 12:30. We were standing at the front gate when they came out of the house. Norma asked Deb if she had her door key. "Yes, thanks, mum," she answered. "Your money for the ice rink is on the mantelpiece," Brian said, before adding: "Be good you two." "We will," we answered in unison, before giving each other a knowing look. We went into Deb's house as soon as Norma and Brian were out of sight, and Deb put the kettle on to make us a cup of coffee. "I'm gasping for a fag," she sighed. "Me too," I lied, and we both started laughing. Half an hour later, Deb and I went along to my house to collect my ice boots and say goodbye. Mum was busy with housework and dad was working on the car out front, and they both told Deb and I to take care and have a good time. We walked in the direction of the bus stop, but once around the corner and out of sight, we crossed over the road and crept through the field that was at the back of our houses, being especially careful as we passed my house that we wouldn't be spotted.

"Stop walking as though you're sneaking," Deb said. "If you're asked why you were going back to mine, just tell them that I forgot my money or something." "Okay," I said, trying now to walk normally. I really hated skulking about and was sure that I looked guilty. Soon we were safely in Deb's with another cup of coffee. We pooled our money, and Deb calculated that we easily could afford cigarettes, a takeaway, and a bottle of lemonade to go with the vodka. I felt both excited and nervous. Deb said that the ice-cream van usually came around 5 P.M., which was fine – we were usually home from the Forum by then.

After our coffee, we decided to go and sit upstairs in Deb's bedroom and look out of the window. She had net curtains up, and we wouldn't be seen, she reckoned. We often sat up there, just looking out of the window and people-watching while listening to the radio. Norma and Brian had separate bedrooms for some reason, and before we went into Deb's room, she suggested that we have a scout around looking for spare cigarettes that her parents might have left lying around. She found a few half-smoked cigarettes in Brian's room, smokes he must have had prior to sleeping. But I didn't really fancy second-hand ones, so we moved into Norma's bedroom. There were none in evidence, so Deb decided to look through her mum's wardrobe – she was sure she would find some. Sure enough, in a handbag on the wardrobe shelf there was a packet of cigarettes with two left in it. "Hey presto – meant to be!" Deb declared. I was a little unsure that it was a good idea to take them. "What if she notices they've gone?" I asked. "She won't – she probably doesn't even remember that she's left them in the bag. Besides, she hasn't used this bag for ages." "Well, if you're sure?" I said.

I had thought about our new smoking habit and I knew that there was no way in the world I would ever dare take cigarettes out of our house. This thought was stupid anyway – mum didn't smoke and dad was then smoking a pipe. He often alternated cigarettes with pipe smoking, depending on his preference at the time. Deb almost made taking these cigarettes a good thing to do, reasoning that we were saving Norma and Brian from smoking even more by taking the odd few off them. I couldn't quite reconcile it in my mind, but went along with her anyway. We took up our positions on her bed and, after deciding to share one cigarette at a time, Deb lit up. "Nectar!" she declared, as she took her first intake of nicotine, before passing it to me. And I have to admit that it didn't taste half as bad as the cigarettes had the previous evening. I didn't seem to feel as dizzy either; perhaps this could turn out to be a bearable habit, after all. We shared our cigarette while singing along to the radio and watching the world go by from Deb's bedroom window.

I could see dad, his head under the bonnet of the car, and a cup of tea by his foot. I saw my brother Mark and his friend Mike as they walked from our house on their way to Mike's, and felt bizarre that while I was watching everything go on, the people that I was observing were totally oblivious to the fact. We watched as several of the neighbours came and went, going about their usually Saturday duties. Deb often commented about those we watched; her unique take on them and good sense of humour always made me laugh out loud.

As we were looking down the road, Deb drew my attention to a woman who had just come into view. She was carrying shopping bags which looked really heavy. "See her," she asked. "Yes," I replied. "She's a witch," she whispered. "A real one." This woman was in her late 30s – she had a pleasant face and long, black hair that matched her long, black coat. I was never sure when Deb was joking and I said: "No way." "She is, honest. Her name is Gina. Her son is in my form at school; they haven't lived here for long. They came from down south." "Wow!" I said, fascinated by this information. "Are you sure, Deb? You're not just saying it because she looks like a witch?" "Swear to God," she said dramatically, and I knew she was telling the truth. This Gina seemed to be walking quite slowly and, despite the heavy bags that she was carrying, she appeared to be really enjoying her journey, stopping to look in gardens, and smiling at the children who were playing out. "I'll show you her son when we get the bus to school," Deb said to further convince me she was telling the truth.

Gina was by now level with Deb's house on the opposite side of the road, and then something really strange happened. We were obscured by the net curtains and couldn't be seen from outside, but this fascinating woman stood opposite and looked straight up into Deb's bedroom window as though she knew we were there, as if she sensed us talking about her. We ducked immediately, and Deb said: "God, do you think she knew that we were talking about her?" "No, silly, how could she?" I reasoned. "Well, if she's a witch, she'll have those special powers – ESP or whatever it's called." After a minute or so, we got up from our crouching positions and gingerly looked out of the window to discover that Gina had disappeared completely. "Where the hell did she go?" Deb asked, her eyes almost popping out of her head. "I don't know; maybe into someone's house," I said. Deb made her own story up about how witches really could make themselves invisible to those that they didn't want to be seen by, and apparently they were able to transport themselves off by thought power. This was an interesting philosophy, but I wasn't convinced. It did seem peculiar, though, that Gina seemed to have vanished into thin air.

The rest of the afternoon passed really quickly after that, and in no time Deb declared that it was time for us to go out and try and catch the ice-cream van. Before we left the house, Deb suggested that I wet the hem of my jeans so that I would look as if I really had been skating. As I did this, she applied some of Norma's peach lipstick, and when I looked at her questioningly, she said: "It's so I look 14 when I buy our fags." "Good thinking," I said. She had thought of everything.

We left by the back door again and traced out steps to the road, where the bus stop was, just around the corner from our house. We sat on the fence and after a few minutes we heard the familiar jingle of the ice-cream van as it came into our road. "It will come round here next," Deb said, rubbing her knees. She had our money in her pocket and as she fumbled to get it out, I asked her: "Are you nervous?" "No, course not," she answered. "I look much older than I am anyway." "What if it's the older ice-cream man?" I said. "Stop being so negative," she frowned. "It won't be." She was right, too. Just a few minutes later, the van appeared, driven by the younger man. As it pulled up, Deb jumped down from the fence and confidently strutted over to where the van had stopped. She then successfully purchased our first ever pack of ten cigarettes. She put them into her pocket, and I joined her as she got up to the fence, and we walked the short distance round the corner to home.

Deb had correctly estimated that this would be the time that we were due home from the ice anyway, and as we turned the corner, I could see that dad was still mending the car. "Now then, what have you two been up to?" he asked as we got level with him. "We've been to the ice," I answered, a little defensively. "I know that," he laughed "Look at you, Deb, with your lipstick on," he teased. "It's not lipstick," Deb lied. "I've just had an ice pop." "Oh, right," dad said, obviously not convinced. "I'll see you later," I said to Deb, as we got to my gate. "I'll be along about seven-ish." "Great," she answered. "I've got some extra pocket money this week, so I'll treat us to a Chinese," she winked. "Oh, thanks, Deb," I said. "See you soon." I was still sucking the extra strong mint she'd given me to mask the smell of our cigarettes. When I got in, mum was ironing and asked if I'd had a nice time. "Great, thanks," I said, before going upstairs to change my trousers.

Later that evening, once Norma and Brian had left for the club, we had our first cigarette of the night. It tasted nicer than the stolen ones that we'd had previously, and Deb explained that it was because the cigarettes that we had bought weren't as strong as the ones that her mum and dad smoked. After a cigarette and a coffee, we walked the short distance to the local village shops where we ordered our portions of chips, curry sauce, and mushrooms – a veritable feast. As we left the Chinese takeaway, we had a busy road to cross. Deb was carrying the takeaway and was babbling on about what we could watch on the television. I wasn't paying much attention, because there at the opposite side of the road, waiting to cross to our side stood Gina. Once the road was clear, we began to cross and as we met, she stared straight at me. Her gaze held mine for what seemed like an eternity and then she smiled at me, smiled as though she had known me a long time. I was a little stirred by the stare, but managed to continue walking across the road, Deb linking my arm. Deb had also stopped talking when she had spotted Gina. Once we were across the road, she looked over our shoulders, and when she was sure that she wouldn't be heard, she whispered: "Well, she's still visible this time, but did you see the way she looked at you?" I didn't reply – I didn't really want to think about what had just happened or how it had made me feel.

Deb's conversation soon returned to our plans for the night, and in no time we were back at her house. We didn't mention Gina again that night, but the memory of her looking deep into my eyes kept coming to me throughout the evening. I had felt a sort of recognition when I had come face-to-face with Gina, as though I knew her from somewhere. I needed to be on my own to think about, it though.

We had another great night at Deb's. We ate, drank, and smoked our cigarettes while watching a Clint Eastwood movie. We had six of our ten cigarettes, and munched our way through a packet of extra-strong mints. I went home at ten to avoid Norma and Brian, and Deb once again said that she was going straight to bed when I left. I managed to avoid too much conversation with dad and mum that night, feigning tiredness, and going straight to bed. Once in bed, I pondered the events of the day, especially the Gina episodes, and before I fell asleep, I remember thinking over and over again: "Where do I know you from? Where do I know you from?' The answer came eventually, from Norman, who, when he answered, said simply: "From the future."

26

IN A KNOT

1976 is remembered by most for the glorious summer that we enjoyed in this country. It was also a very eventful year in my life. My lovely friend Deb moved to Scotland; Norma and Brian separated, and I was devastated to think that I would never see her again. I called for her to go to school one morning, and was surprised when Brian answered the door. He looked really dishevelled and his eyes looked sore from crying, but he managed to tell me that Norma had left him, taking Deb with her, and that she wouldn't be coming back. "Why?" I asked, close to tears. "I don't know, pet. She's just buggered off," Brian said bitterly. I was so shocked, all that I could say was "Sorry, I'm really sorry," before walking away from the door like a zombie. I went back home and cried, telling mum what had happened. She could see how upset I was and suggested that I stay off school. I nodded and walked up to my room thinking that life wouldn't be the same without my best friend. I knew that mum would be sad, too. Deb was a regular visitor at our house. I stayed in my bedroom most of the day and thought about all the lovely times that Deb and I had shared, which made me cry even harder.

While I was in my room, perhaps because I was upset, I felt as if a spiritual storm was brewing. It's difficult to articulate this, other than to say that it feels a little like the weather does before a thunderstorm – all tense and dark with underlying expectations of gloominess. I sensed that there was going to be more happenings in the house and, instead of feeling anxious like I normally did, I felt angry. The more I thought about it, the angrier I got, feeling almost victimized. I had irrational thoughts about fighting these dark presences that spoiled our peace in the house. It was a weird day, and I was loath to leave my bedroom – preferring to be alone. Mum came up a few times to ask if I wanted anything to eat or drink; each time asking me if I was alright. I told her that I was fine, just sad, and she said she understood and left me alone. I spent the day lying on my bed, thinking about all sorts of things, contemplating my existence.

When dad came home from work, he came straight up to my room – obviously prompted by mum. He sat next to me and asked how I was, and then assured me that Deb would be in touch when she was settled. He was sure of it. It was a Friday, and he asked if I was going ice skating that night. "I don't think so, dad." I said forlornly. "I don't feel much like doing anything." "You should go, chick," he said. "Get yourself out with your friends. It will cheer you up. I don't mind picking you up later." He then went into his pocket and gave me two pound notes. "Here, my treat." "Thanks, dad," I said and kissed his cheek. "I'll think about it." "Well, what about thinking about coming down for some tea? Your mum is worried about you," he said before leaving. "Okay, I'll be down in a minute," I said, not realizing that I was causing so much concern. I got up, straightened my bed, and brushed my hair, before making my way downstairs. As I was walking down the stairs, our phone started to ring, and mum shouted that it was for me, that it was my friend Karen from school. Karen was lovely and was concerned that I hadn't been to school that day. I told her about Deb leaving. Karen knew how close Deb and I were, and was sorry to hear she'd gone. "Why don't you come to the ice tonight?" Karen said. "It will cheer you up and we'll have a laugh." I thought about it and decided that she might be right. Karen lived at the opposite end of the town to me, so we arranged to get our respective buses and meet outside the Forum at 6:45.

When I went into the lounge and told mum and dad of my plans, they both thought that it was a good idea. Dad repeated his offer to collect me after the ice, and mum got up to get me something to eat. "No, thanks, mum," I said. "I'm not hungry." "But you haven't eaten all day," she said. "Honestly, I'm fine. I'll get something later," I replied. I decided to have a nice, hot, bubbly bath that always made me feel better. I laid my clean clothes out on my bed while the bath was running and poured extra bubble bath into the tub. While I was laid in the bath relaxing, I meditated and thought about happy things to try and lift this dark cloud that had descended upon me. I would stay in touch with Deb after all and was sure to see her again when we were old enough to travel to see each other. The hot, soapy water was working its magic, so I jumped when suddenly the airing cupboard door flew open. Once again, I felt angry at whatever or whoever had done this and felt glad to be going out of this horrible house. I knew that more things would happen that night and I also felt vulnerable without my clothes on. So I clambered out of the bath, still covered in soap suds, and wrapped the towel around me quickly. I got dressed in double-quick time.

I was at an age where make-up was a must: just subtle eyeliner and mascara with a pale lip gloss made all the difference to one's appearance, and I certainly felt better for wearing it. This particular night, I decided to put my 'face' on downstairs where the rest of the family were gathered. We had a large mirror that was carried from room to room in our house, depending on who needed it. I carried it downstairs to the kitchen and positioned it on top of the fridge. Mum was washing up after tea and she smiled as I put my few make-up items on top of the fridge and plugged my hairdryer in. After drying my hair, I plugged my curling tongs in so that they would heat up while I applied my make-up. I began to put some moisturizer on my face and noticed out of the corner of my eye that something was moving. Sure enough, my mascara was turning around like the hands of a clock; it then rose into the air and hovered a little before falling in between the sink and the fridge. This was a nuisance, and I tutted as I bent down to retrieve it. I heard someone tut and snigger behind me, but when I stood up and looked behind me there wasn't anybody there. I began to tong my hair and, as I did, I noticed my lip gloss started to move in the same fashion as the mascara had.

Mum by now was in the lounge, collecting more dishes to wash and I didn't want to alarm anyone, so I just stood and watched what was happening. Once again, after several rotations, the lip gloss hovered then rose into the air. When it got to just below my chin, I snatched it and put it into my pocket. I felt that if I could get hold of the mischievous spirit that was doing this, I would nicely strangle it. I said very quietly, almost to myself: "Bloody idiot. Get lost!" And, once again, I heard a definite snigger. I was ready in no time and I gave my ice boots a quick rub over with a cloth before putting them in my bag. On my way out, mum told me to have a nice time and dad said that he would see me in the Forum car park later.

Once out of the house and on my way to the bus stop, I felt much brighter than I had all day. I was convinced that staying in that stupid house always brought me down. As I approached the bus stop, I noticed that Gina was waiting there, too. For no reason, I began to feel a little nervous: my heart started to palpitate, and I wished that I could about turn and walk in the opposite direction. But that would have looked stupid, so I carried on walking towards her. I hadn't seen her since the night that we'd crossed the road at the Chinese takeaway months ago, and hoped that she had forgotten the encounter. As I got nearer, she said: "Hello, Julie." Geez! How did she know my name? I thought. "Hi," I said, barely able to utter anything else. "How are you?" she asked, as though she knew me really well. "Fine, thanks," I babbled. "I'm just going to meet my friend to go to the ice rink." What was I telling her all this for? I wondered – damn nerves always made me babble. "That will be nice," she said, still smiling at me. "How do you know my name?" It was out before I'd had time to think about what I was saying, or how rude it sounded. "Oh, my son knows you. He goes to your school. His name's Anthony. He gets the bus here each morning, same as you," she explained. "Oh," I said, feeling foolish. Deb had already told me that he went to our school. "I pass your house on the way to the shops," she said. "Our Anthony told me where you lived." "Right," I frowned. What was the big deal about our house? "I sense things," she said. "And your house has a strange aura about it." I couldn't do anything other than stare at her. "I'm sorry. I've said too much," she added. "No. It's fine," I said. "You're right; it is a funny house." "Mm, I know," she nodded.

I felt really peculiar I didn't have a clue what to say next so I just stood there looking at the floor. "If you ever need any help with that house, I'd gladly help you," she said in her nice, friendly, soft voice. "Thanks," I said flatly. Thankfully, just after, my bus came from around the corner. She wasn't getting the same bus as me, thank God. And as it drew to a halt in front of us, she repeated her offer of help with our house. I thanked her once again, and as the bus doors opened, she touched my arm before I stepped aboard, and said: "Don't get your laces in a knot." I smiled back at her. What an odd thing to say! I'd heard people saying "don't get your knickers in a knot", but not "don't get your laces in a knot".

That meeting with Gina had, like the previous encounter, a profound effect on me, and I couldn't stop thinking about what she'd said. I met Karen at the Forum and made a conscious effort to enjoy the skating that night. We sat in the area to get changed into our boots, and when I took mine out of the bag, the laces were tied together. "Oh, my God!" I said out loud. "What?" Karen said. I'd obviously alarmed her. "My laces are tied together." I said incredulously. "That's not a problem is it?" she asked, looking at me as if I'd lost the plot. "No, of course it isn't," I laughed, realizing what I'd just said, Gina's words ringing in my ears. "Don't get your laces in a knot." I knew without doubt that those laces weren't tied together when I'd put them into my bag earlier. I never knotted the laces, always preferring to tuck them inside each boot. The ice skating session passed without further incident, and I was glad that I had decided to go. Karen was lovely and really good company, the music was good, the atmosphere was great, and I really enjoyed myself.

Dad was outside to meet me after the session and he said that he was glad that I had brightened up. On the way home I told him that I'd had a lovely time and that I was hungry. "I'm sure mum will do you something for supper when we get in," he said. When we arrived home, he called to mum that we were home, announcing: "Our Julie's hungry now." She offered to make me some of her delicious chips. She couldn't cook very well, but her chips were legendary, everybody loved them. I offered to have toast instead, but she insisted on doing me some chips, especially since I hadn't eaten since breakfast. Dad was working the following morning and had a six A.M. start, so he kissed us goodnight before going up to bed. Mum told him that we wouldn't be long behind him – just as soon as I'd eaten, we'd be going to bed, too. I thanked him for the lift and the money he'd given me to go with, and felt very lucky to have such wonderful parents.

I stood with mum in the kitchen, watching as she shook the basket containing the chips. They were turning a lovely, golden brown. "Anything happen tonight, mum?" I asked. "No, I don't think so," she said, thinking about it. "Why do you ask?" "No reason." I decided not to alarm her with my earlier feelings of foreboding. "No, nothing has happened tonight. You haven't missed anything," she said, as she emptied the basket of chips on to the plate. "Do you want bread and butter?" she asked. "No, thanks; just salt and vinegar," I replied, my mouth already watering. I carried my plate through to the lounge, and she followed. "You go to bed, if you like, mum," I said, as I made my way to dad's chair. "Oh no, I'll stay up with you until you're finished." She smiled and sat on the couch. As I went to sit back on the chair that dad always sat in, I was punched in the back. The force of the blow winded me, and I fell forward.

The plate and the chips flew forward, spilling onto the floor. Mum screamed, and I just lay on the carpet, gasping for breath. "Are you alright?" mum kept asking, over and over again, and I nodded, not able to speak for a few minutes. When I could breathe normally, I began to sob. "I hate this house, mum. I'm sick of it. I am going to have it sorted." I spoke out loud, hoping that whoever had just done this was listening. "It's okay," she said, as she rubbed my back. "We'll get it sorted, I promise you."

When I eventually got up, we cleared the mess up and I felt both exhausted and depressed. We went up to bed together, mum still concerned that I was going to be alright. I told her that I would be fine and that I wasn't going to let anything like that happen again. I went to bed wondering how I was going to resolve these attacks. Mum had said that moving house at the moment wasn't an option. That night, as I prayed for help, Gina's words came into my head: "If you ever need any help with that house, I will help you." Perhaps this was my only option.

27

LIVE AND LEARN

I stayed in bed until lunch time the next day, having decided that I was too tired to get up. I also felt as though I needed some time to myself to think. When I eventually got up, dad and mum were together in the kitchen, preparing lunch. "Are you alright, chick?" dad asked. He looked really concerned. Mum had obviously put him in the picture about what had happened the previous evening. "I'm fine, thanks, dad – just a bit tired," I said and smiled. "I don't know what to do," he said, "about this house and the things that happen to you." "Don't worry, dad," I said. "We'll get it sorted somehow." "We don't know where to go next, me and your mum," he admitted, and I surprised both of them, and myself, when I said: "I think I'm gonna go to the Spooky Church to see if they can help us."

Billingham has a small Spiritualist Church just off the Green – a mere stone's throw from St Cuthbert's. It was one of those places that everyone knew was there, but few admitted to going to. When I was younger, myself and friends would walk past it on a Sunday evening, when it was holding a service, and imagine all sorts of things happening inside the building: everything from human sacrifice to séance and black masses. I don't know what made me say that I would go there – the place terrified the life out of me. Dad and mum just stared after me as I walked through to the lounge, my cereal bowl in my hand. The subject of the church wasn't mentioned anymore until later that year. Predictably, the house settled down again, as it did after any sort of attack or event, as if the spirits in the house went back to sleep – lulling us all into a false sense of security.

The following week, I found that going to the bus stop without Deb was really strange and depressing, and I suppose, for the first time ever, I began to notice who else waited for the bus at this stop. Deb and I always had loads to talk about, so we seldom noticed what was going on with anybody else. This was my opportunity to observe. It seemed that the same kids stood in the same positions around the bus shelter with their friends. I noticed Anthony, Gina's son – he was with a girl who I assumed was his sister. They looked alike. It wasn't considered cool at my age (approaching 15) to speak to boys that you didn't know, and, as much as Gina intrigued me, I wasn't about to introduce myself to Anthony or even acknowledge that I knew of him. Instead I smiled at his younger sister, who smiled back at me. She looked bored to be standing with her older brother and his friends, and I felt a little sorry for her. Each morning that week, I smiled at her, and she always smiled back. By Friday, she approached me and asked if she could stand with me. "Of course," I said, and we started up a conversation. She told me how they had moved to Billingham from Kent and that she didn't know very many people yet. I told her that she could come to my house sometime, and she smiled again, telling me that she would love to. The following week, every time I arrived at the bus stop, it was to find Anthony's little sister Dawn leaving him and his friends to stand with me.

Anthony had started smiling at me, too, and I smiled back – he seemed really sweet. By Thursday of the following week, Dawn and I were getting on well, and I offered to call for her after school and take her for a game of tennis at the old tennis courts near us. "Oh, I can't tonight," she said regrettably. "Any night but a Thursday; I'm not allowed out on a Thursday," she said, and I was intrigued. "Why?" I asked, hoping I didn't sound too nosey. "Oh, I do stuff with my mum on a Thursday," she said. "What stuff?" I pressed. "Just stuff." She seemed reluctant to elaborate, and I didn't want to push her. "Not to worry; another night then?" I asked. "That would be lovely," she beamed. "When?" "How about tomorrow?" I offered. "That would be great. Thank you," Dawn said. "Check with your mum that you're allowed," I told her. She assured me that she would, and that it would be fine. My curiosity was getting the better of me; I was dying to know what they did on a Thursday night and felt sure it was something interesting. After all, Gina was the most intriguing grown up I had ever met. As I had been getting to know Dawn, I had tried to draw Gina into our conversation, asking questions about her. But Dawn talked of her as if she was just a regular mum. She had no idea that Gina and I had met, and I didn't intend to enlighten her.

The following night after tea, I walked the few hundred yards to Gina's house to call for Dawn. She answered the door before I even reached it and invited me in to meet her mum. Even though our paths had already crossed, neither Gina nor I alluded to this, and once Dawn had made the formal introductions, Gina said: "Hello, Julie. How are you?" "Fine, thanks," I replied. I was really excited to be invited into Gina's home. It was a larger house than ours and it had a much nicer feel to it. It smelled lovely, and I noticed there was some incense burning on the fire hearth. The lounge was decorated in purple and lilacs with a mish-mash of furniture, and there were unusual crystal-shaped ornaments dotted about. There were two occasional chairs: one purple, one turquoise; and a black leather couch. For all its extraordinary decoration, the house felt lovely – peaceful and calm.

Gina had two cats, one of which slept on the windowsill like a big ginger ornament. There were lots of books scattered about: sewing books, gardening books, and cookery books. Gina asked where we were going, and I told her about the old tennis court that we had fashioned behind our house. "Call in for a cup of tea when you've finished your game," she said. "I'd like that," I said, and we left shortly after.

I wasn't really very focused on the game and was much more excited about having a cup of tea with Gina. Dawn was only two years younger than me, but seemed very childish in her ways. She told me that Anthony and she were the only two children of Gina's that had survived. Survived what? I thought. My heart went out to her – she was a sweet girl. Her dad had died and her step-dad worked away. She was obviously very close to her mum.

Gina seemed really pleased to see us on our return, and I followed her through to the kitchen as she put the kettle on for tea. The kitchen was as interesting as the lounge; all manner of herbs were growing in pots on the windowsill. Three pestle and mortars were lined up on a shelf above the oven, and yet more books lined a shelf in the kitchen. Gina told me that she liked to bake her own bread and pointed to a newly baked loaf cooling at the side of the cooker. It smelled lovely, but looked a little peculiar. It was covered in pumpkin seeds and had a slight green tinge to it. Gina was dressed in a long skirt and a black top, and as she made the tea, I marvelled at her shiny black hair and almost translucent complexion – she was a beautiful lady.

She made us both some tea, and when I looked at it wondering where the milk was, she smiled explaining that it was herbal tea and best taken without milk. It tasted really nice, and I felt very grown up sitting there at the table in Gina's kitchen, drinking this strange brew. Dawn had some orange juice and talked incessantly about our tennis game and anything else that came into her head. When she excused herself to go to the bathroom, Gina thanked me for taking Dawn out. "You're welcome," I smiled. "She's lovely." "She's a little young for you, Julie. You are an old soul – like me. She'll be going to bed soon. Stay and we'll have a chat." I was thrilled. To be invited to stay and talk to this fascinating woman was great. Dawn rejoined us, but then at 9:30 she was reminded by Gina that it was time for bed. She tried to negotiate to stay up for another half an hour, but Gina was firm, and Dawn reluctantly bade us goodnight and went off to bed sulking.

Once she had gone, Gina put the kettle on again and asked me what time I was allowed to stay out until. "Ten o'clock, usually," I replied. "Sometimes I'm allowed out later if mum and dad know where I am." "Do they know where you are now?" Gina asked. "Not really. They know I was taking Dawn for a game of tennis, but that's all." "Fine. Do you want to phone home and let your mum know where you are, and perhaps they will allow you to stay here a little longer," she said, gesturing to the phone on the windowsill. "Sure," I said, and picked up the receiver and dialled our number. Dad answered after a few rings, and I told him that I was up the road at Gina's, who was Dawn's mum. I explained that I was having a cuppa and wondered if I would be able to stay out a little later tonight. "I'm not sure," he said. "I don't know this Gina. Where exactly does she live?" I felt embarrassed talking while Gina was sitting there and I'm sure she must have heard him because she asked me what his name was. "Bill," I whispered, as she took the phone from me. "Hi, Bill. It's Gina – Dawn's mum. We haven't met. I've just moved here. I'm only down the road from you. Julie has been kind enough to entertain my daughter for a few hours, and I'm enjoying her company. Is it alright if she stays for another hour, and I will walk her home? Before dad had time to answer, Gina added: "I'll give you my phone number, in case you want to ring here." "Yes, yes, I think that will be alright," dad said hesitantly. "If you're sure you don't mind seeing that she gets home safe?" "Not at all, Bill," Gina smiled as she spoke.

"Right then, thanks, Gina," dad said, and Gina said goodnight and hung up. "Settled!" she said as she clapped her hands together and put the kettle on for more tea.

She invited me through to her lounge, and I followed her, cup of herbal tea in hand. She put some lovely, relaxing music on – it was a tape that played just music, no words. And as she did, I looked around the lounge again. I noticed that she didn't have a television, and as I was thinking about why, she turned from what she was doing with the stereo and said: "I don't ever watch television, that's why I don't have one in here. The kids have one each in their bedrooms. "Oh," I replied, wondering if it was just coincidence that she had mentioned the exact thing I was thinking about. "Do you like living here?" I asked, merely for something to say. "Yes it's nice. I don't know how long we'll be here, though" she answered, and I frowned. "Maybe just as long as I'm meant to," she added. Then she smiled as she said: "I know enough about life to know that I'll be put where I'm meant to be and be moved when I'm done." This philosophy of hers fascinated me, and I asked her: "Do you work for somebody, then?" She laughed softly and said: "Yes, sort of." I really liked Gina. She seemed to be the most interesting person that I had ever met, and she made me feel very grown up in her company. "You and I were meant to cross paths," she said. "What do you mean?" I asked. "Just that our lives were destined to touch," she elaborated. But I felt none the wiser. "One day, I'll explain it all to you, Julie. You're very different. You have a special gift, and I think I am meant to help you with it." I was getting more confused by the minute, but I was really enjoying listening to her and would have sat there all evening.

Our conversation changed to normal things about home, school, and family. Gina laughed as I gave her a brief synopsis of life in our household: the noise, the different characters of my siblings, mum and dad, and how we all got on. "You're close to your nana, aren't you?" she asked. "Mm. Yes, very close," I said, wondering how she could have known that. I'd never mentioned nana. "Do you know my nana?" I asked, wondering if they had met. "No, but you're evidently hereditary," she said. Not wanting to sound either ignorant or immature, I nodded my head.

Soon Norman appeared at my side. He often did when it was time to go home. I don't think I flinched or even acknowledged his presence, but to my surprise Gina did. Sitting up straight, she looked to where Norman was standing at my right, and said: "Well, well, well. We have a visitor. It must be your home time, Julie." She then gathered our cups together and walked out of the lounge into the kitchen. I followed behind. "It's been lovely having you here," she said, as she put the dishes in the sink. "I've really enjoyed chatting to you. I'll just get my coat and I will walk home with you." "There's no need," I said. "It's only down the road." "No," she said, putting her long black coat on. "I told your dad I would see you home safe, and I will – a promise is a promise." We left her house and walked the short distance to our house. It was a lovely, starry night, and Gina kept looking up at the sky remarking on the beauty of the stars and how wonderful the Moon looked that night. When we reached our gate, she paused and looked up to my bedroom window. "Sleep well, Julie," she said. "Thanks,

Gina, for walking home with me, and the tea and everything," I said. She smiled and gestured for me to go inside. I turned to wave to her when I opened the front door, and watched as she looked up to our roof as though she were surveying the property. Embarrassed, I closed the door behind me and went into the lounge. Dad and mum were still up and, as usual, they asked if I'd had a nice night. "Yes, thanks," I said, before wishing them both goodnight, and going up to bed. I felt that I needed some quiet time to think about the conversation that Gina and I had just had. She was both fascinating and intriguing, and I felt really drawn to her. Once in bed, I asked Norman if he thought that she could see him. He said that he was sure that she could. "How, then, if I've been the only person ever that could see you?" I questioned. "She's a gifted lady," he said, and then suggested that I got some sleep. When I told him that I didn't think I could and that his answers had left me feeling puzzled, he said that I wasn't to worry and that all would be revealed shortly.

I thought about my night at Gina's all weekend, even at church the following Sunday, and I hoped that I would be invited to her house again soon. I felt compelled to get to know her and I somehow sensed that she would bring change to my life or teach me something. On Monday, at the bus stop, Dawn was waiting for me and she enthused about our (boring, if I'm honest) game of tennis, asking if we could play again. "Yeah, sure," I said. "How's your mum?" "Oh, she's fine, thanks," Dawn said. "She really likes you." "Really?" I said. "How do you know?" "She said so," Dawn replied, and then pointed to where the bus was coming around the corner.

The following evening, I had just completed my homework in my bedroom and was packing my bag for school the following day, when I noticed from my bedroom that Gina and Dawn were walking past our house on the opposite side of the road. They were both dressed very smartly. The next day at the bus stop, I mentioned to Dawn that I had seen her the previous evening. "Oh, yeah, we were going out." Obviously, I thought. "Anywhere interesting?" I pushed – my curiosity getting the better of me. She hesitated, thinking about her reply, before saying: "Oh, just church." "St Cuthbert's?" I asked, knowing for a fact that they didn't have a service on a Tuesday evening. "No, the other one," Dawn said, looking a little awkward. "Which one?" I continued my questioning. "I'm not sure what it is called," she said, then changed the subject before I could pry any further. I sensed that she knew which church, but just didn't want to tell me. There was a Methodist church on the village green opposite St Cuthbert's, and I wondered if they would have gone there. "I didn't know that you were religious, Dawn?" I remarked, rather like a dog with a bone at this point, desperate to get to the bottom of the subject. "I'm not – not really. I just go with mum sometimes." "Oh," I said, and realized that I was making her feel awkward.

We got onto the bus when it came, and I must have been a little quiet, as Dawn kept asking me if I was okay. "I'm fine," I told her. "Just thinking." When we arrived at school, we walked through the gates together. Dawn went to a different school to me – there were several on the campus. We reached her school first, and I told her to have a good day, and that I would probably see her on the bus after school. She seemed a little hesitant and then said: "Okay. Thanks, Julie. I'll see you later." I had walked just a few steps from her when she called me. I stopped and turned, and smiled. "Are you okay?" I asked her. "Yes. I've remembered the name of the church we went to," she lied, and then put her head down, before adding: "It's the Spiritualist church." "Oh, right," I said. "I know which one you mean." I turned and headed to my school. As I walked, I thought about what Dawn had said and I wasn't the least bit surprised to hear that was where she and Gina had been; in fact, I think that I had known already. This further little piece of information made Gina and the 'Spooky Church' – as everyone referred to it – even more interesting.

28

TIME FOR CHANGE

Life in 1977 was good. A time of discos, lip gloss, boyfriends, and probably one of the happiest times in my life. My friend Karen and I became really close. I still heard from Deb. We wrote to each other. My letters were full of what was happening with those that we knew, and hers were funny and upbeat. Deb seemed to be settling into her new school and her new life. Norma and she were now living with George, who was to be Deb's future stepfather, and his two children. She was enjoying the company of siblings, and Norma was really happy, which made Deb happy, too.

Karen had a Saturday job working in a record bar in the town centre. Her aunt was the manageress there and had given Karen the job. I envied her and longed for a Saturday job, too. I wanted to be able to earn some money and buy clothes, make-up, and records, too. Karen's mum, Enid, was manageress at a café-cum-cake shop in the town centre, and when a Saturday position became available, she offered it to me. I was ecstatic. Enid and I got on really well and she was lovely to work for. I worked a 12 till 5 shift in the café, waiting on tables, and helping with the cooking and washing up. It was great having my own money and being able to save it until I could afford the things I really wanted. I had also been asked by a number of the neighbours to babysit. I loved this, too; sitting in their houses most Friday and Saturday evenings, listening to records, or watching what I wanted on the television. All of the children I looked after were really well behaved, so it was easy money. I also took the children that I looked after, who were old enough, to Sunday school with me each week.

I hadn't seen much of Gina for a few months. Dawn had made friends with a girl her own age, and I was glad that she had a nice friend to hang around with. I was still fascinated by Gina, but was so busy being a teenager, that I had put our conversations to the back of my mind.

Mum had started work at the local crisp factory. She worked from 5 till 10, four nights a week; and we were old enough to look after ourselves for the short time between her leaving for work and dad coming home. The little bit of extra money that she earned helped out, and everyone seemed happy. In the school summer holiday, I got some extra shifts at work in the café, and the six weeks that I was off school passed really quickly.

One Wednesday afternoon, I had been ice skating, making the most of my last week off school, and when I arrived home that day was surprised to see Gina talking to mum at our front gate. They stopped their conversation when they saw me approach, and Gina smiled and told me how well I looked. I thanked her and asked if she was alright. "Oh, yes, I'm fine, thanks," she said, before saying to mum: "Well, Ena, I'd best be going and get the tea on. Don't forget what I said, just give me a shout if you need me." "Thanks, Gina, I will," said mum, as though she had known her all of her life. "See you next week, Ena. Bye, Julie," Gina said, before heading off. "I didn't know that you knew, Gina, mum," I said as we went indoors. "Oh, yes," she said. "I like her; she's a nice woman." "How do you know her, then?" I asked. "That would be telling," mum smirked. "Come on, you can give me a hand to prepare the tea."

Once in the kitchen, I again asked her how she had come to know Gina. "Well," she whispered conspiratorially. "I've been going to the spooky church with Gwen for a few weeks now on a Wednesday afternoon, and Gina goes, too." Gwen was her friend from work. "What are you going there for?" I asked, surprised that she had been. "It's good, I like it. Gwen suggested it; she's been loads of times before and when I told her about the funny happenings in this house, she thought it a good idea that we go." "Oh, right," I said, a little hesitantly. "What have they said about the house?" "Nothing," mum replied. "I haven't got round to telling them yet. Gina is a really good medium and often gives messages to people," she enlightened me. I must have looked puzzled, because she added: "Gina is a psychic – a clairvoyant – that's what it's called when you can communicate with spirits." I didn't feel very comfortable with this whole situation – the fact that: a) mum was getting to know Gina better than I was; b) my mother was going to the spooky church; or c) all of this had completely escaped my attention. "So have you come up with any solutions for the goings on in this house?" I asked mum. I was aware that I was sounding just like dad. "Well, no, but nothing has happened lately has it? And when it does, then I will mention it. I just enjoy going." She went on to tell me about the service there, which was just like our church. Prayers were said, hymns were sung, and then whichever medium was taking the service would pass on messages to the congregation from their families and friends who had 'passed over'. Good God! Mum was even using the spooky lingo. "Passed over what?" I almost spat. "You know – passed over to the other side. Heaven, I suppose, or wherever you go when you die." "Oh, right. And do you believe in all of that stuff?" I asked her. "Yes, I do now. Some of the proof those mediums give is astonishing, and you have always been able to see dead people, Julie, so why shouldn't I believe?" "Mum, you haven't told anybody about me have you?" I asked her – panic starting to set in. "No, of course not," she said. "Besides, you told me that you don't see anything anymore." "Yes, well, that's right," I lied. "I tell you what; why don't you come along one Wednesday afternoon with us?" she said, making it sound a good idea. "They make everybody welcome – even Gina's daughter goes sometimes, and she's younger than you. "No, thanks," I said, dismissing the whole idea. "I'm not really interested in any of that stuff," hoping that I sounded more convincing than I felt. "Well, one day you might," she said, as she started peeling the potatoes." "No, thanks," I repeated, trying to sound nonchalant. I carried on helping get things ready for tea, all the while trying to work out why I felt so put out about mum's new found interest.

The following morning, I went to the local shops to get some groceries for mum. I had only just set off when I heard somebody call my name. It was Dawn and her friend. "Hiya, Julie, where are you going?" she asked. "Just to the village to get some stuff for my mum," I said. "Can we walk with you?" she asked. "We're going there, too." "Sure," I said, and we continued on together. I asked her what she had been up to in the school holidays, and she told me that she and her new friend, Sharon, had been swimming, skating, and had enjoyed spending most of the weekends at Sharon's caravan. Dawn was her usual bubbly self and Sharon joined in with the conversation, and seemed to be a really nice girl. She had a smiley, open face and was obviously very fond of Dawn. "What you up to tonight?" I asked them, and looked to Sharon for an answer, thinking that it was probably the only chance she would get to speak. "Oh, nothing tonight," Sharon said. "Dawn always stays in on Thursdays.""That's right, I remember," I said. "What is it you actually do on Thursday evenings?""Oh, nothing really," Dawn answered. She looked uncomfortable and seemed reluctant to talk about it. There followed an awkward silence, before she added: "Just stuff with mum." Sharon looked at me, and I shrugged. Dawn quickly changed the conversation as we continued to the shops. Once there, we separated and went in opposite directions. "Enjoy the rest of the holidays," I said. "I'll see you at the bus stop next week." "Okay, Julie – you too," she waved, and off they went.

After tea that day, mum got ready and went off to call for Gwen to catch the bus to work. Dad came home soon after, and I gave him his tea. There was nothing on television that evening, and I was bored, so decided to go out for a walk. I headed off in the direction of Gina's, not really having a clue as to where I would end up. As I got up to Gina's house, I noticed that the curtains in the lounge were closed. It was only early and there was plenty of daylight left in the day. This puzzled me. I continued walking, and after about ten minutes, realized that I had nowhere in mind to go, so decided to re-trace my steps and go back home. When I got to Gina's house, I felt compelled to stop. The need to know what went on there on Thursday evenings was all consuming. I found myself walking down the path and knocking on the door, clueless as to what I was going to say when someone answered the door. For a split-second I regretted my impulsiveness. I heard the door to the lounge opening, and Gina answered the door. She smelled lovely – of incense – and she looked awesome, dressed in a long black dress with burgundy velvet patches on it. "Hi," I said, and then just stood there dumb struck. "Hello Julie, nice to see you. I expected you to call one of these evenings. Come on in." "I'm sorry if you're busy," I hesitated. "No, it's fine. Come and join us," she said, and held the door open. I stepped in and took my shoes off in the porch, before following her into the lounge.

Gina had guests, and I felt embarrassed at having disturbed her evening now. She had moved the furniture in the lounge, positioning the chairs so that they formed a circle, and, sitting in one of the chairs was Dawn, who said hello and looked a little sheepish at me, before looking to Gina for explanation. "Everyone, I would like you to meet Julie," Gina said, as though she were expecting me. "She is gifted and will be joining us tonight." I smiled and felt myself blush, thanking God that the room was in semi-darkness and that my embarrassment would be spared. Dawn jumped up, got another chair from the dining room, and placed it between hers and Gina's for me to sit on. I sat down, aware that everyone's eyes were upon me.

The lounge had a strange feel to it. The curtains at the rear of the lounge were closed, too, so there was no natural light in the room whatsoever. In the middle of the circle of chairs was a small table with candles on it. The candles were different shapes and sizes, and had all been lit – casting an eerie glow on the faces of the people sitting around them. Gina introduced the people sitting in the circle: an older lady with very black hair and bright red lipstick, wearing black and red clothes that matched her hair and lipstick, was called Mercedes. Sitting next to her was a man, probably in his late thirties with thinning sandy-coloured hair. He was dressed like a teacher and his name was Brian. Next to him was a plain-looking woman, with a page-boy haircut, who had a nice, friendly face. This was Carol, Brian's wife. Finally, George, the oldest in the group. He was lovely – like a jolly Father Christmas, he had a grey beard and spectacles that sat on the end of his nose. His hair was wispy and out of control, and he oozed warmth and friendship. I immediately connected with George, and he winked as we were introduced.

After the introductions were made, Gina announced that it was time to get on and connect to meditate. This meant that, after she had put on some soft music and rejoined the group, we were to hold hands, close our eyes, and meditate. I was completely taken aback by the surrealism of the situation, and was glad to close my eyes to ponder on what was happening. Nevertheless, I was enjoying the whole experience immensely. After several minutes of listening to the music, my curiosity was getting the better of me, and I felt that I just had to open my eyes, in case I was missing anything. This also gave me an opportunity to study these strange people, while they couldn't see me doing so. After all, it would be the height of rudeness to stare at them! Brian's eyelids appeared to be flickering madly, while Carol sat with a soft smile on her lips. George looked almost angelic as he sat; his face looked almost line-free in the soft focus that the candles created. And then I looked at Mercedes. She looked very dramatic; her brow was furrowed and she looked troubled. Her lips seemed to be moving 50 to the dozen, as though she was talking at speed to someone without making a single sound. Gina looked peaceful and serene, and Dawn looked much older than her years as she sat there with her eyes closed.

The meditation lasted about 15 minutes, and during that time, I opened and closed my eyes several times. Norman appeared and drew my attention to the activity in the lounge going on around the circle. As the rest of the group sat in peaceful meditation, there were numerous shadows moving around the lounge. Some of them very animated, and they seemed to be both unconcerned and affected by the presence of the group. The room had turned much cooler and visibility was difficult due to the smoky grey mist that seemed to have descended in the last quarter of an hour. I was particularly drawn to a large spirit man who stood against the lounge door. He had a long black coat on and he held an old fashioned lantern. He reminded me of a railwayman that I had once seen in an old movie. He was the only spirit who seemed to be keeping an eye on the proceedings. I felt safe and calm in his presence, despite the absurdity of this situation, or the strangers that I sat amongst.

The music came to a crescendo and then ended; signalling the end of the meditation. Everyone opened their eyes. We broke free from each other's grasp and sat for a moment in silence. The spell of silence was broken by gorgeous George, who declared that he had a message. I already knew that he had. I had watched as a levitating spirit had earlier landed and whispered something in his ear. I also knew that the message was for me. "Julie, my dear," he began. "I have been instructed by my guide to offer you some healing. Your spiritual energy is low and if your guide will permit," he actually pointed to where Norman, who nodded, was standing, "then I would like to pass on to you some divine energy." I just sat and nodded, feeling unable to say or do anything else. George looked at Gina, who nodded. Then he got up from his chair and came and stood behind me. He placed his hands on my shoulders and took a deep breath. The feeling of his hands was amazing. Warm energy seemed to radiate from him, and I felt myself relax immediately. I hadn't ever felt anything like this before. As George stood with his hands on my shoulders, the other members of the group passed on the messages that they had received in meditation to one another.

Mercedes, in a surprisingly soft voice, told Gina that there were five little angels around her, each growing in spirit. Gina confirmed that she had lost five babies and thanked Mercedes for the message. Brian had a message for Mercedes, mentioning that he had been instructed by a lady with a Spanish name (her mother apparently) to tell Mercedes that she would move before the end of the summer. The message seemed to please Mercedes immensely. Carol recited a poem that her spirit guide (a native American Indian) had given to her about the circle of life. It was really good, and I felt sure that she couldn't possibly have made it up. Gina gave messages to Brian, Carol, and Mercedes; and I could tell from their reactions that they were very accurate. She then told George, as he was healing me, that his guide was more in evidence than ever while he was healing. Dawn stayed surprisingly quiet for once, and when Carol asked her if she had anything to give after her meditation, she just said" "No, not tonight, thanks, Carol. But I really enjoyed the meditation."

It fell quiet once again, and then Carol asked: "What about you Julie? Did you hear, see, or feel anything?" I was dumbstruck – unsure as what to say, not really sure that I was expected to be fully participating in the evening's events, but quite honoured that she had asked me anyway. "I'm not sure," I began. "I saw lots of things." I went on to explain the various activities that had gone on. I was really pleased that when I described the guide that I had seen giving George his message, he confirmed that my description was amazingly accurate. I also spent time talking about the man with the lantern standing at the lounge door. Brian listened intently, and then looked at the others with a smile on his face before declaring: "Yep, that's our doorkeeper. He's here each time we meet, keeping our circle safe and guarded." Wow, this was brilliant! Nobody questioned what I said or what I had seen. It was as though I was part of something that brought together like-minded souls. I felt euphoric and energized. George's healing power was certainly working for me.

Once my healing was finished, I thanked George, and he went back to his chair. I loved this gathering. I felt completely at ease and glad that I had been cheeky enough to knock on Gina's door. I wouldn't have missed this experience for anything. When all the messages had been discussed, Gina told us to rejoin hands, and we said some healing prayers. Each of the circle members asked for healing for specific friends or family members who were out of sorts. We then gave thanks to our guides for their divine guidance and intervention in our lives. These prayers seemed to matter to me more than any prayers that I had ever said before. Gina closed down the circle and announced that there would be tea and cakes coming up shortly. We broke free from each other's hands, and Gina and Dawn excused themselves and went through to the kitchen to put the kettle on. Brian and George began to put the chairs back, and Carol opened the curtains. Mercedes sat in her chair, once it had been moved to its normal place, and I felt that I, too, should be doing something. I asked Carol if I could help, and she suggested that I put the candles on a tray and take them through to the kitchen for Gina. I did, and once in the kitchen, I helped put biscuits and cakes on to plates, while Gina and Dawn made the tea. Gina asked if I had enjoyed the evening, and I told her that I couldn't explain just how much I had, and thanked her for the opportunity to sit with the group. As usual, she just smiled.

We carried plates of goodies through to the lounge, and it struck me that with both sets of curtains open, how normal everybody seemed – even Mercedes, despite her heavy make-up, looked fairly normal. Carol and Brian seemed to sit or stand together all of the time and they made me feel really welcome. They asked me how long I had known Gina and how long had I been psychic. Mm, I would have to think about that one. I blagged my way through the conversation, pretending to know far more than I did, and they seemed to accept what I said. I reasoned with my conscience that, if I pretended to know more than I did, then perhaps the group would accept me better and invite me again. I wanted to be accepted by them all – badly. George also came over and kindly asked how his healing had made me feel. I couldn't articulate strongly enough just how wonderful it had felt. "You needed it, young lady," he said. "You were drained." I wasn't really sure what he meant, but thanked him profusely anyway.

Each of the group seemed to be very respectful of Mercedes. Dawn told me that she was a very well established medium, who always stayed with Gina when she was in the area. Apparently, she was just here for the evening, and they were all really pleased to have her sit with them. Gina, in particular, seemed to look up to her, so I was delighted when she came over to me, touched my shoulder, and in her broken English accent told me: "You will be a good medium one day, my dear. A very good one." All of this was said with her eyes closed, and I felt that I had had a reverential blessing. "Thank you. Thank you very, very much," I babbled. I was on cloud nine. She just nodded and went back to her chair.

This meeting came to an end far too soon for my liking. I wanted the night to last forever. As each of the guests left, they thanked Gina for her hospitality, and Mercedes for coming, and every one of them mentioned that they hoped to see me again. Apparently, this meeting took place every Thursday. So this was why Dawn didn't make arrangements for anything. I didn't blame her. I wouldn't have missed a night such as this for anything. Naturally, I was the last to leave. I helped clear up and wash the dishes, and when I couldn't find another excuse to stay longer, I announced that I'd best go home. "Thanks for a lovely evening, Gina," I said, as I was getting my shoes on to leave. "It was great. Your friends are lovely, and I loved every minute of it. Can I come again?" I asked, with a note of desperation in my voice. "We'll see," she said noncommittally, and I impulsively hugged her before dashing off, embarrassed by my show of affection.

I almost danced home that evening and arrived just before mum got in from work. "You look happy," dad remarked, when I got in and offered to make a cup of tea. "I am, dad – very happy." "Glad to hear it, pet," he smiled, and I hugged him, too. As I lay in bed that night, I replayed the evening's events over and over in my mind, each time remembering another little detail. I really hoped that Gina would allow me to go again. When I thought about why I had enjoyed the night so much, I couldn't explain it, not even to myself. Norman told me that he thought that being with like-minded people had opened up a channel of education. I didn't really understand what he meant. Shortly after, I fell into the best night's sleep I had had for months.

29

SATURDAY NIGHT AT 'THE SPOOKIES'

I called at Gina's house the next day to thank her once again for the previous evening. I also hoped to cement a position in the group a little by letting her know how much I had enjoyed it, and how effective George's healing had been. She invited me in for some tea, and we sat at her kitchen table. She laughed as I became excited and very animated while talking about the group; after all, she had been there, too, and I was only telling her what she already knew anyway. When I asked if I was allowed to come again, she hesitated before explaining that, because I was only 15 years old (albeit a very mature 15), I really shouldn't be there without parental consent. "What about Dawn. She's only 13," I said defensively. "Yes, but Dawn is my daughter, and I allow it," she reasoned. "So if I ask dad and mum if it's okay to come, then I'll be allowed," I pushed. "We'll see," she said. "We'll see." I sensed that I was becoming a nuisance and was disappointed by her reply, but determined to do something about it. When I left Gina's, she told me to trust that if I was meant to sit in the circle, then I would. It seemed that I had to just make do with that for now.

After working on the Saturday of that week, I came home tired. It had been a busy day, and by now I was working 9 till 5:30 in the other end of the shop, selling cakes, bread, and other bakery items. We had been kept going all day, and I was looking forward to a hot bath, pyjamas, and an early night, as I travelled on the bus home from work. Mum had made a nice salad for tea, and I sat and ate it while watching her apply fresh make-up. Dad was watching the television, so she was obviously going out without him, which was rare. "Where are you going, mum?" I asked. "Spooky church," she said. "Where?" I asked, not sure that I had heard her correctly. "Spooky church. There's a really good medium on tonight, and Gwen and I are going." "Can I come, too?" I asked. She stopped applying her mascara, thought for a while, and then said: "Yes, yes, of course you can – that would be lovely." "Great. I'll finish tea and be ready in a jiffy." "Gwen will be here in half an hour," mum said, looking at the kitchen clock. We want to get there early to get good seats." "No problem. I'll be ready for then," I said, and felt a rush of energy that dissolved the earlier tiredness that I had felt. I quickly got washed and changed, took my ponytail out and combed my hair, before adding a touch of lip gloss. When I got downstairs, dad asked: "Where are you off to, pet?" "Spooky church with mum," I answered. He shook his head and laughed. "Bloody hell," was all that he said. Gwen arrived right on schedule, and the three of us set off to walk to 'the Spooks', as most people called it.

We soon reached the church, and I found myself standing in front of the big red doors of the building that had scared the life out of my as a younger kid. I got a shock when I went inside, though – it was really nice. It felt cold inside, but it seemed just like a normal little church. There were pictures of Jesus on the walls, and wooden chairs were set out in rows, with an aisle down the middle of them. The carpets were patchy and ill-fitting, forming a kind of mosaic effect that made walking on them uneven. The windows in the church were small and high up, and they obviously didn't open. There was a musty smell in the room. The chairs all faced the front of the church where, instead of an altar, there was a sort of stage (or rostrum as they called it) with two chairs, a small table with glasses of water on it, and an organ in the far left corner.

A lady came towards us as we entered the church, and spoke to mum and Gwen, before welcoming me, once mum had told her that I was her daughter. She was about 5 feet tall and quite stocky, with lovely yellow hair that matched her gold glasses and pink lipstick. She was dressed in a nice floral blue dress and smelled of lavender. Once we had sat down in the front row, mum told me that her name was Isabelle (Belle for short) and that she was the president, caretaker, and practically ran the church single-handedly. My God! Gwen and mum were regulars! Belle kept coming over to them and talking in between greeting her other guests. They would be standing for positions on the committee before long it seemed.

I shuffled in my chair, thinking that perhaps I would have preferred to sit nearer the back of the room, and when I mentioned it to mum, she told me not to be daft and that these seats were the best in the room. So we sat like the three wise monkeys in the front row. Each time somebody came in the room, Gwen and Mum would turn around in their chairs and usually greet the visitor by name. I figured that they either: a) came here a great deal more than they let on; or b) being in church was making them over-friendly.

I remained facing forward in my chair, looking towards the rostrum, feeling sure that I wouldn't know anyone that was coming here tonight. So I was surprised to feel a tap on my shoulder. I turned to see Gina sitting in the row behind me. "Hello, what are you doing here?" she asked, with a big beaming smile on her face. "I just thought I would come with mum and Gwen," I smiled back. "You will really enjoy it tonight, Julie," she continued. "The medium – Mrs Gregory – is excellent!" "Oh, right, thanks," I said. Gwen and mum quizzed Gina some more about Mrs Gregory, and Gina responded by giving an account of her as though she was her PR manager, enthusing about how amazing she was.

Not long after the service began, Belle stood up from her chair on the rostrum and welcomed everybody to the Church, commenting on how nice it was to see the church full that night. I looked around and, sure enough, every chair was taken – some people were even standing at the back of the room. She gave a brief address about the order of service, and then welcomed the revered Mrs Gregory onto the rostrum. Mrs Gregory appeared from a side door straight onto the stage to a round of applause. She had come all the way from Tyneside, some 40 miles away, and looked pretty normal to me. I didn't see what all the fuss was about: she looked like somebody's nana in her floral skirt, pale blue twinset, and sensible shoes. We sang a hymn, said a prayer, and then it was announced by Belle that the next hour would be given up to Mrs Gregory and her spirit guides.

I warmed to Mrs Gregory the minute she started to speak. She was like a female version of George. She had a lovely face and seemed to give her messages kindly, making the recipient feel comforted and comfortable. She pointed to a lady in the audience and asked if she knew of a Stan in spirit. The lady confirmed that Stan was her father. Mrs Gregory then gave a message to her from Stan that made her cry. As she finished her conversation with the lady and her late father Stan, she said: "God Bless". I liked that. Mrs Gregory said "God Bless" to everyone that she spoke to that evening. She continued the service, giving astonishingly accurate messages to people. I watched and saw as different spirits came to her with their messages. It was wonderful. The only spirit she seemed not to acknowledge was a small lady who stood to her left the whole of the time, slightly behind her. Norman told me that this little spirit lady was called Mary, and that she kept saying that she was there for Gladys. The tension in the room between each message was tangible – each person in the audience hopeful of a word from their loved ones in spirit.

When the service eventually ended, Mrs Gregory thanked everyone in the audience for giving her their attention and for welcoming her into their church. The whole audience seemed to relax. She turned to sit back on her chair, heralding the time for Belle to stand and close the service. But Mrs Gregory thought better of it, and asked Belle if she had time to give out one more message. Belle, of course, said yes. She turned, looked straight at me, and said: "I need to speak to the young lady at the front here. Would you stay behind please? I need to see you." I was speechless. My cheeks were on fire, and I couldn't speak for the lump in my throat that seemed to be choking me. I just nodded inanely. Speak to me? What could she possibly have to say to me? It must be serious, I fathomed, or else she would have told me in front of everyone. Mum nudged me, saying: "Eeh, I wonder what she wants you for." Gina patted my shoulder and, as I turned, she smiled. I knew that something important was going to happen, and my legs were shaking.

After the service, most of the congregation stayed behind. The chairs were stacked neatly against the wall, and Belle and another lady disappeared to make tea and coffee for everyone. The refreshments were just 10p per cup, and for that you got a custard cream biscuit too! I couldn't manage to eat or drink anything, and managed to manoeuvre myself so that my back was to the rostrum. I was standing with Gwen, Gina, and mum, who were each talking about how good Mrs Gregory had been, and how amazing her messages were. My heart started to beat really quickly when Gina looked over my shoulder and announced that Mrs Gregory was on her way over. "Hello, Gina," Mrs Gregory said, as she kissed Gina on the cheek. "Nice to see you again. How are you?" Gina said how well she had settled in the area, before introducing mum, Gwen, and me. She shook hands with us all, and mum and Gwen congratulated her on such a good service, saying how it was the best demonstration of proof they had ever seen. Mrs Gregory seemed a little bit embarrassed, but thanked them graciously, before turning to me. "Hello, my dear. I'm sorry if I embarrassed you earlier, but I felt that I must speak to you. Have you been to this church before?" "No, this is my first time," I managed to mutter. It was only Norman's order to breathe that made me stop holding my breath. "Well, I have to pass on a message to you," she said, before pausing. "Thank you," I replied, before I had even heard what she was going to say. "How old are you?" she asked next, and I told her that I was nearly 16. "She's my daughter," mum butted in. "My, my; just 15 years of age," she said to herself. "You are very, very psychic, and one day soon you will be up on that rostrum," she said, pointing to where she had just given an amazing performance. All I could say was "Oh." "I knew it," mum was saying. "I said to you, didn't I Gina, I said our Julie was psychic." "Yes, Ena, you did," Gina confirmed. "I'm surprised you aren't aware of it," Mrs Gregory said to me, and I just shrugged. Then the most awesome thing happened – Norman spoke to Mrs Gregory and she heard him. He told her that I was just a little overwhelmed by the whole evening, and Mrs Gregory said "Right", in response. She nodded her head in agreement. "Right, what?" I asked her. "Your guide has just told me that you are just a little overwhelmed," she explained. "Yes, yes. He did just say that," I said excitedly. "And you heard him?" "He has just told me that you call him Norman." "That's fantastic," mum said. "Nobody could have known that, could they Julie?" I just shook my head, dumbstruck. Mrs Gregory smiled at me and Norman confirmed that she could indeed hear him. He then encouraged me to tell her about the lady I had seen her with as she worked the rostrum that evening. I was reluctant, but, with his gentle encouragement, I told her. "There was a little lady standing behind you tonight, Mrs Gregory. She was even smaller than you, and her name is Mary. She kept saying that she was there for Gladys." I was glad that I had managed to pass on the whole message without stuttering. "I'm Gladys," Mrs Gregory said smiling. "And Mary is my mother – a very good medium, too, so thank you for that." I felt elated that she could understand the message. She then repeated her earlier message to me and told me to pursue my gift, and help others. She wished us all goodnight and retreated to the little room at the side of the rostrum.

Gina, Gwen, and mum all congratulated me, and I felt really strange. Something had happened to me this week; what with the meeting at Gina's on Thursday, and now this. The four of us left church together, passing and thanking Belle. Was it my imagination, or did she stare at me for longer than seemed polite? She told mum and Gwen how good it was to see them, and how she expected to see them next Wednesday afternoon. It was evident that she knew Gina very well, and told me that she hoped I had enjoyed my first experience at the Spiritualist church. I told her that I had.

As we walked home together, poor Gina was questioned mercilessly about the different mediums and church services. She answered all the questions with patience, as though it was part of her job to spread the word. When mum eventually stopped quizzing Gina, she then went on to repeat once again the message that Mrs Gregory had given me. Gina and I glanced at each other and she smiled at me. Mum was lovely and so proud of the fact that I had given off an accurate message, and she kept shaking her head in amazement. Gwen left mum and I at the gate, and continued the journey with Gina after wishing us goodnight. There was to be no early night for me that night, though. Mum insisted on a re-enactment of the evening's events for Dad, making me join in at the relevant times with the things Mrs Gregory had said to me, and more importantly, the message that I had given to her. Dad seemed genuinely interested and commented: "Well, we always knew you were different, Jue. And now we know why." "Yeah, I suppose," I answered, before making my excuses and going up to bed, leaving them to talk about it. Before I left the room, dad asked: "Are you going to church in the morning?" "I dunno," I said. "I'm really tired." "Okay, pet. I'll not bother shouting you up in the morning." I had a lot of thinking to do, and knew that I wouldn't get to sleep for some time that evening. I also felt that going to St Cuthbert's didn't seem to be a priority for me anymore. This left me confused. I had lots to think about.

30

CLEARING THE HOUSE

I missed church the following day. In fact, I slept till after 11 A.M. Another really good night's sleep left me feeling a little bit disorientated. When I woke up, I went downstairs and mum asked me if I was alright. "Yes, I'm fine, thanks," I said looking puzzled as to why she would be concerned. "Oh, just checking. By the way, Gina rang for you earlier and asked if you were okay. I told her that I would get you to call her when you got up." "Thanks, mum," I said, and went to ring Gina, wondering if she was okay. "Hi, Gina," I said when she answered. "Oh, hello there – how are you?" she also asked. "I'm fine, thanks, I think," I replied. "Did you think that I wouldn't be?" "Oh no, not at all. It's just that sometimes when you start to channel spirits and give off messages, it can leave you feeling drained," she explained. "I'm fine, thank you. Honestly," I said, thinking that having done this for years that I was quite used to it. "If you ever need any help or advice on all of this, I am here for you," Gina offered kindly. "Thanks, Gina," I said. "Does that mean I can come to your circle on Thursday?" I asked. She laughed as she said: "I expect so. Just check that it's okay with your mum, first." "Thanks Gina. I will, definitely. And thanks for calling," I added. "You're welcome. We'll see you on Thursday, if it's okay with mum." "Great. I'll be there," I said with confidence, never doubting for a minute that I wouldn't be allowed to go.

I went back into the kitchen after the phone call to find mum washing up, as usual. "I like Gina," she announced, as I picked up the tea-towel to dry the dishes. "It was really kind of her to call and see how you were, Julie." "I know. She's lovely," I said. "I have seen her give messages out on a Wednesday afternoon at church, and she seems a very good medium, too," mum added. "Yes, I know. Mum, Gina has a group meeting on a Thursday evening at her house," I said, as casually as I could. "Just a small group of mediums and healers, and she said that it is okay for me to go, if it's okay with you and dad." I waited with baited breath for her reply. "What do you want to go for?" mum asked, while drying her hands. "Well they sit and meditate on things, and pray and it's a nice evening...I think," I said, thinking that it was best not to push it too much. "I don't know, really – I'm not sure that it's a place for kids." "I'm not a kid," I said indignantly. "And I really would like to go, mum." "I'll tell you what," she said, as though she was about to negotiate a deal, "I'll speak to Gina about it when I see her on Wednesday afternoon, and let you know." Mum didn't often refuse us things, so I knew better than to push the issue. "Okay," I said. "But I really, really would like to go, mum." "We'll see then," she said.

I reminded mum each day leading up to and including Wednesday not to forget to ask Gina about the group when she saw her at church. She assured me that she would. When I got in on Wednesday afternoon, mum was getting ready for work.

"How was church today, mum?" "It was a lovely service," she said. "Belle asked about you." "Really?" I said. "What did she say?" "Oh, she just said that Mrs Gregory had mentioned how much potential that she thought you had, and how it was unusual to see a girl of your age with such a gift." I glowed with pride. I really liked Mrs Gregory and was grateful for the kind words. "Did you see Gina?" I asked tentatively. "Oh, yes, she was there, too" "And?" I said – this was like getting conversation out of a stone. "Oh, her Thursday night group seems really interesting, and I told Gina that I was worried that you were at an impressionable age and therefore perhaps a little too young to go." I was about to say something scathing, when Norman shushed me. "Gina thinks you will be fine, though." I breathed a sigh of relief. "But I still wasn't sure," she said, and I tensed. "So Gina has invited me along, too." "What? Why?" I said. "Well, she thought that if I came along, too, I could see what went on and keep my eye on you at the same time." "I don't need babysitting," I sulked. "Maybe not Julie – but after all the things that have happened to you, I don't want you getting into something that you don't understand," she reasoned. I knew there was no point arguing. Once mum had made her mind up, that was it. I knew that if I was to go to Gina's group, then the only chance I had now was to accept that mum was going to tag along. And as much as I didn't want her to, the desire to go back to the group was greater.

So on Thursday evening, the two of us walked together to Gina's. I could tell that mum was excited about the prospect of sitting in a circle. She was really in to all things spooky lately, and I didn't say much. I wasn't sure if she knew already that I had been at Gina's the previous Thursday. We were the first to arrive, and helped Gina and Dawn set the room up. The furniture was positioned as it had been the previous week, only this time a larger dining table had been put in the centre of the chairs. There were no candles on this table, and I wondered whether tonight's meeting was going to be different. Brian and Carol were the first to arrive, closely followed by George. They all said hello to me and were formally introduced to mum, who didn't seem to notice that they knew me already. Another lady arrived a little later. Her name was Avril, and she had apparently been on holiday the previous week. Gina introduced her to mum and me – explaining that Avril was a church medium, well versed in rostrum work. She, like Mrs Gregory, just looked like an ordinary housewife. It was hard to believe that she had psychic powers. In fact, the only psychic-looking person in the room was Gina. She had plaited her hair this evening and looked lovely in a green velvet top and black trousers. After the initial pleasantries were exchanged, we were invited to take our seats at the table. Gina closed the curtains to the front and rear of the lounge, and lit some candles on the mantelpiece. I made a beeline to sit next to gorgeous George. Mum sat on the other side of me, and Gina was to sit next to her. Avril was given a chair at the head of the table, and we were told that we were going to hold a séance, and that Avril was excellent at channelling spirit, so she would be the hosting medium that night.

I was so excited and sensed that mum was, too. Gina, once back at the table, got us to join hands together and remain linked in order to combine our energy. This, she said would help us communicate with spirit. It was different to last week; it sounded much more dramatic. We were to meditate before we started the séance, to ensure that we were protected and were "working in the light", Gina explained. There were sighs of relaxation as we all settled down to meditate. Once again, I felt compelled to open my eyes after a few minutes and looked first at mum; her brow was creased in concentration. Everyone else looked as they had the week before. Carol sat with her lovely smile of serenity. I watched as the atmosphere in the room changed, and saw again our protector – the man with the lantern, who appeared at the door to guard us and keep us safe. Norman stood a little away from the group, surveying the proceedings, and I knew that while he was there, we were safe. Once again, lots of different spirits seemed to gather in the room, and I was dying to look behind me. I felt as though someone was standing between mum and me. I didn't dare turn my head, in case the movement would alert the others to the fact that my eyes were open. I closed my eyes to continue my meditation.

After about ten minutes of meditation, I opened them again, and was amazed at what I saw. Avril had not moved from her position at the table, but it wasn't her sitting there – it was a man. Her whole features had changed into those of a very masculine- looking, square-jawed man. I was completely amazed; I had never seen anything like it. I blinked several times to make sure that my eyes weren't playing tricks on me, and, sure enough, this apparition was still there. I closed my eyes, knowing that very soon Gina would open hers and tell us to open ours. I didn't want to be caught. When she told us to open our eyes, I looked straight to Avril and noticed that she still sat there, with this funny projection of a man on her face. She was the only one around the table with her eyes still shut. Mum looked around and gasped as she looked towards Avril. My God! Even she could see it! "Don't worry, Ena. It's just transfiguration. Avril has taken on the appearance of her trance guide," Gina explained. "That is completely amazing," mum said, and the other members of the circle nodded their agreement, with George telling us how good Avril was at channelling. We stayed there with our hands all linked together.

Gina had told us not to break the circle, explaining that it was dangerous for the medium if we did. We were to stay with our hands joined together until she told us when to break, explaining that if we sat for long enough, we were sure to get some messages from spirit. We sat and stared at Avril for what seemed like an age, watching the differing expressions of her guide. The whole time, her eyes were closed; yet open eyes appeared on her eyelids – those of her guide, apparently. As we were watching her in silence, she began to mutter in a voice that sure didn't sound like hers. We couldn't understand what she was saying, and Gina explained in a low voice that her guide spoke the tongue of Christ – Aramaic. This was awesome! I felt privileged to witness such a wonderful thing. After a few moments of chanting, Avril's face returned to normal; that is to say that she started looking like her usual self. She opened her eyes and declared herself ready to work, then immediately closed her eyes again.

We all sat expectantly with bated breath, looking at Avril, and I became aware that a spirit that had been standing between mum and I, left and walked towards Avril. I watched with astonishment as this little lady seemed to step into Avril's body, and it made Avril jump. Gina asked out loud: "Hello and welcome. How can we help you?" Avril didn't respond, she just kept sighing and saying she couldn't hear. She seemed to be getting quite agitated and pulled her hands free from the group, and started to make as though she was writing on the table. Gina told us that we were fine to break hands, and then put some white paper in front of Avril and a pencil in her right hand. Avril started to write and all she seemed to draw were 'Xs' all over the page. She then spoke in her own voice and explained, still with her eyes shut, that the lady who was with her couldn't write. She told us that this lady wanted help for someone in the room, and then drew 164. Mum gasped – we lived at no. 164! She told Gina this, and whether Avril heard or not, I am not sure, but immediately she started talking in a broad Geordie accent that Mum immediately recognized as that of her mother – my grandma, who had died when I was just two. She was saying over and over: "Let these people help you with that house, hinny. There's evil at work there." Mum looked at me, and I was as shocked as she was. Passing on this message seemed to distress Avril, and when she finally said goodbye to it and opened her eyes, she looked more drained than anyone that I had ever seen.

She asked mum why it was that her mother wouldn't write anything other than Xs and 164, and even I was amazed to hear that my grandma had been completely illiterate and could only sign her name as an X. Mum also confirmed that 164 was our door number and told the whole group about the things that had happened in the house since we had moved there. I sat and listened as she gave her account of the events that she and I had endured in the last five and a half years. And, all put together, I realized that we had been through a lot. Avril thought that the amount of activity was probably due to the fact that I was very psychic, and explained that at my age it was normal for paranormal activity to increase. Gina looked on thoughtfully and declared, after mum's catalogue of events, that it would be best if we had the house cleared. Mum explained that we had already had prayers said there and blessings from our lovely vicar at St Cuthbert's. "That won't have helped," said Avril, quite coldly. "How can those that can't see spirit get rid of them?" Logical, if you ask me!

Gina asked the group to rejoin hands, and ask for protection and healing for mum and me. Lovely George explained why he thought I had needed the healing that he had given me. "To live in a house with that amount of activity would pull the life out of you," he said. Once the circle was closed down, and we were enjoying our tea, the matter of the house clearance came up. "How would you feel if a group of us came and tried to rid the house of the bad spirits there, and perhaps close down the vortex that they emanate from?" Gina asked. That was a no-brainer! "That would be marvellous, wouldn't it, Julie?" mum said, and I agreed wholeheartedly. Gina told her to talk to dad about it; and although mum told her that he would be more than happy for their help, she insisted that he was agreeable to it. I asked what would actually happen, and it was Avril that answered me. "We will come and open ourselves up to the spirits in the house, and then one by one we will rescue them and send them to where they should be." It sounded as though it was all in a day's work for her, and I couldn't wait for this to happen. My next question was: "When can you come?" "It will take a couple of weeks to organize," Avril said. "But trust that we will come and sort it out for you." She then looked at mum and said: "It might be an idea if you and Julie could take part, in view of the fact that the majority of happenings are around you two." "Yes, of course, Avril," mum replied. "We will do whatever is necessary to sort it, won't we, Julie?" I nodded my agreement.

"What a night!" mum remarked as we walked home together that evening. I couldn't think of anything to say. I was amazed at what had happened: Avril's trance guide, my grandma's appearance, and the forthcoming rescue of spirits had all been a little bit too much for me to take in. Mum was elated that her mother had come through to her and reasoned that, if her mum had asked the group to help us, then we would be alright – her mum was, evidently, watching over us. Once in, she told dad what had happened that evening, and even he was lost for words. She mentioned that we needed his permission to clear the house, and he remarked that he didn't care who did what, so long as we could live in peace. He mentioned that I looked a little pale and asked how I felt about it all. I was both excited and scared at the thought of being involved in this 'clearance', and was afraid to dare to hope that I would be able to relax and not worry about every shadow I saw.

Over the next few weeks, we continued going to Gina's on Thursday evenings. There weren't any more séance nights, but lots of lovely meditations followed by messages. I was gaining confidence steadily and, encouraged by the rest of the group, I began to deliver my own messages from spirit. Mum and I never discussed the events at circle outside of the group, and she marvelled at my accuracy and ability to connect to spirit. Two weeks after Avril's trance, we were finishing off circle for the night, when Gina asked that instead of holding circle at her house next week, how about we hold it at our house and get a feel of the vibrations there. Mum was in complete agreement, and the rest of the group seemed keen, too. As we walked home that evening, mum was more concerned about what biscuits to buy and whether we had enough cups, rather than what might happen when the spirits were summoned. I couldn't wait to get started with the whole process of living in a normal house; so next week couldn't come soon enough for me. The fear that I had felt initially had abated after Norman told me that I would be fine, and that nothing would harm me while I was with these experienced mediums who knew what they were doing. When I mentioned to him that night that the house seemed to have been quiet lately (there had been no scary moments), he explained that the low spirits – those with evil intention – were probably storing up their energy for a fight. This made me fearful again.

It was arranged that the following Thursday, Dad would take the kids out, so that we could get on with sorting the house without worrying about protecting anybody not in the circle. The group arrived early, and Avril asked if she could walk around the house to survey the different rooms. She did and, amazingly, picked up on the areas where most of the events had occurred. She sensed energy points and vortexes. She said that she could feel the anger of the spirits and their dislike of me and mum. It was fascinating to watch her. Gina was good, too; explaining about the open doorways that these bad spirits came through – pointing out the one on the landing and another in the bathroom, she explained that the staircase was a prime place to attack us, as it was just outside the vortex. It was starting to get dark, and Gina suggested that we get together and link up in the lounge. We all sat on the floor in a circle. George, for once, was dressed really casually. Apparently, he did when he was doing 'rescue work'. And Carol and Brian were very reassuring to mum – they had done lots of work like this before, and guaranteed that the house would be fine when they had finished.

After we had sat for just a few minutes, it began to feel icy cold in the room, and we began to hear a low droning noise that we couldn't ascertain the essence of. The room started to get foggy – like at Gina's when we meditated, only this time there was no door keeper or protector, just lots of dark shadows milling around. Gina alerted us to Avril, who once again seemed to have taken on a different appearance. Gina told us not to break the circle while we tried to rescue. It was very frightening – Avril began to growl and snarl, and an awful smell began to pervade the air. Gina kept telling the spirit to go back, and was reciting what sounded like Latin in a kind of mantra. After what seemed like ages, but was probably only five minutes, I watched incredulously as this dark spirit left Avril and dissolved into a million little particles. Avril fell forward with a gasp. No sooner had she recovered, than Gina told us to watch George, who appeared to be straining against something. The veins on his head were standing out, and he was making choking noises. Gina told us to push good energy towards George, and he appeared to struggle to break free of a malevolent presence. Once again, I watched in wonder as a rush of white substance dissolved into thin air as the spirit left him. These rescues went on and on, each of the group sending these trapped earthbound spirits to where they belonged. The presence that had breathed on mum's neck so many times appeared behind her, and she cried out that she could feel him behind her. Brian shouted at him, and we watched in awe as the spirit whizzed from behind mum and into Brian. His lovely, soft face became distorted with anger, and we each pushed energy to him until this spirit left, too. Each time a spirit was released, the room felt lighter, almost brighter in spite of us sitting in darkness. It was evident that the group was getting tired, but they were all committed to sorting things out for us. After discussing the energies in the room, the group were in agreement that there seemed to be just one bad spirit left. "He's elusive, this one," Avril said. "I have only ever seen him bobbing behind Julie." "Yes, I have noticed him there, too," said Carol. "It's almost as though he is hiding behind her. Do you feel okay, Julie?" "Yes – just cold and I can smell something horrible," I said. At that, I was really not prepared for what happened next. I felt an enormous pressure pressing on my back, forcing my face to the floor. I heard Gina shouting instructions to send energy to me, and was aware that mum was getting upset. Then I heard George saying: "Listen to me, Julie. Do what I say and you will be fine." He summoned Norman to draw close and help me, and then told me not to try and fight this presence – just to go with it. I was then thrown back, and felt as though this man – I was sure it was a man – was trying to break my hands free from the rest of the group. Gina was shouting to stay linked, and I prayed that they would not let go of me. I was terrified. This felt worse than anything I had ever experienced before. I could feel this horrible man around me, and he was smelly and evil and perverse. It seemed that the more scared I became, the more empowered he seemed. I was trying desperately to listen to George's instructions, but could barely hear him for this awful, filthy-mouthed spirit, who was spitting out obscenities, telling me what he was going to do to me. Gina was reciting her mantra, and I remember mum being even more alarmed. Then I felt this horrible spirit put his hand on my breast and squeeze hard. Something happened in that moment. I stopped being scared and became really, really angry. I shouted at the top of my voice: "Get off me, you scum! Get off me!" "That's it," I heard George say. "Channel that anger, and send him from you. Push all that negative energy towards him. Fight with fight, good girl." I did, and as I pushed my anger towards him, I felt him weaken. I wasn't getting weaker – I was getting stronger. Norman was behind me, spurring me on. I felt an enormous release of pressure as he left my body through the top of my head, and heard his screams as he was cast back to where he belonged. I started to shake and cry once he had left, and was told how well I had done.

Soon after, it was declared that the house had been cleared. Mum made some tea, as Avril and Gina wandered from room to room, closing down the now smaller vortexes that would prevent spirits coming through. I was exhausted, but felt completely at peace and, for once, useful. Each of the group congratulated me, and Avril said that she hadn't ever seen anything like the fight I had put up. We went, and joined mum when our tea was made. She kept on repeating her thanks to the group. They all agreed that the house had been full of bad spirits and marvelled at how resilient we had been to put up with it. I noticed that she asked Gina a few times if I would be okay; each time to be told that I would be. "Thank God," was her reply.

The group left as dad and the others returned, and I asked mum if it was okay if I went up to bed. I couldn't face going over the events of that evening. Dad remarked that the house felt so much calmer – so that was progress indeed. In bed, I thanked Norman for his enduring protection and kindness, and was amazed that I no longer felt afraid of anything. He said that he was glad that I had successfully conquered my fear by fighting for good. This was just another thing he said that I didn't understand. I knew that night that things were to change for me. I also realized that I had little control over what would happen, but reasoned that with Norman by my side, I would always be alright.

31

ONLY ONE GOD

Sure enough, over the next few days, the house took on a different vibration altogether. Gina came the following day to check on us all, to make sure that the energy flowing through the house was good. I knew it was; the rooms were warmer and brighter, and there wasn't a constant low hum either. She congratulated me on my rescue and said that she felt sure that I would do more of the same in the future. This really appealed to me. In a perverse way, I had enjoyed the experience of rescuing that horrible spirit, even though he was malevolent and meant me harm. When I went to work the following Saturday, a few of the girls remarked that I looked different – fresher and brighter, they thought. I felt happier than I had in ages, and felt that I had grown up so much in the last few weeks. I sensed that now I would have a good year, and felt excited about the future. I bought some cream cakes that day out of my wages, and took them home for tea – much to the delight of everyone.

I decided to have an early night that Saturday and make an effort to go to church the following day. I hadn't been for a few weeks, and felt guilty. I went up to bed at ten o'clock and asked dad to shout me in the morning, in time to go to church. I had slept like a log since the healing I had got from George earlier that month, and not long after climbing into bed, I fell into a restful slumber. Dad gave me a shout the next morning, and I got up and had an early bath before getting ready for church. It was a lovely crisp, autumn morning, and I was filled with the same lightness of heart that I had experienced the previous day. As I walked to St Cuthbert's, I passed the road that lead to the Spooky church, and made a mental note to visit there again soon. I walked into church and made my way to the front pews. I always sat with Mrs Brown, the vicar's wife; but this morning, I noticed that she was sitting with a lady. The Browns often had visitors who would join them for the Sunday morning service. Not wanting to intrude, I sat a few rows behind against the stone pillar. The service was as it always was, and I noticed that when we all went down to receive communion, that Mrs Brown's guest didn't join the line to receive the communion or a blessing. As the final verse of the final hymn began, I watched as Mrs Brown left, as she always did, and made her way to the church hall to light the boilers to prepare the morning's tea and coffee. I followed her and watched with some surprise, as she seemed to ignore the lady that was walking with her. Then I noticed that this little lady in a long blue coat turned and walked to the vicarage, not bothering to accompany Mrs Brown.

When I got into the church hall's kitchen, I greeted Mrs Brown and she said how pleased she was to see me, saying that she had missed my help for the last few weeks. I made excuses for not going and got on with the task of helping plate up the biscuits. "Why didn't you join me in church?" she asked as we were working. "I didn't want to intrude," I explained, and she looked at me with a puzzled expression on her face. "I saw that you were with that lady and I didn't want to intrude," I reasoned. "What lady, Julie?" "The little lady with the grey hair, blue bag, and long blue coat," I said. "I'm sorry, dear, I don't know what you mean," she said. "The lady that was sitting next to you – she went up to the vicarage after church." She shook her head, and shortly after when Vicar Brown came into the kitchen, she asked if he had noticed anyone sitting next to her in church that morning. "No, dear – not even Julie," he said as he smiled. I was confused and started to feel quite tearful. "She was there – I saw her go up to the vicarage," I said. They looked at each other and, for some reason, I burst into tears. Mrs Brown immediately came to my side and put her arm around me, and apologized if she had upset me, saying that she could have been mistaken and that perhaps she hadn't noticed anyone. Mr Brown looked puzzled and left us to join the waiting congregation for a cup of tea. After the kitchen was cleared and the morning's guests had dispersed, Mr Brown asked me again what I had seen in church. I explained in detail the lady who was sitting next to Mrs Brown. And, as we were locking up the church hall, I looked towards the vicarage and noticed the same lady upstairs in the vicarage. She was looking out of one of the bedroom windows.

"Look, there she is!" I pointed to the upstairs window that I saw her looking out of. "Oh, well, we better go and investigate," the vicar said to his wife, and the three of us walked towards the vicarage. The front door was open, and once inside, the vicar asked which room I thought she was in. What was wrong with them – surely they had seen her looking out of the bedroom window, too. "Upstairs, to the right of the stairs," I said, and he invited me to join him and his wife. As we were going up the stairs, Mrs Brown remarked that that was their room. I loved the vicarage – it was a beautiful old house, and Mrs Brown had filled it with lovely, tasteful furniture. Committee meetings were often held there, and a few times I had helped her in the kitchen as she baked for the numerous church fares and Sunday school parties. The whole house had a lovely warm feeling, and upstairs was no different. This was the first time I had ever been upstairs. We walked into what was their bedroom. It was a pretty room, dominated by a large wooden bed. There was a matching dressing table and wardrobe in a light wood that matched the bed head. The bedding was white with pretty flowers on it. A Bible stood on a small bedside table that I presumed to be the vicar's. Sunlight poured in through the windows, and there, in the large bowed window, sitting in a rocking chair, holding a baby, was the lady I had earlier spied in church. "There, look!" I said pointing to her in the chair, amazed that they weren't acknowledging their guest. "Where, dear?" Mrs Brown asked. "Can't you see her, there in the rocking chair?" I asked. By now, I was really exasperated by the whole thing. "No, sorry, I can't," she said, and then adding: "But look, John, the rocking chair is rocking on its own." "Oh, yes – so it is," he confirmed.

I then realized that I was seeing the mere spirit of a person. Granted, it was very clear to me – I had never seen anything quite so clear before. I then heard myself telling them that her name was Mary and that she had been a midwife. They stood in silence, listening as I gave an account of her. Mary was telling me the year was 1906, and I passed this on to them, too. When I had finished talking, I felt foolish, and my head and shoulders dropped. Mrs Brown suggested that we all go downstairs and have some tea.

We sat in the living room of the vicarage, the room where I had sat in endless committee meetings and had endless fun, and practically told the Browns my life story: about Norman and my early days, and about how hard I had tried to fit in and act normal; also about the recent events that had made me question my faith and my path. They were very patient and let me ramble on and on. What lovely people – they didn't sit in judgement or interfere as I tried to articulate as best I could what my life had been about. When I had finished, Mr Brown said that he thought I was an extraordinary girl with a special gift, and that he trusted that my belief in God would sustain me in life, irrespective of the path I chose. He agreed to be there to help me with anything he could. I felt as though I was saying goodbye to them, and this made me sad. I also felt that I needed a blessing to move forward into the unknown quantity that was my future. Mr Brown drove me home and this gave me chance to tell him how I felt. "You don't need my blessing to follow your path, Julie. God will bless you." "Will he always be there for me?" I asked. "Always – for as long as you need him, wherever you look for him, you will find him. And whenever you want him, he will be there." "Even in Spooky church," I laughed, almost too embarrassed to ask. "Wherever, Julie – there is only one God." He dropped me off a few yards from home, and as I waved to him, I felt even lighter than I had earlier that morning. I knew from that moment, I would be responsible for all my own decisions, and that I could find direction in lots of different places. I pledged to try and help others, and felt excited about the future. Little did I know what it had in store for me!

This book was only ever written to entertain my family and perhaps help those who know me well, to understand what it was like to be me as a child. I intended it to be a nice story for my grandchildren to read. My lovely little mum read my book chapter by chapter, and declared that it was worth publishing – rich coming from a woman who had only ever read one other book in her life. The fact that she featured on nearly every page may have had something to do with her interest in it! Unfortunately, she passed away in January 2012 before I ever had chance to finish writing, and had only read as far as chapter 15. Her wish for me was that I would try and get it published. So, if you are reading this – then I was successful. I hope that you have enjoyed reading about my life, as much as I have enjoyed writing about it. As for the rest of the funny and sometimes tragic events that helped shape my life – well there lies another story.

ABOUT THE AUTHOR

Julie Savage realized at a young age that she was different. Her ability to feel, hear and see dead people pretty much set her apart.

This candid account of her early life details what happened when she formed a relationship with her spirit guide, Norman.

Made in the USA
Charleston, SC
09 February 2014